"The personal stories—yes, they do matter—collected in this volume present a narrative about how the tide has been rising, perhaps still too slowly. To paraphrase the poet, even for PFM 'the times they are a changing.' It was about time."

Marco Cangiano, *Former assistant director of the IMF Fiscal Affairs Department and currently an ODI research associate*

"These stories need to be read by researchers, practitioners and policy-makers. The collection should inspire young women into a career that can make a massive difference in people's lives and further discussion on how to make public finance space more inclusive."

Michaela Lavender, *Managing Editor: Public Money & Management*

"By giving voice to the many women leaders in public financial management from around the world, this book explores the many persistent challenges to making gender-budgeting a critical reality. The personal accounts featured also help identify key opportunities that can drive progress in both 'women in public finance' and 'public finance for women.'"

Carmen Niethammer, *Senior Gender Specialist at the European Investment Bank*

"The breadth of regions covered will resonate with women everywhere, as we see ourselves in these stories and relate to the policies that need tending. I congratulate the authors and hope this book gets disseminated widely and talked about for years to come."

Therese Turner-Jones, *Former IMF Staff, CARTAC Coordinator, and Interamerican-Bank General Manager for the Caribbean*

Women in Public Finance

Public finance is often considered a discipline in which numbers, efficiency, and productivity talk. And while gender budgeting, a field of public financial management (PFM), has gained increasing attention in recent years, the personal stories of the women driving this work have remained largely invisible. This is the first book to share unprecedented insider narratives from the women shaping public finance and public policy.

It brings together the stories and conversations of 22 professional women from around the globe who are all working in the fields of PFM and gender budgeting, a space largely dominated by men. These authentic first-person accounts provide rare insights into both the barriers and breakthroughs experienced by women in a field traditionally dominated by technical discourse and masculine perspectives. It demonstrates how women's presence at decision-making tables directly opens the discussions on inclusive, sustainable, and effective public finance outcomes. It provides:

- Authentic insights into gender representation in PFM and how it can be advanced within the structures of public finance—from ministries of finance to donor agencies and civil society.
- Encouragement and strategic guidance in navigating leadership, reform fatigue, and institutional resistance, particularly for women and underrepresented groups.
- A storytelling approach, helping readers to relate to this largely technical area.
- Concrete examples of successful reform and personal stories of resilience, valuable for professionals creating capacity-building programmes, applying change management, or shaping institutional culture.

This important book is for public finance professionals, civil servants, economists, gender policy advisors, donor agency staff, civil society organisations, and graduate students in gender studies, public policy, governance, and development programmes, providing both inspiration and practical pathways for creating more equitable financial systems worldwide.

Maja Bosnić is a senior economist with over two decades of experience in public and corporate financial management, specialising in gender and climate-responsive budgeting.

Manal Fouad is a former Assistant Director and Division Chief at the IMF's Fiscal Affairs Department, with over 30 years of experience in fiscal policy and capacity development in the public financial management and budgeting area around the world.

Women in Public Finance

Stories of Gender *in* Budgeting

Edited by
Maja Bosnić and Manal Fouad

Routledge
Taylor & Francis Group
LONDON AND NEW YORK

Designed cover image by Heba Khalifa

First published 2027
by Routledge
4 Park Square, Milton Park, Abingdon, Oxon OX14 4RN

and by Routledge
605 Third Avenue, New York, NY 10158

Routledge is an imprint of the Taylor & Francis Group, an Informa business

Library of Congress Cataloging-in-Publication Data
A catalog record has been requested for this book

ISBN: 978-1-041-22490-7 (hbk)
ISBN: 978-1-041-20213-4 (pbk)
ISBN: 978-1-003-73253-2 (ebk)

DOI: 10.4324/9781003732532

Typeset in Times New Roman
by Taylor & Francis Books

Contents

Acknowledgments

First and foremost, our deepest gratitude goes to our friend and editing coach Sharry Lapp. This book would have not been the same without her endless support. Her thoughtful guidance, encouragement, questioning, insightful wit and generosity have shaped not only the pages of this book but also contributed to our growth as creative writers. Sharry's enthusiasm for the project has been a constant source of strength and motivation, especially during the most challenging moments.

We also wish to extend our heartfelt thanks to Sureni Weerathunga, whose invaluable help in getting us organised, keeping us on our toes with deadlines, and uplifting moral support enabled us to finish the book on time. Thank you also to Laura Wahlandt who contributed valuable support in the first phase of this book. And special thanks to Lesley Fisher for her support and friendship through the final process.

Thank you to the Routledge team who supported us in this endeavour: Rebecca Marshall (for believing in the book), Zoe Everett, Dominic Corti our production manager, and Fleur Kinson our copyeditor; your responsiveness and flexibility made the process smooth and enjoyable.

To all the formidable women in this book: thank you for accepting the invitation to be part of this adventure, for sharing your compelling stories, for your patience and for the grace with which you met all our requests and suggestions. We know that for many of you, stepping out of your comfort zone was testing, and we are grateful that you took this risk with us! Your stories are a true inspiration.

To the other women *not* in this book: thank you! We extend our acknowledgement to all the women shaping public finance, gender budgeting, and gender equality globally. While not every voice could be included in this book, the work being done in these fields—and the experiences of women behind it—remain essential and has deeply inspired us in our journeys.

We also want to thank allies and colleagues of all genders who make our professional lives so enjoyable.

On a personal note, we want to thank the men in our lives for their patience, love and support!

Maja: Thank you to my ever supportive, trusting husband Dino Zulumovic and sons Andrej and Jan who are now very tired of listening about gender equality.

Manal: Thank you to my husband, Eric Mottu for his unwavering support and patience during all this project. And to my sons: Rami, the first person to read my chapter and my fiercest critic and supporter, and Nadim, my cheerful technical advisor.

A final word: during the preparation of this book, some of the women featured in its pages were living directly or indirectly through war, bombardments, displacements, and terror. We stand in solidarity with them and with all those whose lives have been affected by war and violence.

Foreword

Those of us who have had the privilege to serve in government understand that public finance is not simply about figures on a page. It is about choices. It is about what we build, who we protect, how we prepare for the future, and whether the people we serve can feel, in their daily lives, that the state is working for them.

A budget is one of the clearest expressions of a country's priorities. It tells a story about what we value, what we are prepared to defend, and what kind of society we are trying to become. When properly used, public finance can open doors, correct unfairness, strengthen communities, and give people the chance not only to survive, but to live with dignity and possibility.

That is why this book matters.

I have learned in public life that the hardest decisions are rarely about numbers alone. They are about people. They are about the mother trying to keep her family together after a storm, the young woman seeking opportunity in an economy that was not always designed with her in mind, the public officer trying to stretch limited resources to meet urgent needs, and the country that must find a way to protect its people while still investing in their future. In those moments, public finance becomes deeply personal.

Across the world, women working in ministries of finance, treasuries, audit institutions, parliaments, and public agencies have been helping to shape decisions that affect millions of lives. Many have done so without fanfare. Many have entered rooms where their presence was once unusual, and in some cases, unwelcome. However, they have stayed the course, bringing discipline, judgement, courage, and a fuller understanding of how policy touches people.

Their stories remind us that public financial management cannot be treated as a narrow technical exercise. The management of public resources is deeply human work. It determines whether a child has access to opportunity, whether a family can recover after a shock, whether a country can protect the vulnerable, and whether development reaches those who have too often been asked to wait.

For small island and vulnerable states, this truth is even more urgent. We live on the front line of a climate crisis we did not create, but which demands from us constant preparation, adaptation, and resilience. We are being asked to plan differently, borrow differently, invest differently, and protect our people differently. These are not abstract policy debates. They are matters of survival, fairness, and national dignity.

We know, too, that the burdens of crisis are not carried equally. When families are displaced, when livelihoods are interrupted, when social protection is stretched, and when communities are forced to rebuild, women are often among those who carry the heaviest responsibilities. Any fiscal system that fails to see this reality will fall short of the people it is meant to serve.

Gender-responsive budgeting should never be interpreted as placing women in a separate category of concern. It is about making better decisions, and asking sharper questions. Who benefits? Who is left out? Who carries the cost? Who is in the room when choices are made? Whose experience is trusted as part of the evidence?

I recognise something familiar in the women whose stories are gathered in these pages: the quiet discipline of those who know that serious work is not always glamorous, but it is necessary. They have worked within complex institutions, pushed against old assumptions, and helped to show that fiscal responsibility and social justice are not enemies. Indeed, the strongest societies are those that understand that prudence and fairness must walk together.

Their journeys also remind us that leadership does not always announce itself loudly. Sometimes it begins quietly, in the willingness to do the difficult work, to challenge what has become comfortable, and to insist that institutions must serve people better. That kind of leadership is no less powerful because it is steady. In many ways, it is the leadership that changes nations.

I welcome this volume because it gives rightful space to voices that public finance needs to hear. It does not only ask us to celebrate women in the field. It asks us to listen to what their experiences reveal about the systems we have inherited, the reforms we still require, and the future we must build.

May these stories encourage more women to see themselves not only as participants in public finance, but as leaders, reformers, and architects of more just societies. May they remind all of us that the purpose of public finance is not the balancing of accounts alone, but the building of lives, the protection of dignity, and the creation of opportunity for all our people.

The Hon. Mia Amor Mottley, S.C., M.P.
Prime Minister of Barbados

Preface

Is your story worth telling?

Your professional story, your personal story, your life story?

Two years ago, I was sitting on a plane somewhere over Indonesia, thinking about all the women I've met over my 20-year career in public financial management (PFM) and gender budgeting. In that deeply male-dominated PFM world, every time I met a woman, I was struck. Struck by how quickly we would 'click' and connect, how fast we would sit and talk about our lives, our paths, our reasons for being in that room. I was also impressed by how hard she worked, how educated she was, how rich our conversations could be. And yet—those conversations always stayed between us because our stories just didn't belong in the serious world of our professional duties. Or so we thought.

On that very flight I was also thinking how I wanted to know more about Manal Fouad. At the time, Manal was working with the IMF as a Division Chief in the Fiscal Affairs Department of the IMF. I had only met her once years earlier, and since then we had collaborated indirectly. Manal would sometimes like my social media posts. Why did liking my posts matter to me?

Because after years of posting only work-related technical updates, I began writing more about gender equality, reflecting on the state of international development, and occasionally sharing something personal, even a random selfie. I felt the need to challenge the topics and the 'professional' persona we are expected to show in our professional settings and networks. And Manal always liked those reflections.

So, I was thinking: *I would really like to know more about this woman. I want to hear her story.* All I knew was that she was an Egyptian woman working in a powerful institution traditionally shaped by masculine norms. I was sure her story would be interesting. And I realised I wanted to know it—and tell it—because I knew she herself probably never would. Because we rarely do. And by 'we,' I mean women working inside bureaucracies around the world, especially in public finance. I have always believed that our stories matter and deserve a place in professional discussions on PFM because they help show whose lives are reflected in fiscal decisions, whose are left out, and why paying attention to these experiences matters for building PFM spaces that are fairer and more inclusive.

So I reached out to Manal and the idea for this book was born.

Maja

An anecdote comes back to me. I had newly joined a PFM division at the IMF in a managerial role. On International Women's Day (March 8) I organised a PFM women's lunch for the two PFM divisions. It was an opportunity to get to know each other (some of us had never spoken together), chat in a relaxed setting, and just have fun. We must have been around eight women or so, and everyone seemed to enjoy it. But as we walked back to the office, I was puzzled when one of the women expressed guilt that we were betraying the 'guys.' No one questioned the exclusion of the 'others' (women, and national minorities) when our male colleagues played squash together, went for drinks, sat with their feet on the desk, and gave each other the best assignments. Yet when we just ventured to lunch together, some of us felt like traitors.

When I joined the IMF, in the early 1990s, I was one of the very few Arab (men and women) economists. Two decades later, when I began working in PFM, the sense that I was an intruder was even sharper. It was not just that there were so few women like me. It was an atmosphere heavily dominated by men and deeply steeped in Anglo-Saxon traditions (not just culturally but also intellectually, which impacted the advice we gave to countries). Years later, the women's lunch, a small gesture towards creating a space for ourselves, left some worried about betraying the boys' club.

All this left me perplexed.

My first encounter with gender budgeting was in 2016 when Maja Bosnić came to present the Ukraine gender budgeting project to us (see her chapter in this book in which she describes her trepidations stepping into the IMF space). Finally, here was a field that could open up so many opportunities and reflections to elevate our PFM work to explicitly support equality, and impact women and girls. I continued to follow Maja on social media, and was charmed by her free thinking, authenticity, and her generosity in sharing her enthusiasm.

So, a few years later, when Maja shared with me her idea to do a book on women in PFM and gender budgeting, I enthusiastically agreed without fully knowing what this adventure would turn out to be. I just knew that such a book would provide some answers to my perplexity. A year later, with the manuscript in hand, I know I was absolutely right.

Manal

We hope that in reading this book, you will find it as inspiring and resourceful as we have.

Manal and Maja

About the Editors

Maja Bosnić is a senior economist with over two decades of experience in public and corporate financial management, specialising in gender and climate-responsive budgeting. She led one of the world's largest projects on gender budgeting, the Gender Budgeting in Ukraine Project, funded by the Swedish Government, from 2013 to 2020. She has collaborated with major international financial institutions, including the International Monetary Fund (IMF) and the World Bank Group. She is the co-founder of *Claim. Impact*, a consultancy firm specialising in green and gender budgeting. She is a sought-after speaker on the intersection of gender and finance, delivering a highly viewed TED Talk at the TEDWomen Conference in Palm Springs in 2021, which has garnered close to 2 million views.

Manal Fouad is a former Assistant Director and Division Chief at the IMF's Fiscal Affairs Department, with over 30 years of experience in fiscal policy and capacity development in the public financial management and budgeting area around the world. She has numerous publications including as co-editor of the book *Well Spent: How Strong Infrastructure Governance Can End Waste in Public Investment*. She has represented the IMF in various international fora, including the G20 Infrastructure Working Group.

Contributors

Amina Bambara Billa is a former Minister of Budget of Burkina Faso and is currently a public financial management advisor working internationally.

Hajar Ben Ameur is responsible for budget reform at the Ministry of Economy and Finance in Morocco, specialising notably in gender-responsive and performance budgeting.

Maja Bosnić is a gender budgeting and public financial management expert working in international development with international financial institutions, including the World Bank and the International Monetary Fund.

Nordia Campbell, a Jamaican national, is a former Budget Director at the Turks and Caicos Islands Ministry of Finance, and currently a public financial management advisor working internationally.

Lekha Chakraborty is a professor at the National Institute of Public Finance and Policy, New Delhi, a research faculty member at the Levy Economics Institute of Bard College, New York, and a board member of the International Institute of Public Finance.

Marine Destrez, a French national, is a public financial management advisor and governance specialist working globally.

Diane Elson is a feminist economist and an Advisor to the UK Women Budget Group. She is currently Emeritus Professor at the Department of Sociology of the University of Essex, and a Visiting Professor, at the WiSE Centre for Economic Justice, Glasgow Caledonian University.

Manal Fouad is an Egyptian public financial management expert and a former Assistant Director and Division Chief in the Fiscal Affairs Department of the International Monetary Fund.

Ayesha Javed is a civil servant and public financial management expert. She currently holds the position of Deputy Secretary at the Ministry of Finance of Pakistan where she manages the federal budget and leads strategic budgeting reforms.

Sepideh Labani Motlagh is the founder of Equalab Consulting and a Senior Consultant specialised in gender equality and social inclusion, with experience supporting governments and multilateral organisations globally.

Ermira Lubani is an Albanian gender budgeting expert working with UN Women on public finance and gender equality.

Thokozile Madonko is a researcher and policy analyst at the Southern Centre for Inequality Studies, University of the Witwatersrand (Wits) in South Africa, where she manages the Public Economy Project.

Lamia Moubayed is President of the Public Finance Institute in Lebanon and Vice-Chair of the United Nations Committee of Experts on Public Administration.

Ana Patricia Muñoz, an Ecuadorian, is the Executive Director of the International Budget Partnership. She previously served as Assistant Vice President at the Federal Reserve Bank of Boston and as Executive Director of FARO, a leading Ecuadorian think tank.

Scherie Nicol is a Senior Policy Analyst at the OECD, working internationally in the field of public finance.

Angela O'Hagan is Professor Emerita at Glasgow Caledonian University whose work focuses on public finance, gender budgeting, and feminist analysis in public policy. She is a founding member of the Scottish Women's Budget Group.

Trinish Padayachee is a South-African/Canadian public finance professional currently at the Ministry of Finance of Canada, as Gender Budgeting Lead.

Maya Rostanty is an Indonesian public financial management expert with focus on gender responsive budgeting and fiscal decentralisation. She is a Senior Advisor at PATTIRO, Indonesia's first governance-focused civil society organisation and consultant to several development partners.

Catharina Schmitz is a Swedish consultant specialising in gender-responsive budgeting and public finance advisory work, with extensive experience in international development cooperation, and is currently working with the Asian Development Bank.

Oksana Tsiupa is a professor of public finance and is a driving force behind Ukraine's efforts to integrate gender-responsive approaches into its budgeting processes.

Sureni Weerathunga is a Sri Lankan economist currently pursuing a PhD in Economics at the University of Glasgow. She previously worked as a Research Analyst at the Fiscal Affairs Department of the IMF, and as a Senior Research Analyst at Verité Research in Sri Lanka.

Urška Zrinski, a Slovenian national, is a Senior Public Sector Specialist at the World Bank. She led the development of the PEFA Gender Framework, a global tool for assessing how public financial management systems support gender equality.

Chapter 1

Introduction

Looking Inside Public Financial Management and Gender in Budgeting

Maja Bosnić and Manal Fouad

Introduction

Much has been written about public financial management (PFM) and its role in managing government resources efficiently and responsibly to deliver services to citizens. Most publications come in the form of reports, manuals, handbooks, and technical notes. The literature is rich and detailed, but it is also almost exclusively about numbers, efficiency, and scorecards: how to reduce fiscal deficits, improve accounting systems, strengthen budget credibility, or manage public debt. These are necessary and important topics, but are only part of the larger context of who public finance is for and who gets to shape it.

This book wants to tell a missing piece of the story: the 'inside' story of PFM—reflecting on the people working in the PFM world, and, more specifically, women. Starting from the premise that personal stories matter, the book provides first-person accounts of women's lived experiences in seeking to shape decision-making and impact public finance outcomes. Why women? Because in a field dominated by men, having a seat at the table and framing the policies from the perspective of equality is the only way to ensure that policies do not only reflect the perceptions and biases of the dominant group. Women share their experiences in persistence, reform, and resistance, reinforcing the idea that PFM cannot be understood as a purely neutral or technical field: it is inherently political. To quote from Thoko Madonko in the last chapter of the book, "These perspectives expand our frameworks and remind us that economics and PFM are not neutral—they are deeply political disciplines with histories of inclusion and exclusion."

In parallel, the book also focuses on gender responsive budgeting (GRB)[1] which represents a clear example of how PFM can connect with broader social and gender equality objectives. In this sense, GRB is not an 'add-on' to PFM, but part of its evolution toward people-focused, outcome-oriented public finance for fairer and more equitable societies.

DOI: 10.4324/9781003732532-1

Looking Inside PFM: Institutions, People, and Power

In its traditional definition, PFM refers to the set of laws, rules, systems, and processes used by governments to mobilise revenue, allocate public funds, undertake public spending, account for funds, and audit results (Box 1.1).[2] PFM is the enabler of fiscal policy strategies and objectives.

More recently, the conversation has started to shift. Increasing attention is being paid to what and how PFM institutions deliver services to citizens. Greater emphasis is finally being given to issues such as the impact of policy priorities on various population groups, whether spending is equitable, and whether public finance policies effectively address development needs, gender equality, and environmental concerns. With this nascent shift in focus from purely technical to addressing more political and social concerns, PFM spaces are becoming more attentive to outcome-based reforms.

But like in many other 'rules-based' institutions, one critical dimension remains conspicuously absent for the PFM literature and debates: the 'inside.' By inside, we mean the *people* within the institutions that think about, design, redesign, support, and implement PFM reforms. These include the leaders and staff of ministries of finance, international organisations, expert communities, capacity-building teams, and reform support teams. PFM is often presented as a world of rules and systems, yet those systems are conceived, interpreted, and enforced by people, and they impact people's lives.

Despite this, a deeply rooted assumption persists in PFM: that the personal (i.e. lived experiences and the social setting and structures of class, race, and gender that shape them) are separate from the professional and therefore irrelevant to technical work. As in other areas of public administration, bureaucrats are often expected to serve the system, not to reflect on how the system shapes them, or how they, in turn, shape it.

When we look inside the public finance space, we find institutions that are often rigid, closed and traditional, shaped by unchallenged legacies and groupthink. And while there has been progress, the world of PFM, in conceptual frameworks, practice and institutional reform design and support, remains largely dominated by men, who disseminate the Western models they are familiar with, failing to recognise the specificities of political and cultural contexts and the reality of capacity constraints.

Many influential PFM books are authored by men, often native English-speakers from the Global North. High-level discussions, expert panels, reform missions, and working groups, even those tasked with 'rethinking PFM,'[3] remain male-dominated with few women represented. To discuss the achievement of PFM objectives, it is important to acknowledge this reality and discuss whether this also impacts the design and implementation of public finance policy objectives, including when it comes to gender policies. Within this context, GRB can hardly succeed if it ignores the gendered reality of the PFM world itself.

Box 1.1 Some Definitions

Public Financial Management (PFM) refers to the set of institutions, laws, processes, and procedures through which governments plan, direct, control, and account for public financial resources—covering revenue collection, budgeting, spending, accounting, reporting, and auditing—to support sound fiscal policy, efficient resource allocation, transparency, and accountability (Cangiano, Curristine, and Lazare, 2013).

Budgeting is narrower than PFM. It refers to the formulation process through which governments translate policy priorities into a financial plan by allocating resources in the annual budget and medium-term plans. It involves preparing, negotiating, and approving expenditure and revenue plans that give effect to government policies and priorities, and can be expanded to include budget execution and ex-post reporting.

Gender Responsive Budgeting (GRB) recognises that state budgets impact men and women differently and thus need to be formulated and analysed through a gender lens. It is defined by UN Women as "an approach to systematically integrate gender equality objectives into government policy, planning, budgeting, monitoring, evaluation, and audit. It aims to highlight the distributive impacts of the budget (revenue and expenditure) on women and men and adjusts [or reallocates] resources to ensure that both benefit equally from government resources." (UN Women, 2022)

Gender Budgeting Within PFM

GRB has been part of PFM reforms for well over three decades. At its core, it recognises that budgets impact women and men differently and requires budget analysis through a gender lens—examining how public finance decisions affect groups of people differently and gender equality more broadly. It emerged in the mid-1990s and gained institutional force through the 1995 Beijing Platform for Action, which called on governments to integrate gender analysis into all stages of policymaking, including budgets.

Pioneers of the GRB concept in the 1990s were feminist economists and activists who sought to make public finance responsive to women's lived realities. Key contributions were made by women such as Debbie Budlender, Diane Elson, and Rhonda Sharp, who helped establish the foundations of gender budgeting. Debbie Budlender played a central role in developing and documenting some of the first gender budget initiatives, particularly through practical analysis and advocacy in South Africa. Diane Elson contributed important theoretical frameworks, emphasising the need to assess how macroeconomic policies and public budgets affect gender equality and unpaid care work (see also Chapter 17). Rhonda

Sharp advanced gender budgeting by linking feminist economic theory with public finance, highlighting how government spending and taxation can be evaluated through a gender lens to promote equity. Taking the analytical frameworks into practice from the 1990s to the early 2010s, much of this work—particularly in Eastern Europe during periods of transition—was led by NGOs, research institutes, think tanks, and later UN Women. While essential, this work often took place outside ministries of finance, limiting its systemic impact.

Ten years after the Beijing Platform for Action, another pivotal moment for gender budgeting came with the United Nations Member States adoption in 2015 of the Sustainable Development Goals (SDGs), as part of the broader 2030 Agenda for Sustainable Development. SDG 5 focuses on achieving gender equality and empowering all women and girls, ensuring full and effective participation at all levels and eliminating discrimination and gender-based violence. With countries required to report on their progress towards achieving all SDGs, this gave an impetus to adopt GRB. Thus, gender budgeting entered mainstream PFM reform agendas. International organisations such as the IMF, World Bank, and OECD increasingly framed it as a natural extension of results-oriented PFM.[4] This shift brought gender considerations, which were previously under the authority of social or 'women's' ministries, and largely unfunded, into budget systems and under the purview of ministries of finance, giving them greater technical legitimacy, funding, and hopefully making the reform more sustainable.

Yet even as gender budgeting has become institutionalised, it remains largely discussed in technical terms. The people dimension—who works on it, under what conditions, and within what power structures—remains under-explored.

Gender, Resistance, and Representation in PFM

An Atlantic Council study from 2023 highlights the extent of the gender imbalance in economic policy making. Only 26 of the IMF's 190 member countries had women appointed as finance ministers and just 17 had women as central bank governors. This means that only 11.3 percent of policymakers in these two roles are women, compared to a global average of 22.8 percent for women serving as cabinet ministers overall.[5] The reasons for this disparity are multiple: male dominance in the study of economics, structural barriers to promotion, and persistent social perceptions about women's abilities in finance and economics. These dynamics shape not only who leads PFM systems, but also whose perspectives are reflected in policies and outcomes.

The lived reality of PFM capacity development and reform support has long been highly gendered, reflecting and reinforcing unequal gender norms. For many women, going on PFM missions means travelling and working in teams dominated, if not entirely composed, of men. North–South dynamics further complicate this picture, intersecting with gender to determine whose expertise is valued, who designs reforms, and who implements them.

Why Women's Stories in PFM Matter

This book shares unprecedented insider narratives from women shaping PFM and GRB. In doing so, it challenges two assumptions that have long shaped the field. First, that women in PFM do not have distinct experiences, that PFM is a gender-neutral technical field where practitioners do the same work based on training and merit regardless of their gender. In reality, and as chapters in this book relate, many women describe having to do twice as much to 'get there,' precisely because they are minorities in a field that renders them invisible.

Second, it challenges the persisting notion that the personal is irrelevant to professional, technical work. This book takes the view that the personal is political *and* professional. Personal stories matter. They cannot simply be buried under technical reports and policy briefs. As the chapters show, many contributors entered the field of public finance driven by major historical ruptures and marked by the political environment they grew up in, a social conscience, and reactions to inequality, civil unrest, dictatorships, or wars. These motivations shape how they understand budgets, policy priorities, and reform outcomes to effect change for better, more people-centred public policies that promote human rights. The authors clearly articulate how these moments shaped fiscal institutions, budget norms, and the policy space for gender-responsive approaches, rather than leaving these connections implicit.

By centring women's experiences, their lived realities and perspectives, the book connects the internal dynamics of PFM institutions with the external outcomes of PFM systems. Who designs budgets, who implements reforms, and whose voices are heard all matter for whether public finance systems deliver more just and inclusive results. It also highlights the importance of building alliances and collaboration to advance social and economic progress.

Who We Are

This book follows the journeys and reflections of 22 women who either narrate their stories or converse with each other. Many of them work in government or international organisations and are accustomed to drafting technical and policy documents. Yet when given the pen, they tell powerful stories of achievements, challenges, aspirations, grit, and resilience and they do so with honesty, humour, and lucidity.

The women in this book span generations, from baby boomers to millennials, and come from Europe, Africa, Asia, North and Latin America, and the Caribbean. We meet women who grew up in Burkina Faso, Ecuador, India, Jamaica, Pakistan, Sweden and other countries. The barriers they faced are distinct with relation to race, class, geography, upbringing, and life chances in general. The differences are also compounded by stark Global North–South differences in living conditions.

They studied economics, law, accounting, development, and social sciences. Some were first in their families to study at university and secure a government job. Some were raised by parents with little or no formal education while others had parents with PhDs. Most talk about the importance of and support from their family (or lack thereof). For many women, studying and making a career meant leaving behind the familial home and facing a big city alone, in what many describe as a pivotal moment in their life.

Contributors to the book have pursued careers paths taking them through ministries of finance, central banks, international organisations, civil society organisations, consultancy firms, academia, research institutes and policy think tanks. Some identify as activists or feminists; others do not. Many reflect on patriarchal societies and institutions as they are now and how to adapt or effect change from within. Their stories are also about the importance of support systems, mentors, and solidarity in the workplace.

One theme that resonates across the narratives is the influence of the political context women grew up in and how this shaped their ambitions to make the world a more equitable and inclusive place. Whether it is in Apartheid South Africa, post-communist Albania, or war-torn Lebanon or Ukraine, the profound commitment to improve lives is present throughout the personal stories, highlighting how these intersect with professional trajectories.

Structure of the Book

With the rich diversity of intersecting themes emerging across chapters, we explored a number of potential structures for the book. We opted for four parts that focus on the main resonances in the respective trajectories, while keeping a diversity of space and time.

Part I, "Women *in* PFM: Navigating the Boys' Club" relates the stories of women whose careers focused on broad PFM issues, with a determination to drive transformative, power-shifting agendas within established and often resistant institutions and institutional frameworks. In this part, the authors navigate their professional journeys in male-dominated institutions and networks where men maintain exclusive influence and privilege, highlighting entrenched patterns of gendered access and power.[6] Sometimes unable to read the unspoken codes and feeling out place, each in her own way finds a pathway through the long-standing 'rules of the game,' paving the way for more inclusive and dynamic approaches to public finance.

Ana Patricia Muñoz opens the storytelling in **Chapter 2**, with an essay on growing up in Ecuador where she observed from an early age the pervasive effects of inequalities. Through a career that takes her from the Federal Reserve Bank of Boston to leading a global civil society organisation devoted to fiscal transparency and equity, her story is a quest for and commitment to social justice.

In **Chapter 3**, in a piece resonating with Ana Patricia's, Manal Fouad offers a frank and pithy account of how an Egyptian woman navigates a powerful global organisation such as the IMF while trying to reconcile her personal and professional personas. She describes the challenges of grappling with issues of gender and race in an organisation lacking racial diversity, offers insights on how to run a harmonious work environment, and reflects on PFM as an instrument to enable social justice and human rights.

With Amina Bambara Billa in **Chapter 4**, we are immersed in the story of how a successful student who had to sell street food to make ends meet becomes a Minister of Budget. Amina also provides insights on reform and change management, emphasising the need to build bridges across stakeholders and the identification of champions who can lead and sustain transformative change.

In **Chapter 5**, Urška Zrinski, whose professional experience takes place a few years after the preceding authors, relates with humility, curiosity, and optimism her journey from Slovenia to the World Bank. Like Manal, she reflects on how to navigate male-dominated environments while remaining authentic. Like others, she pushes for change from within, including through tools to include gender budgeting in PFM. She places a strong emphasis on networking and solidarity.

In the subsequent two chapters we read the accounts of women who spearheaded transformations within national institutions and governments. In **Chapter 6**, Ayesha Javed brings alive the story of how a girl born in the mountains of Kashmir scales to the heights of the Ministry of Finance of Pakistan through persistence, determination and the support of allies. She deliberately works to increase women's recruitment in government institutions and becomes a role model for other girls.

Chapter 7 follows Oksana Tsiupa's journey to become an influential voice that combines analytical precision with a sensitivity to societal needs in a country where (familiarly) a woman often had to prove her competence twice over. At the heart of the story lies the evolution of GRB in Ukraine, providing an example of sustaining reforms durably in a country facing war while protecting its acquired institutional achievements.

Part II, "Finding Ourselves *in* Gender Budgeting" shifts the narrative to a greater focus on how gender budgeting impacted the life of the authors at a profound, almost visceral level. These are stories about the indelible role gender budgeting played in the life and life choices of the authors. This part explores feminist responses (whether implicit or explicit) to orthodox professional expectations.

In **Chapter 8**, Lekha Chakraborty offers a candid personal glimpse into the emotional experiences and traumas that have led her to find solace in GRB.

She shares how her mother's life story drove her relentless desire to work on gender equality and how this inspired her academic work to become a leading economist in the field.

Maja Bosnić reflects in **Chapter 9** on her 'infatuation' with gender budgeting, set against the patriarchal world of international development and PFM. She traces her journey from childhood during the civil war in Bosnia and Herzegovina to leading one of the world's largest GRB projects in Ukraine, while navigating the tensions of motherhood and career, and ultimately sharing her message through a TED Talk with two million views.

In contrast to Lekha and Maja, the discovery of GRB comes to Hajar Ben Ameur later in her career as a defining moment of self-reckoning, as she relates in **Chapter 10.** Constantly torn by the need to reconcile the traditional role expected from her and the professional life she aspires to, GRB transforms her professional mandate into a deep commitment to gender equality.

Closing Part II, Ermira Lubani recounts in **Chapter 11** that when she stumbled into GRB, it felt both unfamiliar and urgent all at once. What started as a job quickly became a mission: to turn public finance into a tool for equity. From student protests in Albania in the 1990s to UN programmes, she has carried her lived experience into a world of budgets and systems, proving that behind every number is a story that can make the world fairer.

Part III, "From Margin to Mainstream: Gender *in* Budgeting" relates the lived experiences of women in what O'Hagan and Klatzer[7] observe as the shift of GRB from the margins to the mainstream of public finance that took place in the early 2000s. Authors recount the transformational nature of their gender budgeting work within institutional settings, influenced by feminist economists and gender budgeting pioneers, as well as by the new interest of international organisations in GRB.

Chapter 12 opens this part with a crisp interview with Maya Rostanty from PATTIRO, a civil society organisation working with local communities across Indonesia. Compelled by a commitment to reduce inequalities and improve the poor living conditions observed around her while growing up, she dedicates her career to improving citizens welfare through advocacy, public participation, and collaboration with the government to make budgets more gender responsive.

'Academic activist' Angela O'Hagan gives an account in **Chapter 13** of the feminist gender budgeting movement in Scotland, starting in the late 1990s with the establishment of the Scottish Women's Budget Group, and progressing over time, facilitated by Scotland's innovative experience with the devolution of public finance institutions to the sub-national levels. Her commitment to activism, advocacy, research, and policy implementation presents a unique blend that exemplifies how the personal is political.

Nordia Campbell recounts in **Chapter 14** her experience growing up in rural Jamaica, moving to the city, raising a son by herself, and pursuing opportunities through risk-taking and hard work. Her narrative provides vivid examples of coping with personal and professional challenges, including when integrity in civil service is threatened. Nordia's reflections on the role of gender and opportunities for young men offers both resonances and dissonances with other contributors, pointing to some challenges for GRB.

Catharina Schmitz reflects on the development cooperation world and its handling of PFM and GRB work in **Chapter 15**. Influenced by her upbringing in rural Sweden, a relatively egalitarian society with an established feminist movement, she feels compelled to support gender equality elsewhere in the world.

In **Chapter 16**, Lamia El Moubayed shifts gears with a critical examination of PFM reforms in Lebanon, where the institutional setting is marred with dysfunctionalities, disillusions, and a strong patriarchal system. A defining moment of 'victory' is when she establishes collaboration with a CSO to publish a Citizens Budget. She is candid about disappointments, setbacks, and accomplishments and successes.

Part IV, "Reflections and Conversations" both concludes the volume by offering critiques and reflections on feminist journeys, and opens up conversations on strategies forward, particularly at the current crossroads, when progress on gender budgeting remains politically fragile or even at risk of reversal.

Diane Elson, a gender budgeting pioneer whose influence is demonstrated across several chapters in the book, opens up the conversation with **Chapter 17**. She gives a concise reflection on her early involvement in gender budgeting as a feminist economist, and highlights the importance of working with allies. She offers a blend of pessimism and optimism in her thoughts on ways forward.

In **Chapter 18**, Trinish Padayachee offers a profound reflection on how lived experiences are closely intertwined with the professional, based on her comparative PFM work from South Africa to Canada. Apartheid showed her how budgets entrenched racial and gender inequalities and PFM offered her a chance to use fiscal policy as a tool to reduce inequality and strengthen accountability. She offers incisive insights on how, by lacking diverse perspectives, public finance risks crafting policies that prioritise dominant groups while neglecting the most vulnerable.

Angela O'Hagan weaves together in **Chapter 19** the various threads of the authors' explorations through the lens of key feminist theories and analytical frameworks, emphasising the various approaches to gender mainstreaming as an institutional turn in feminist public policymaking. Highlighting the high degree of thematic coherence across chapters, despite the wide range of geographic, institutional, and political contexts, she demonstrates that the shared experiences of reform, resistance, and persistence create a consistent narrative across the volume.

Chapter 20 departs from the storytelling approach and offers a refreshing and stimulating discussion by five women around the topics of feminism, PFM, GRB and international development. In a free-flowing roundtable format, Maja Bosnić facilitates an exchange with Marine Destrez, Sepideh Labani, Thoko Madonko, Scherie Nicol, and Sureni Weerathunga that is filled with authenticity, depth, and camaraderie. Through resonating anecdotes, they reflect on what it means to be a working mother, to navigate patriarchal institutions, to raise global awareness about gender equality, and to persist, particularly in today's increasingly hostile and regressive political environment. The conversation addresses strategies for adapting to changing contexts, mechanisms for advancing power-shifting agendas and reforms, and the importance of solidarity, role models, and women's networks. Above all, the conversation is about making women's contributions visible, ensuring that their voices and achievements are recognised.

Notes

1 In this book, we use the concepts of gender budgeting and gender responsive budgeting interchangeably, depending on the context.
2 Cangiano, Curristine, and Lazare, 2013.
3 See for example, Tim Williamson, Paolo de Renzio, Jordi Baños-Rovira, 2025, Reimagining Public Finance – Clarifying the Agenda, IMF PFM Blog, https://blog-pfm.imf.org/en/pfmblog/2025/11/reimagining-public-finance
4 See for example IMF, 2017, Alonso-Albarran et al. (2021), and PEFA Gender https://www.pefa.org/gender
5 Yin (2023)
6 We want to clarify that in global organisations, not all men are part of the boys' club. The boys' club entails strong bonding and networking related to language and culture, often excluding men from the non-dominant culture. Likewise, we have also seen many women find their way into the boys' club.
7 Klatzer, E. and A. O'Hagan. 2020.

References

Alonso-Albarran, Virginia, Teresa Curristine, Gemma Preston, Alberto Soler, Nino Tchelishvili, and Sureni Weerathunga. 2021. *Gender Budgeting in G20 Countries*, IMF Working Paper 21/269. Washington DC.

Cangiano, Marco, Teresa Curristine, and Michel Lazare (Eds.) 2013. *Public Financial Management and Its Emerging Architecture.* IMF, Washington DC.

International Monetary Fund. 2017. *Gender Budgeting in G7 Countries*, IMF Policy Papers, April 19. Washington. DC.

Klatzer, E. and A. O'Hagan. 2020. "Moving Boundaries with Gender Budgeting: From the Margins to the Mainstream" in Marcuzzo, Maria Cristina, Ghislain Deleplace, Paolo Paesani (eds.), *New Perspectives on Political Economy and Its History.* London: Palgrave Macmillan.

PEFA Secretariat. 2020. *Supplementary Framework for Assessing Gender Responsive Public Financial Management: Guidance for Assessment Teams.* Washington DC: PEFA Secretariat.

UN Women. 2022. *Action Kit: Engaging Parliaments in Gender Responsive Budgeting.*
Williamson, T., P. de Renzio, & J. Baños-Rovira. 2025. "Reimagining Public Finance – Clarifying the Agenda." 17 November, IMF PFM Blog.
Yin, Jessie. 2023. "Only 11 Percent of Finance Ministers and Central Bank Governors are Women." *Econographics, Atlantic Council*, June 2.

Part I

Women *in* PFM: Navigating the Boys' Club

Chapter 2

An Unconventional Path from Central Bank to Civil Society

Ana Patricia Muñoz

Where it All Began

I was born and raised in Ecuador, a small, diverse, beautiful Latin American country. Ecuador has a rich cultural heritage, but as I grew, I also witnessed the terrible effects of intergenerational inequality. We had so many natural resources, yet that starkly contrasted with the awful levels of poverty I saw around me.

Both my mother and father migrated to the capital, Quito, when they were young to look for better opportunities. Both had lost one of their parents at a very young age. My mother had 12 siblings and has always been an important pillar of my extended family. My father was a judge, and many relatives on my mother's side were activists and politicians. My father's and my uncles' roles in seeking social justice shaped my view on the importance of public service. Witnessing the infinite generosity my mother always had to welcome and help family and friends without asking anything in return influenced how I saw life and the responsibility each of us has to support each other.

One early memory that stands out is when I was about seven years old. One of my uncles was the president of a public university's student association and in that role he used to work with activists fighting for better workers and students' rights. After a family gathering, I went with him to pick something up from the tiny apartment he shared with his siblings, and when we walked in, everything was in disarray. The police had raided the apartment without notice or authorisation. I felt confused and physically ill. Why did the police do this? My uncle was just fighting to ensure people who needed the most had better opportunities.

This experience, coupled with seeing my father tirelessly work to improve the justice system, instilled in me a deep desire to understand the root causes of exclusion and inequality and to actively seek solutions.

This passion led me to pursue a career in economics, where I could combine mathematical rigour and analytical skills with my commitment to addressing social issues. However, I quickly learned that no theoretical

DOI: 10.4324/9781003732532-3

framework or analytical tool could fully capture the complexities of the world or correct the power imbalances that underpin many of its injustices.

In my final undergraduate year, I served as an economic advisor in the Ecuadorian Congress, focusing primarily on promoting a fair distribution of revenues from the extractive industries—and strategies to mitigate disparities. For decades, oil has been Ecuador's primary export and source of revenue—but the territories where oil comes from were among the poorest and didn't get even the most basic services.

My visit to the Amazon during this time was eye-opening. I remember how isolated local communities were from the capital and the people who were making decisions that would affect their lives. We had to drive for nine hours then take a small plane and then a canoe for another four hours just to reach them. A human rights activist came with us, and I remember how impressed I was when I saw her interviewing not only the area's leader but also local residents to get a deep understanding of the problems they were facing and hearing about the pressure they would get from private companies to let them drill for oil on their land.

This exposure to the inequalities faced by these communities that had been marginalised filled me with rage and frustration. When I returned to Quito, I directly engaged with legislators, advocating for evidence-based public policy and the integration of research with advocacy that included affected communities. A barrier I faced then was the dismissive way male legislators treated women advisors. At that time, only 16 percent of congressional members were women, and it was rare to find a female advisor specialising in economics. In meetings with congressmen (all men), as I was trying to make the case for a better way to redistribute the oil revenues that mainly came from one of the poorest provinces in the country, I was never acknowledged as an economist, despite my rigorous analyses. It was disheartening to experience that, but it did not stop me from pursuing what has become my life's passion—bringing economics together with public policy to change people's lives, particularly in crafting structural solutions that account for entrenched interests and power dynamics.

The experience also showed me how important it is to adopt a gender-intersectional lens in public finance (though I didn't know what to call it at that time). In these historically marginalised communities, I saw that women disproportionately bore the brunt of socio-economic challenges, facing higher rates of disease, limited access to basic services, and gender-based violence.

Full of dreams and seeking answers, I was fortunate to get an academic scholarship to pursue a graduate degree, first in Economics of Development in Canada and then in Public Policy in the US. After completing my graduate studies, in the wake of the 2008 financial crisis, I joined the Federal Reserve Bank of Boston as a research associate, eventually becoming one of the first Latina Assistant Vice Presidents. But it certainly wasn't a smooth ride. English was my third language, so I wasn't fluent when I arrived, and I needed to wait nearly two years for a job promotion due to red tape in the immigration system. When I saw the job posting I wasn't sure they would even consider non-US candidates. I clearly remember reaching out to a research assistant who had also migrated to the US to ask if I could apply, and she encouraged me to do so. After a few years, my boss asked why I had applied for that job for which I was overqualified. My answer was simple, I was eager to learn and take advantage of all the opportunities and I also knew I needed to prove myself.

I was incredibly lucky to find a mentor in my first boss, another woman economist. Like all economists at the Fed, she was very strong on quantitative analysis and in presenting her findings. She expected no less from me. She would correct my write-ups and ask me to write them again. She had the patience to provide continuous feedback. She always had faith in me to succeed.

I co-authored several papers with her and presented at several high-level conferences (something that was not very common for a research associate). She helped me gain the confidence to be comfortable speaking to a room full of PhD economists and I just jumped into the pool and fell in love with public speaking. She also listened attentively to my desire to go beyond analysis and support real change in people's lives. My drive and her support led me to shift gears in my area of focus as I started working more directly on issues that affect underserved communities.

I focused on cities with the highest concentrated poverty rates in Massachusetts. I would drive for hours to reach places that had seen deep economic decline and spend the day talking to mostly immigrants about the harsh challenges they faced. Seeing that huge gap of growth and prosperity within the US was jarring. And I thought the Fed should do more, I should do more. I eventually moved to the community development department as a policy analyst where I worked with colleagues who supported my ideas even though they seemed risky for an institution such as the Fed.

One of my first projects in this new role was to co-lead an initiative to bring together the banking industry (an industry in which most leaders are still men) and local housing organisations to reduce the number of foreclosures in the aftermath of the 2008 financial crisis, one of the worst financial crises the world has ever experienced.

Later on, I joined a group of groundbreaking researchers such as Darrick Hamilton who were working on measuring and addressing racial wealth disparities. I proudly co-authored "The Color of Wealth in Boston" report that became one of the most viewed publications from the Boston Fed. Yet, for me, that wasn't enough. Once the evidence was out there, I led a multi-sectoral group (including the private sector, community-based organisations, policymakers and academia) that generated concrete proposals to reduce racial wealth inequalities. These were included in the City of Boston's resiliency strategy. It has been very rewarding to see that, even after ten years, the national public radio reported that this research had one of the "most repeated statistics in Boston."[1] This wouldn't have happened if I hadn't had the support from senior leadership to take risks and run with it. I am forever grateful for that.

Slowly, my focus was shifting from pure analysis to impact.

Going from studying economics in the Global South to working at the most influential central bank in the world was a dream come true. However, for me, purpose and family come first. Working on racial wealth inequality changed my life forever. It convinced me that reducing inequalities is a moral imperative and that to do so effectively one has to recognise one's own privilege, my own privilege. I was also shocked by the gaps that existed even in wealthy countries. I couldn't stop thinking about the bigger challenges that developing countries faced, including, and especially, my own.

Coming Back to My Roots

In 2017, my family and I returned to Ecuador—a decision made with no job prospects at the time. Driven by strong family ties and the conviction that we could contribute meaningfully to our country, we embraced the challenge. It was also a wonderful opportunity for our two children to connect with their roots. I was fortunate to assume the role of executive director at FARO, a prominent Ecuadorian think tank. I led a team of brilliant young leaders and worked with organisations across Latin America on issues including the improvement of labour conditions for informal workers, education, democracy, fiscal and economic issues, and inequality. Building a shared agenda for social change showed me that the traditional economic models and ways of measuring growth and well-being have important structural weaknesses that need to be addressed.

My contributions extended to national and international forums with multilateral institutions, UN agencies, and the OECD, where I was often the only woman addressing economic reforms from a civil society perspective. I was invited by the Ecuadorian National Assembly to comment on proposals for tax reforms and public-finance-related issues. And yes, most of the time I was the only woman talking about economic reforms. This might sound disheartening, but it only strengthened my resolve to take up space in those rooms and pave the way for other women to follow.

Full Circle

In 2023, I joined the International Budget Partnership (IBP) as its second executive director (and first woman to lead the organisation), completing a full-circle journey that began with analysing public budgets in Ecuador's National Assembly. My career has consistently straddled research, advocacy, and collaboration with civil society and grassroots organisations. At IBP, I am well-positioned to influence public resource governance on a global scale, especially as we confront rising inequality, shrinking civic spaces, and escalating climate crises that disproportionately affect communities that have been excluded. Transformative change is possible by advocating for equitable and efficient public resource allocation, addressing power imbalances, and ensuring that budgets reflect community needs. As an organisation we are also committed to ensuring everything we do is through an intersectional gender lens. We firmly believe that giving a voice to the traditionally voiceless and inviting women and groups that have been marginalised to the table where decisions are being made is the only way to achieve true equity. I think back to those women in the Amazon just trying to survive. And I'm even more determined to right those intergenerational wrongs and continue to work with and learn from our partners across 125 countries.

I am continually inspired by the collaborative efforts between technical civil society organisations and grassroots movements, often led by women, to identify and address bottlenecks in public debt accountability, taxation systems, public finance management and service delivery, resulting in improved agricultural, healthcare, and sanitation services.

Does Gender Matter?

Has my identity as a woman shaped my perception of my role and work? Has it complicated my success in a predominantly male field? There are both subtle and overt challenges. Seemingly small things such as the lack of a breastfeeding space at work while I was nursing my firstborn showed me first-hand that women's priorities were not the priorities in the workplace. On a larger scale, the fact that I need to continually articulate how important it is to include gender in policymaking shows that the work for gender parity is far from over.

On a personal level, I vividly recall being elected president of the National Federation of Civil Society Organisations in Ecuador, composed of over 100 organisations. During a photo opportunity, a male counterpart turned to me and said, "You look like a Christmas princess." Those kinds of chauvinistic 'compliments' are not only unwelcome, but they also insult the leadership role that I was undertaking.

On another occasion, I was invited to speak on a high-level panel about fiscal conditions. After I spoke, another panellist grabbed my arm and said (on live television), "Let me explain to you how this works." Even though I was confident of my presentation backed up by data and research, internally I froze. This kind of 'mansplaining' needs to stop. In many societies, it is still rare to have a woman commenting on fiscal issues. The fact is, on most panels discussing economic themes, I have been the only woman. It is frustrating but not very surprising when around the world, only 11 percent of the heads of ministries of finance or central banks are women.

We need to make sure that diverse views are part of policymaking.

While women bring unique perspectives, it is essential to recognise our diverse abilities and interests. I often received invitations framed through a lens of social analysis rather than economics. Gradually, I hope to have demonstrated that one can embody both roles—engaging in rigorous public finance analysis while advocating for social justice.

Representation matters, and it is our collective responsibility to address both conscious and unconscious biases that limit women's engagement in fields that remain predominantly accessible to men. This endeavour is not only beneficial for women; it is advantageous for society as a whole.

Balancing Family and Professional Life

I have been fortunate to have a robust support system that has allowed me to pursue my professional path and take risks. However, I still grapple with 'mother guilt.' The thought of missing a doctor's appointment or my children's school performances weighs heavily on me, especially when my work requires me to travel extensively. Talking to other women who share similar experiences has been invaluable. Research indicates that working mothers positively influence their children's development. Still, that is easier said than done. I am also very conscious that not all women have the family support that I have.

Beyond the personal impact, motherhood has illuminated the intergenerational effects of public policies and how opportunities are often dictated by factors such as birthplace, gender, or skin colour. The privileges some enjoy can profoundly shape future generations unless intentional fiscal, economic, and social policies are enacted to facilitate genuine transformation.

My Inspiration and Drive Come from My Family

My career was on the rise and life felt perfect when at 24, my father was killed inside a local bakery where he had gone to buy bread. A thief entered and tried to rob the owner, my father tried to intervene and was killed instantly.

My father was a good person with a huge heart. And part of what he instilled in me is that everyone deserves dignity and respect. Both he and my mother were always concerned with supporting others. At one point or another my mother welcomed at least six family members to live with us when they needed it and she will always put others before herself.

Just recently, we also learned that my father's uncle helped 200 Jewish families flee the Holocaust, giving them Ecuadorean passports while he was ambassador to Sweden. It caused him to lose his post, and he died in obscurity until researchers recently discovered what he'd done.

Learning about my great uncle connected me again to my own father. Even if he never knew what his uncle had done, he was the same kind of person, the kind of person I also hope to be.

Something I have always asked myself is "How can I make a difference?" You see missionaries travelling to distant countries. You see others creating innovations with their hands. I always have that kind of guilt, "Am I doing enough." One thing I've realised is that as the head of an organisation committed to structural change at the national and global level, I have the privilege and the opportunity to help make lasting change. Scaling is important; sustaining change is important. Through public policy, through economic changes, through pushing through as a woman in a world that still mainly belongs to men, that's how I can contribute. And that is incredibly gratifying.

Final Thoughts: Gender and Budgeting in Civil Society

Having worked across various sectors—public, legislative, civil society, and academia—I find profound fulfilment in influencing public finance from a civil society perspective. A civic space that encourages participation is fundamental to the functioning of inclusive democracies. Working within a mission-driven organisation alongside like-minded entities is both challenging and rewarding. The innovation, creativity, and commitment inherent in the third sector are vital for challenging the status quo.

While there are significant challenges, particularly related to fundraising pressures, organisations such as the IBP provide the freedom, flexibility, and opportunity to innovate. Our sole agenda is to enhance opportunities for communities that have been systematically marginalised, ultimately benefiting society as a whole, and that is invaluable.

Note

1 Rios, S. (2021, July 8). *$8: The Complicated Story Behind One of the Most Repeated Statistics About Boston*. WBUR. https://www.wbur.org/news/2021/07/08/greater-boston-black-families-net-worth

References

Munoz, A. P., Kim, M., Chang, M., Jackson, R., Hamilton, D., & Darity, W. A. (2015). *The Color of Wealth in Boston*. Federal Reserve Bank of Boston, Duke University, The New School. https://www.bostonfed.org/publications/one-time-pubs/color-of-wealth.aspx.

Rios, S. (2021, July 8). *$8: The Complicated Story Behind One of the Most Repeated Statistics About Boston*. WBUR. https://www.wbur.org/news/2021/07/08/greater-boston-black-families-net-worth.

Chapter 3

Finding Solace in Public Financial Management

Manal Fouad

February 2, 2011. I am sitting in a restaurant in Damascus with my four male colleagues, having a quick bite following our day-long meetings. I am watching CNN on the muted TV screen in the restaurant and see distressing scenes of men on horses and camels trying to crush protestors in Cairo.[1] I am speechless and consumed with worry while my (Western and very kind) colleagues explain to me what is happening in my own country and why the uprising is dangerous for regional stability. We are on a work trip in a country where social media is banned, and all I want to do is to go back to my hotel room, use my VPN, and follow what is happening on the ground. In Egypt, the 'Arab spring' protests had been going on for nine days, every one bringing its share of hopes, worries, and frustrations. I try to act cool but also try to convey to my colleagues that this is not their story and that whatever the outcome, agency should be given to the people protesting in the streets, disappearing, and getting arrested, just because all they want is a future with dignity for themselves and their kids.

When uprisings started, first in Tunisia, then in Egypt, my friends at home and I thought this was a life-changing moment. The youth were demanding bread, freedom, and social justice, and were giving older generations a lesson in peaceful protests and courage. It was something we and our parents had aspired to, and which was present in our subconsciousness throughout our upbringing, though we never thought it would materialise. When the Tunisian dictator Ben Ali left in exile, we all cheered and realised it was feasible to topple a dictator. It opened a whole realm of dreams and trust in the future. When my friends and colleagues at the IMF worried about the chaos that would ensue or when the IMF started to think of new 'programmes' to support regime change, emulating those following the fall of the Berlin Wall, I felt alienated: it was such a hopeful moment, and it was not about an IMF programme! How could I ever explain to them the euphoria? On a personal level, I felt distraught and could not reconcile my professional persona and the real me.

During this period, I was on leave without pay from the IMF, accompanying my husband on an external assignment in Lebanon, during which I

DOI: 10.4324/9781003732532-4

was working as a consultant for various international organisations. It was a welcome break to be away from the IMF for two years, reconnecting with the Middle East, spending time with my young boys and trying to figure out what I want to do 'when I grow up.' It is during this period that I started to work on capacity-development in public financial management (PFM) and discovered that this was a field that closely aligned with my values and ethical aspirations. PFM, as a field that recognises the budget as the most important policy document for a government, opened prospects that enthused me. This was an area where I could help build capacity in formulating policy, managing resources, reporting on outcomes, and above all, holding governments accountable to their citizens. While I could not necessarily influence government policies, I could at least help provide tools that could lead governments to use their budgets to address inequalities, tackle climate change, while being transparent about their policies. That was something that motivated me profoundly.

Growing Up

I had a comfortable and happy upbringing. My parents, both of a middle-class background, came from Assiut, the largest city in the south of Egypt. Nothing had prepared my father to be a diplomat: no one had done it in his family, he had never travelled abroad, and he had no connections. It was by chance that he heard about and took the exams to enter the Ministry of Foreign Affairs. Months later, my parents would be travelling to Lisbon for my father to take up his first post as an attaché at the embassy of the United Arab Republic (the short-lived union between Egypt and Syria). They would spend five years there, and this is where I was born.

Growing up in different countries during the late sixties and seventies with a left-leaning father created my political consciousness and formed my commitment to social justice. I was born a few years after the 'Year of Africa,' when sub-Saharan African countries gained independence from colonial rule. With Portugal being among the last powers to hold colonies in Africa, and Egypt's Nasser's strong role in supporting independence movements, stories about this period marked my first encounters with political engagement. When I was two years old, we moved to Cambodia. This was during the Vietnam war, and my first political recollections were about Vietnamese resistance. The Vietnam war was very present in our conversations, values, and even daily lives.

As an only child who never spent more than four years in the same school, I learned to adapt and be flexible. I was lucky to always go to small French schools where it was easy to make friends. I think this is where I learnt to 'blend,' which would come in handy later at work. Ironically, though, it is in my own country, when I went to the Cairo French Lycée for two years of secondary school, that I discovered discrimination and post-colonial behaviour. I was one of the first 'local' students to be admitted in the Lycée, and while nothing was personal, I was confronted constantly with prejudiced remarks about my country. It was hard to integrate.

It was perhaps during this period that I began to be extremely shy; my desire not to be noticed became very acute and stifled me. While I learned to live with it, it never went away, and I would always suffer from being labelled as "too reserved" in my professional life. It is much less excused to be quiet for a woman than for a man. I noticed at work that a soft-spoken man would be considered as a "wise genius" if no one could hear what he was saying, while a similar woman would be considered weak, unassertive, and perhaps someone who has nothing to say. However, experiencing shyness is also something that shaped me as a colleague and later as a manager: I think it made me more empathetic as I also felt for others in uncomfortable situations. I learned to read the room (as I was trying to hide) and make appropriate and well-thought decisions that were more focused on impact for others.

Sitting at the Grown-ups' Table

When I joined the IMF in 1992 and was assigned to the Middle East Department, I was its only 'professional' woman (i.e. holding a non-administrative position). Arab men were also very few, so I was a good combination of both minorities. The explicit excuse for not hiring women until that time was that it was difficult to send them to Arab countries, an excuse as pathetic as the decision itself. Fortunately, as I joined, there was a change in the department's management, and a restructuring that led to having more women in the department. Still, throughout my career, I cannot count the number of instances I went on an all-male missions or when I was the only woman in the division.

Early in my career, I joined the Fiscal Affairs Department (FAD), which was to become what I consider my home for the rest of my IMF career. It was in FAD that I first experienced working with women bosses: first, my division chief Adrienne Cheasty, and then the department director Teresa Ter-Minassian. Both were inspiring women from whom I learnt a lot. From Adrienne, I learned how to evolve in a male-dominated world, what are the things not to do (e.g., "do not use the adverb 'very,' which demonstrates emotion and is thus too 'feminine'," "do not send unpolished documents, as first impressions count") and the things to do ("always know what you are talking about, be thorough so that you are not vulnerable"). From Teresa, I learned how to be a leader who cared about her department, who knew every single staff member, and who drove the contributions of the department to respond to institutional needs and at the service of the member countries. It was quite difficult to adapt to the particular nature of the institution, and I felt quite lonely, even though I made friends quickly. Ydahlia Metzgen, was my friend, my mentor, and my support system; she is from Belize and had joined the IMF a couple of years before me, coming from Wall Street. We never worked together, but she helped me decode the unsaid and the unwritten and to navigate the boys' club. We understood each other, and I could not have made it in my early years at the IMF without her friendship.

One of the types of assignments that I most enjoyed was to be the fiscal focal point in country teams negotiating IMF programmes.[2] I liked the long meetings with staff of the ministries of finance when we worked together as a team trying to find solutions and do the best for the country. I spent a long period working on Jordan and I believe this is where my knowledge of budgets and interest in fiscal transparency all started.

One thing that marked me was my participation in a working group on improving gender diversity within IMF staff, which was a welcome eye-opener. This group comprised men and women from all nationalities; it met regularly and candidly discussed issues related to gender diversity. It was similar to group therapy! We would share stories, laugh and feel desperate about the patriarchy. The most vocal staff were women, and I realised we all had commonalities, but we just did not share them publicly. The big realisation was that we were all experiencing pressure to fit in a mould—that of the Anglo-Saxon male. The onus was on us to emulate our male colleagues and not on them to change the system to find a place for everyone. My personal experience was telling: there was a total lack of sensitivity of senior white men towards how this work environment could be something unfamiliar and intimidating to a woman like me. No one asked my opinion, encouraged me to speak up or gave me the floor if I didn't impose myself.

The accepted fact of fitting the mould was something I tried to fight constantly on a personal level. I proudly thought of my cultural heritage, the richness of my history (both national and personal), the diversity in my upbringing to centre myself and feel comfortable with who I am. I decorated my office with pictures that reminded me of where I came from and that brought me immense comfort. I did not fit the mould, but in the end I was appreciated and remained true to myself.

Like many people in big organisations, after about ten years in FAD, I started to feel restless and stuck. It was the 2008 global financial crisis; work was intense and interesting but not necessarily going the way I wanted. I wanted to change and didn't know what to do next. This was when the opportunity to take leave and follow my husband for an overseas assignment in Lebanon arose, something I never regretted. Leave without pay is a great institutional benefit that provides a welcome breather and an opportunity to see the world from a different angle. To me, it was turning point that allowed me to recharge my batteries, reinvigorate me professionally, and increase my self-confidence.

PFM as a Way of Life

In Lebanon, I worked as a consultant, providing 'macrofiscal' advice and training for a couple of international organisations. Many of my assignments were 'hands-on' capacity-building, mostly on strategic budgeting. I helped the staff of ministries of finance of various Arab countries to prepare medium-term fiscal projections, draft a Budget Strategy document, or simply report transparently on fiscal outturns. Once again, I was back to what I enjoyed most: spending days in their offices and working in partnership to improve capacity.

I also worked for about four months at the UNICEF Lebanon office as a Social Policy Advisor. I was charged with establishing a dialogue and presenting a roadmap to the Ministry of Finance on children and women-friendly budgeting. This was in the late 2000s and was still considered a new area for UNICEF. This was a wonderful opportunity to work on something with a strong social justice component without the limitations I faced in other organisations. UNICEF considers respect for human rights as part of its mandate, and it encouraged the use of a human rights narrative in developing capacity, something that would have been considered too political in Bretton Woods institutions. I also met fantastic colleagues working on health, education, and sanitation for children and women, including refugees, and consider that this experience was full of enriching lessons for the manager and PFM practitioner I would later become.

When I returned to the IMF Headquarters, I took up positions fully devoted to capacity-development in two different departments and worked mostly on fiscal policy and PFM. By that time, I had obtained a managerial position in which I could autonomously provide intellectual and strategic direction with impact while aligning with the corporate objectives. The last seven years of my IMF career, when I headed one of the PFM divisions in FAD, were the most enjoyable and fulfilling years of my career.

First, I was working on topics I liked. As mentioned earlier, I thought PFM was as close as one could get in the IMF to advocating for social justice, equality, good governance and accountability. Second, I had a brilliant team, with great country diversity, and at many times full gender parity; they were creative, motivated, and passionate about their work. Third, we worked on innovative topics, putting PFM forward at the service of development and SDG needs, gender equality, climate adaptation, and infrastructure governance for the efficient, transparent and accountable use of resources for public investment. Fourth, I had the privilege of building bridges with other organisations, forging partnerships and promoting our complementary work. Here, I would mention that—again going back to my commitment to my personal values—one of the most rewarding experiences was to collaborate with the Global Initiative for Fiscal Transparency (GIFT) and the International Budget Partnership (IBP) where for some moments I could feel I was part of civil society. When we developed the PFM online course (PFMx MOOC), we gave GIFT and IBP a voice and centred the main messages towards an audience of civil society holding governments accountable, in addition to training government officials. I believe that this contributed to the huge success of the course, and it made me feel that I could be an 'activist' while working at a mainstream organisation.

The Joy of Leading a Diverse and Passionate Team

I enjoyed people management, which was a blessing given that I led one of the largest divisions in the IMF (with a lot of staff in the field). I had the reputation of being a good leader and I owe this to my excellent team and my upbringing. As I said, I had a very large 'dream team.' They had more technical expertise than I could ever have, and I saw my role as a facilitator and coach rather than as a boss. After all, many of them had already had accomplished careers in their countries and most were working in a capacity-development division because they had a passion for transferring knowledge and know-how. I knew how the organisation worked and was good at anticipating areas that would become strategically relevant. My commitment was to IMF country members, how to help them and raise their capacity. I believed that every staff member had something to provide and that my role was to find the right assignments, challenges and matches. A division needs all competencies to be successful, but the key was to work together as a team to complement each other and ensure high quality outputs. I also thought language skills were key to building relationships with government counterparts, and when recruiting staff, I attached high importance to this—from personal experience, I could see how much can be 'lost in translation' and how much trust can be gained when you can communicate in the same language.

I also did not shy away from taking risks and charting new ground, and this usually turned out for the best. I listened and let people work on topics they liked, just ensuring a link with the broader corporate mandate and how it could fit together. It is in this vein that we started work on gender budgeting, green budgeting, digitalisation, governance, and other topics. I guess I can summarise my management style as relaxed and empathetic, which I could afford because I was a 'child' of the institution, knew the nuts and bolts, the requirements, the leeway and the boundaries, which made me confident enough to manage the division in the best way I saw fit.

Lately, when my father passed away, and I read tributes written by his colleagues, I realised that a lot of who I am as a manager was inherited from him subconsciously. I always knew that my father was considered a mentor by many younger colleagues. Like me, he liked managing down more than up. Cohorts of younger diplomats considered him a mentor or coach. He provided them with support, advice and comfort. Once, a friend told me that in the Ministry of Foreign Affairs, my father was viewed as an example of how to make an impactful career and successfully represent your country abroad when you do not always support your country's policies and international positions and while remaining true to your values (without 'selling your soul'). He always stood in favour of those treated unfairly, or not given equal opportunities, many of whom were women. When I read these tributes, I recognised myself. Like him, I made the best out of working in an imposing institution, feeling like a 'rebel' but not really being seen as such.

Blending and Survival

I often look back in wonder at how I made it for 30 years in an organisation such as the IMF. When I joined, I thought I would be there to gain experience for a few years only. Coming from a minority background, I suffered from impostor syndrome and constantly felt that I was different and that I didn't fit. But the reality was that I was torn between two worlds. On the one hand I was working in one of the most prestigious international organisations, very white and male-dominated, where, especially in my early years there, neoliberal economic policies were considered sacrosanct. On the other hand, I hailed from a social network in Egypt with artists, academics, and activists who considered the IMF to be 'evil.' I wanted to tell the latter that, no, the IMF is not so bad, that it is full of good people who are trying to do their best to help countries grow sustainably and without escalating debt. And I wanted to tell the former: what are you doing, why are you lazily repeating economic mantras without thinking about the consequences on people's lives and livelihoods?

I think there were two reasons I managed to stay that long and have a successful career: first, as I mentioned above, I had a gift for blending naturally given my upbringing in different countries and schools. I was a 'cool person' and a cool person goes with what is given, does not complain, and navigates without creating waves. I did not like conflict and avoidable confrontation, and I used humour and sarcasm to survive in the most uncomfortable situations. I put up stoically with various annoyances and microinequities, trying not to be drawn down by it. The second reason I survived is that the IMF itself evolved in 30 years. When I joined, it was an austere, dark-suit, white, male-dominated organisation, only promoting structural adjustment and economic efficiency; it was all about numbers as if real people did not exist. But gradually, the organisation opened up, both in terms of staffing, with a more conscious effort to diversify, and of policy recommendations, with an honest introspection on past mistakes, more focus on inequalities, gender inclusion, and more equally distributed growth. I felt the reconciliation between my two worlds starting to succeed when my Egyptian activist friends thanked the IMF for being the only organisation able to hold the government accountable and more transparent. It is still not perfect, but we are getting there.

Being able to blend and have cordial relations and lasting friendships worked well for me, but the flip side is that the so-called 'white passing' does not protect you from micro-aggressions and experiencing prejudice. I believe these unconscious biases were not intended, but they shook me every time I was confronted with them, especially the stereotypes about Arabs. Sometimes in meetings, I played a game in my head categorising people in the room: how many were white men, how many were white women, how many were from Africa or the Middle East, and of those, how many were women. I most often ended up with the ratio 1 over n. If I was lucky there could be two people of colour. Such situations lead to self-consciousness and often discomfort.

Recent studies also show that people thrive best when they work on topics they know: it makes them confident and gives them a sense of adding value. In my case, I took the conscious decision that I would like to work on areas where I can deliver at my best and have an impact: public finance and capacity development. I did not do what is expected to climb the ladders of promotion quickly, I knew I would be delayed as a result, and I accepted it for the sake of my well-being. I took leave without pay, and I did not lead programme negotiations and surveillance work because I knew I would not enjoy it. I was privileged to have a husband and two boys who supported me, and I made the conscious decision that work would not be the only thing in my life. I do not take my path to a successful career for granted and in many ways, I was privileged to have a support system that helped me.

I should emphasise, however, that working at the IMF, you get to interact with people who are very smart, professional, and competent. The strong focus on high quality analysis, data and policy messages is in the organisation's DNA and it is what makes it a respected place to work and learn. I have worked and made lifelong friendships with men and women from all over the world that I will always respect and cherish.

The Ethical Meaning of PFM

I often referred above to PFM allowing me to align my values to the work I was doing. This is the field where I felt most comfortable and true to myself. As mentioned above, my upbringing and personal values evolved around the commitment to social justice, human rights, gender equality and generally progressive ideas. When you get to know colleagues at the IMF, you find out that many hold the same values and tend to identify with left-leaning politics, which may come as a surprise. But many are not politicised and think only in terms of numbers and economic efficiency. This often astounded me because I believe one cannot thrive professionally without a political and social conscience. This is why I managed to mostly avoid work where numbers tended to prevail over political economy realities and difficult policy choices. With public finance you could hope to influence social policies through the budget, or at least you could give the chance to governments to conduct the policies they wanted provided they were sustainable—I do recognise the importance of debt and deficit figures. With PFM work, one could focus on what is ultimately the best the government could do institutionally to be at the service of citizens and be held accountable.

When I retired, I wrote a blog entitled "PFM and human rights" in which I tried to explain this idea and link the broader technical issues to the social and political contexts.[3] I argued that PFM plays a crucial role in supporting human rights. A number of human rights are directly related to fiscal policies and institutions: the right to social security, to participate in public affairs, to health and education, to adequate standard of living, and to access to information, to name a few. Additionally, PFM provides a bridge between the government's fiscal policies and its citizens.

The whole PFM cycle provides tools that will ultimately empower citizens and help them to hold governments to account. Obviously, the budget is the most important policy document that the government produces. But there are many other instruments that are crucial for social justice. For example, incidence analysis of new tax and expenditure policies provides information on the impact of policies on incomes and inequalities, including gender-related policies. The gender budgeting framework and related capacity development of course contribute to closing the gender gap, and the intersectionality with climate and green budgeting go a long way to help climate justice. Fiscal financial and statistical reporting allows citizens to understand whether policies were implemented and why there have been deviations. Public debt management and its sustainability show the impact of future tax obligations of young generations. Fiscal transparency of course is a fundamental tool to ensure government accountability. Strong PFM also plays a key role in reducing vulnerabilities related to the corruption of public officials, and the embezzlement and misuse of taxpayers' money, including by state-owned enterprises and non-budgetary sectors.

Information produced by PFM systems allow supreme audit institutions (SAIs), parliament, and civil society to exercise scrutiny over government policies. They cannot discharge their role of holding the government to account and speak truth to power if the government does not ensure public participation in the discussion of policies, explain strategic policy choices and priorities, and report on outcomes and deviations from intended purposes.

At the same time, a good PFM system cannot function in the absence of a healthy human rights environment. Freedom of expression, a fundamental human right, will allow citizens and civil society organisations to speak truth to power, challenge the government, and result in a more efficient use of taxpayers' money and better service delivery. These are the fundamentals of a well-functioning PFM system that brings the best out of public resource use. In the absence of freedom of expression, government accountability is not only weakened, but also undermined with institutions such as SAIs, and the legislature unable to discharge their duties, and citizens have no voice.

In Conclusion

As I am trying to finish writing my story, the brutal and oppressive regime in Syria has fallen in early December 2024. I watch in awe and joy as prisoners are liberated from prisons, families find out the fates of their disappeared loved ones, and people celebrate. Western media reports on the atrocities of the regime, governments acknowledge the good news about toppling "one of the cruellest regimes" and yet, there is difficulty in letting go of the worries about what the future holds for the "stability of the region." Suddenly, I remember my last mission in Syria during the Arab spring that opened this chapter. I remember working with brilliant young staff at the budget department building capacity on fiscal forecasting. I remember how difficult it was to obtain data on budget execution. They had access to the documents for only a few hours a day and had to photocopy pages to then input numbers in their spreadsheets. The same feelings overwhelm me: why can't you allow people to rejoice about their own liberation, give them agency, credit for what they achieved, and empathy for what they suffered. Yes, tomorrow may be full of disappointment and suffering, as it happened in many Arab Spring countries. But was it worth the sacrifices, the ephemeral moment of pride and sense of freedom? Yes, any time.

Notes

1 This was the so-called 'camel battle' in which thugs paid by the regime were called to disband protests in the city centre.

2 Through such 'fiscal economist' assignment, you integrate into the team from the geographic department working on a particular country (usually but not necessarily a country that receives IMF lending) and get to be the focal point for everything fiscal and budgetary (both in terms of the budget outturns and projections and suggested policy design), work collaboratively with official counterparts and help in programme negotiations.

3 Fouad, Manal, 2023, *PFM and Human Rights*, https://blog-pfm.imf.org/en/pfm blog/2023/03/pfm-and-human-rights IMF PFM Blog, March, Washington DC.

Chapter 4

'Madame Budget-Programme'

Amina Bambara Billa

Introduction

I really wanted to study medicine. But resources were stretched thin in our household and my parents could not afford the luxury of enrolling me in medical school at their expense. So, after obtaining my high school degree (baccalaureate) in 1991, I studied economics instead.

In my studies, I was very curious and my contributions were considered pertinent. A quote from one of my professors, Gueda Jacques Ouedraogo, a Public Finance lecturer at the University of Ouagadougou stuck with me: "Tell me what budget you have, and I will tell you what economic and social policy you have."[1] There and then, my passion for public finance and budgeting was born—together with my secret desire to one day become the Director General of the State Budget. Little did I know that I would one day be Minister of Budget, a role far exceeding my initial dream.

The student '*débrouillardise*'

At university, I had little financial means. So, I decided to apply the economic principles we were learning to real life and generate some income. I joined countless other '*débrouillardise*'[2] entrepreneurs in Burkina Faso's informal sector. I sold groundnuts, bread, and cold water that I froze in plastic bags overnight.

After obtaining my Masters degree in 1995, I struggled to find a job because I did not have the necessary political or social connections; I survived thanks to my small informal street business. In 1997, I was hired part-time by the Burkina national TV as a junior professional in charge of translating the news from French and presenting it in a local language (Bissa). I was overqualified for the job but hoped this would be a back door that might one day help me fulfil my persistent dreams. In the meantime, my informal sector job had expanded into a food kiosk, not quite two square metres in size, selling homemade yogurt, sandwiches, cooked rice and spaghetti. My small business in the informal sector enabled me to live comfortably and with

DOI: 10.4324/9781003732532-5

dignity and kept me happy. Because I was overperforming in my junior TV job, I was soon assigned to an economic desk in the news. This would come in handy later in my career.

After several years, I decided that I needed to more proactively align my actions with my aspirations. So in 2002, after my stint with national TV and my kiosk, I studied for and passed the entrance exam to the National School of Financial Administration (ENAREF) in Burkina Faso. In choosing my field of study, I opted for my dream, public finance, rather than taxation or accounting, even though many of my colleagues preferred the latter options because those fields offered better financial remuneration.

Before graduation at ENAREF, students do an internship, and fortunately mine was at the Ministry of Finance in the Directorate General of the Budget (DGB). I was convinced that this was the royal path to becoming the Director of Budget, especially since I had the chance to be mentored during the internship by an official who was himself passionate about budgeting and who fed my own nascent passion. However, my first disappointment came there and then. As I requested to be assigned to the DGB, specifically to the Budget and Accounts Directorate, I was categorically turned down by the director at the time. For a reason I still do not know, he declared that I could be assigned anywhere I wished except in his directorate!

So I found myself in the Directorate of Payroll and Authorisations, once derogatively nicknamed the 'garage' directorate—as it was considered one of the least interesting directorates in the public financial management (PFM) sector. But I rejected this—I always believed that there is no such thing as a 'garage position,' only 'garage officers'! In this Directorate, as the name suggests, we worked on managing payroll—the most complicated and complex types of expenditure and one that is mastered by very few civil servants. I quickly demonstrated my ability to meet the responsibilities the position required, and I was soon assigned to the Permanent Secretary's office. There I became engaged in macro-budgetary planning, preparing the overall Medium-Term Expenditure Framework (MTEF), and organising budget negotiations with line ministries before the DGB takes over the process of preparing the quantified part (the expenditure allocations) of the draft budget law. From there I was asked to take a position leading the implementation of Burkina Faso's programme-based state budget.[3] One position led to another and, in 2014, some ten years after I first stepped foot in the Ministry of Finance, I had worked my way to becoming the Minister of Budget!

'Madame Budget-Programme'

It was my perseverance through tough times, and tough "No's" together with some luck that brought me to the place where I am today. Three years after my appointment at the Permanent Secretary's office, I attended one of the most transformative trainings I would ever have: a result-based budgeting course in Canada. Canada is one of the leading countries on result-based budgeting, so this provided a unique opportunity to learn first-hand from global leaders in the field. I was one of about 20 participants from several African countries trained in Canada at the time. I was determined to make the most of it. While other participants pursued one certification course, I chose to pursue three courses and managed to be the only one to complete three courses in a single year. So, I worked three-times as hard! Because I only received funding from my government for one certificate, I had to cover the costs of training and of my stay for the other two certificates myself. But I viewed this as an investment in myself and was convinced that the return on that investment would come very soon. I was determined to maximise the benefits of this training. My focus and diligence earned me the nickname "the library mouse." True to my nickname, lunch breaks or between classes found me in the library, captivated not just by the practical and theoretical reading for lessons covered in class, but additional complementary reading.

Upon returning to Burkino Faso, I enthusiastically worked with a critical mass of stakeholders well-versed in the subject, to produce a mission report with recommendations for accelerating the national transition to a programme-based budget. It was 2009—a year that emerged as one of the most pivotal in my life. Just one week after presenting the advocacy report to the Minister of Economy and Finance, and as I was preparing to take up the position of Director of Programming and Financial Policies, the Minister decided to put me in charge of implementing the state's programme-based budget. To persuade me, he challenged: "Do you want to achieve results in a pioneering field at the level of West Africa and even Central Africa, with your name remembered in history since you would have designed everything from start to finish? Or do you want to achieve results in an existing, routine field—certainly with fewer difficulties—where you could be easily forgotten?"

Later, I learned what the Minister reported about our meeting: "I have just found the long-sought person to lead the programme-based budget reform. She has just left my office. It is Mrs Bambara Billa." And so started my long-dreamed-of career in public finance. I was entrusted with the responsibility of implementing the programme-based budget in Burkina Faso. My exciting journey into programme-based budgeting was underway.

After five years of successful implementation, Burkina Faso became the first country in West Africa to transition from an input-based budget to a results-based budget. And I had been affectionately dubbed "*Madame Budget-Programme.*"

Madame Ecofinances

Financial matters are often not easy for the public to understand and learn. They are even less easy to teach through the media; journalists tried, but often with quite glaring mistakes. But after a short time working at the Ministry of Economy and Finance, I was convinced that many problems could be solved or even avoided altogether through improved communication with the public on budget issues. Hence came my idea for a television programme, "Ecofinances," a programme I would host while continuing my senior role at the Ministry. My main guests always included a minister, a director general responsible for the day's topic, a member of parliament, and a representative of civil society, along with an audience of at least 50 multidisciplinary participants, including students, academic researchers, and civil society organisations.

My early passion for and experience in economic journalism, including my job at the national TV station, along with my background in budgeting and finance, proved to be a popular combination and the programme enjoyed high audience growth rates. The programme became a landmark of national TV and ran for 14 years, during which I developed more than a hundred topics on public finance, budgeting, the economy, development, and issues across all sectors of Burkina Faso's economy.

This critical debate programme helped strengthen the capacities of public finance officers, as well as those in the economic and other sectors. Through the critiques and proposals presented, the show contributed to improving public services and further increasing transparency in public management. It also helped drive reforms within public administration and enhanced the image of the administration in the eyes of citizens. My TV programme was really 'running the show' on economics and hence my second nickname came about: "*Madame Ecofinances.*"

While preparing an Ecofinances programme on the 2012 Budget Law, I discovered a quote that encapsulated my choice of a career in budgeting: "Nothing in the workings of the State, and almost nothing important in the country's economic and political life, occur without some budgetary impact."[4] I was thoroughly enjoying my work both on personal and professional level; my conviction that a career in budgeting is not just a profession, but a concrete way for me to contribute to state-building and improved governance in the service of society was strengthened by my experience in the Ministry. And my television programme, Ecofinances, served to guide economic and political choices well beyond public administration, reaching a wider, even international, audience.

Lessons from Budget Reforms and GRB in Togo

After my career in national government, I started working internationally. My engagement in gender responsive budgeting (GRB) began in 2016 in Guinea Conakry, in my role as Team Leader for a technical assistance programme funded by the World Bank (PASAG agricultural sector project).[5] It culminated in 2018 during my tenure as Resident Advisor in PFM in Togo under a donor-funded project. Work on budget reforms was not without challenges, and it allowed me to learn some fundamental lessons on leading reforms of such magnitude.

Finding Champions for Programme and Performance Budgeting[6]

Togo had experienced delays in its timetable to introduce programme-based budgeting. Given the delays, the highest authorities were increasingly invested in accelerating the transition to a programme-based budget when I began my secondment there in 2018. After numerous follow-ups, and with the strategic and diplomatic support of the President of the Republic, we decided to convene a government seminar on the programme-based budget in mid-October 2020 under the direct supervision of the Minister of Economy and Finance with the aim of bringing all the various stakeholders on board. I had the honour and privilege of coordinating the preparation of the intervention modules for the technical directorates. Just several months later, on January 1, 2021, the Togolese state budget was launched in programme-based mode, and the first quarterly implementation report showed very satisfactory results.

But what fear preceded the launch! The day after the government seminar, I was informed of the decision to switch to programme budgeting in the new year. Given that the necessary capacities were not fully in place and the very limited time remaining, I was not confident I was up to challenge. There were barely two months to submit the state budget in a programme-based version to the National Assembly. There also happened to be a new government with many new ministers who did not necessarily understand the input-based budget, let alone the programme-based budget.

Thanks to an organisational plan I had established upon my arrival the country was able to rise to the challenge and produce a high-quality programme-based budget. The plan relied on programme-based budget champions identified within each ministry, a core team of national experts, and targeted capacity-building based on skill transfer through a 'learning by doing' approach. One of the greatest champions of the switch to programme-based budgeting was the Minister of Economy and Finance himself, who regularly participated in workshops to provide input and ensure technical supervision of the work.

Advancing Gender Budgeting

Following the successful implementation of results-based budgeting, I proposed supporting the Ministry of Finance in highlighting the country's efforts to integrate gender into budgeting. Indeed, I had the opportunity to witness on the ground what I had learnt from my readings: Togolese women are an essential pillar of Togo's development. This all started with the example of the pioneering '*Nana Benz*' women of the 1940s. Despite their limited literacy, they demonstrated admirable skills in international trade through the sale of traditional fabrics. They became, in fact, the first wealthy businesswomen in Togo and even in West Africa. Many of them invested in healthcare facilities, culture, and the development and protection of children. Others invested in real estate. My argument for continued gender budgeting work was built around this unique example, complemented by favourable conditions at the time for the promotion of gender in Togo: the first country in West Africa to have a National Assembly led by a woman, a government led by a woman, strategic government positions held by women, a minimum 30 percent gender quota respected in government, and a whole range of other complementary policies supporting girls and women across multiple socio-economic planning sectors.

The challenge was how to integrate gender considerations into the budget process and into budget documents. The programme-based budget successfully implemented provided a major opportunity for GRB in Togo. Within just two budget cycles, the country would become a reference point within the West African Economic and Monetary Union (WAEMU) and in peer-to-peer international training programmes.

Gender budgeting was a new practice with numerous challenges, notably adopting gender-responsiveness in budget design, programming, and monitoring/reporting tools, as well as capacity-building for both the government and non-governmental actors, from the National Assembly to private sector to civil society to carry out these tasks. The main difficulty, beyond technical challenges, is that gender is often considered an abstract rather than a concrete subject.

When it comes to gender, stereotypes, traditions, and customs often lead some civil servants to resist or outright reject the concept, and those who have the power to allocate resources to budget programmes may not be generous enough in funding gender-related actions. Public finance, on the other hand, is widely known and generally accepted by all—it is viewed as a technical area, after all. However, despite challenges, we were able to make recommendations for the inclusion of gender considerations across the budget cycle so that, just like other development initiatives, priorities such as gender could receive full attention in terms of resource allocation. With persistence and several years of hard work, mainly under my technical guidance, we succeeded in introducing GRB ministry by ministry. Since 2025, all

Togolese ministries and national institutions are implementing GRB. We are already seeing the first results and this is very encouraging, especially considering the initial challenges.

Introducing Green Budgeting

In addition to gender budgeting, the programme-based budget also brought a window of opportunity for green budgeting. With climate as a clear development priority to be integrated into the budget, the Togolese government, with my technical and organisational support and guidance, has now embarked on green budgeting—also called climate- and environment-sensitive budgeting. Togo launched its first phase of green budgeting in fiscal year 2024, with nine pilot ministries. The number of participating ministries doubled in 2025.

You Can't Hide the Sun with Your Hand: Reflections on the Evolving Role of Women in Burkina Faso

Reflecting on how I rose to my role, I can say these were eventful years in changing landscapes for women in Burkina Faso. After being largely confined to junior roles for a long time, women have, over the past two decades, begun to occupy increasingly more senior leadership and policymaking positions: minister, technical advisor, director general, and service directors. In the past, women were more likely to be given responsibilities in 'social' ministries. But in the government, women are now appointed to leadership positions in budgetary roles because they are increasingly considered good managers of the budget and payroll. Of the last six ministers of budget[7] positions in Burkina Faso, five were held by women. This increasingly reflects a growing awareness of the role women should play on a par with men in public finance and society in general. Women certainly hold positions of responsibility in public finance. Some directorates, such as the Tax Directorate and the Financial Intelligence Processing Unit (CENTIF), are now led by women as well. However, only one woman has ever been appointed minister of economy and finance among the last six officeholders. And there are other key positions that are rarely held by women. For example, no woman has ever held the position of First President of the Court of Accounts, President of the National Assembly, President of the Supreme Audit Authority, or even President of the Chambers within the Court of Accounts.

In my country, as in many African countries, customs and traditions have so disadvantaged the advancement of girls and women that they are often compelled to exert more effort and invest more than men to achieve the same results. This is true in public service in general, and particularly in the field of public finance. It is also true that from a young age, under the pretext of preparing her to be a good wife, a girl is tasked with household chores even while she is attending school. Meanwhile, the boy is allowed leisure activities or to study after classes.

Moreover, I have often said that society is quicker to tolerate or accept a lack of performance from a man than from a woman. A woman does not have the right to fail and then bounce back, learning from her mistakes. In response, I told myself I have a duty not to fail. I have a duty to succeed—even at the cost of sacrificing those dear to me, who may not have the chance to have me by their side at certain times—for the honour of my country and, above all, for the honour of women. Women's advancement has very often been the driving force behind my struggle, my determination, and my sacrifices to succeed. That is why succeeding in public finance positions is for me not just a sacrifice—it is an objective. Fortunately, it pays, and most of the time, the feedback I hear is a clear "At least you, you deliver results…"

One should also not lose sight of the political contexts in which very difficult and bold reforms, including those on gender and public finance, can be undertaken. Change is much easier when the highest authorities of the country are strongly encouraged to enact laws in favour of gender equality and ensure their implementation. In turn, strong empowerment of women in the National Assembly or in the government will certainly have a future impact on society and the economy. Women's capabilities are abundant; what remains is to empower them through equitable appointments to positions of responsibility. For my generation, appointing women merely to satisfy a gender quota or parity requirements risked stigmatising women. I support the recruitment principle used by many international organisations that favour women: "For equal competencies, female candidates are given preference." If I were not a woman, it is possible that I would not have succeeded in the various positions I have held in public finance. The point is that given opportunity and time, a woman will be recognised and entrusted with responsibility, because, as our proverb says, "You cannot hide the sun with your hand."

Part of this is also recognising that women sometimes decline to take on responsibilities because, even from an early age, their education undermines their self-confidence. Isn't it said in our countries that a woman's success in society is measured in her household? In African societies, there is maternity leave, but no paternity leave. There are also no facilities in administrative buildings for babies to be close to their mother so she can breastfeed during breaks. In the 1980s in Burkina Faso, a pregnant schoolgirl could be expelled from high school and boarding school, while the boy—her classmate and the father of the child—was not excluded. This blatant injustice revealed deeply rooted gender inequalities, even within the education system. Women who make unconventional career choices also encounter significant social pressures, unwarranted criticism, and lack of support in their family, community, educational and professional settings. Naming these barriers is critical to understanding why women are sometimes reluctant to take up professional advancement opportunities.

I take advantage of my success and the praise I receive to educate and raise awareness around me, even often at the highest levels of the state by asking critical questions. Do you really know why some women are reluctant to take on professional responsibilities? Have you tried to understand why some fail—and indeed, just like men? What is being done to support them and lighten their other burdens? I have found that when you ask the pertinent questions, men are more likely to stand in solidarity with women and support us. In fact, pertinent questions are all too rarely asked.

A Balancing Act

Balancing professional and personal life is almost never easy, and one side of the equation often feels more compromised. My personal experience of this has sometimes been bitter. With full candour, I can say that I have sacrificed time with my children for my contribution to the success of public finance, both in Burkina Faso and internationally. These were difficult choices, but success required them. Having held pioneering positions and frequently being the first to introduce key budgetary reforms with no prior experience to draw on at the national or even regional level, I often had to work well beyond regular working days and hours.

This disrupts family life, and not just for the children—spouses also bear the cost. There were times when I was called away, requiring frequent and often long separations. I was apart from my second son for 18 months when he was just one year old because I was training abroad. I had to have him live with a sister in a precarious area without water, electricity, or phone. Fortunately, the love and presence of my sister, who has always motivated and supported me, compensated for my absence. Moreover, my heavy workload in public finance led me to limit the number of children I would have—specifically two, with a ten-year gap—this keeping in mind that in my country the fertility rate at the time was around 6.5 children per woman.

I have always made every effort, during my limited free time, to fully play my role as a wife and especially as a mother. Specifically, I made it a commitment to be present on weekends, cook the children's favourite meals, and attend to their needs. The combination of offering them a powerful role model and consistent commitment to their care at the same time, has, I believe, encouraged my children to become eager defenders of women's causes. They tell me this constantly and demonstrate it in their daily encounters, to the extent that some of their friends do not fully understand the support and advocacy they show for women.

Fortunately, the specific challenges women face in navigating a work–life balance was long anticipated by my father, who was quite visionary regarding gender equality. Although my father was illiterate, he set a single condition for giving his consent to my marriage, addressing his future son-in-law: "It is often observed that young girls are assigned in marriage to men under many customs and traditions. I have never done this, and I will not do so for Amina. I have educated, accompanied, and supported her so that she could reach this level of education. My only condition is that you do not prevent her from completing her university studies and that you commit never to be a barrier to her professional career choices." Thus, I was very well protected by my father, both in my choice of study and in the countries where I would work: he has been and remains my main advocate and advisor.

Lessons From the Eagle: Rising Through the Storm

There are not many shortcuts to succeeding in public finance, especially as a woman. Any woman who wishes to pursue a career in this field must first have self-confidence, technical skills, a satisfactory level of education, and strong interpersonal qualities—and generally at higher levels of all of these than her male peers. A woman who stays technically ahead of the team she will lead or work with will have a solid foundation for success in the field. To achieve this, she must continuously strengthen her skills. She must be an expert in public finance as well as in related fields. She can simultaneously be a mother and wife, a civil servant, a technical advisor, a minister, a prime minister. Simply put: the woman that she wants to be. And she must also understand that success and rest do not go hand in hand: "No one can reach dawn without passing through the night." Leadership positions are ones of struggle and constant challenge. Given an overall context that is not naturally favourable to the promotion of gender equality, a woman must adopt the behaviour of an eagle: "The eagle does not escape the storm; it uses the storm to rise higher." She must turn each difficulty into an advantage and an opportunity.

Women should also insist on living according to their principles and always be guided by their ethical and professional convictions. In my case, I was identified early on as a young staffer who, in handling allocations, was neither pliable nor lenient with public entities that were not in urgent need of public resources. With this reputation, I was often sought after for delicate and technically demanding missions. In a fragile state such as Burkina Faso, given the trade-offs between the limited funds and the expensive needs of the population, these assignments are fast-paced and draining. It is also for this reason that I was nicknamed "*Madame Budgetary Austerity*," but this is a story for another day!

Notes

1 I was inspired by many readings that guided me through my career in public finance, such as: Paul Samuelson's classic *Economics*, published in 1948; Aaron Wildavsky, *Budgeting: A Comparative Theory of Budgetary Processes*, 1975; and Charles E. Lindblom, *Politics and Markets: The World's Political Economic Systems*, 1979.

2 Note from the editor: *débrouillardise* in French literally means 'resourcefulness.' It indicates small jobs in the informal sector, loosely translated here as street peddling.

3 The OECD definition of programme-based budgeting is "the systematic use of performance information to inform budget decisions, either as a direct input to budget-allocation decisions or as contextual information to inform budget planning, and to instil greater transparency and accountability … by providing information to legislators and the public on the purposes of spending and the results achieved."
4 Nathalie Carré de Malberg (éd.), *Le grand état-major financier: les inspecteurs des Finances*, 1918–1946, IGPDE, 2011.
5 *Projet d'Appui au Secteur Agricole de la Guinée* (PASAG), Funded by the World Bank.
6 All the reflections below are from my personal perspective.
7 In many Francophone public administration systems, the Minister of Budget is considered a more junior minister compared to the minister of finance (*ministre délégué.e au budget*). The minister of budget typically handles all the entities in charge of expenditure and revenue (including tax authorities), as well as procurement.

Chapter 5

From Slovenia to the World

Urška Zrinski

Finding My Path

A few summers ago, I was back in Slovenia, enjoying the familiar rhythm of home, when I ran into an editor I knew from the time I worked as a journalist during my university days. He was now leading an online news outlet and told me over coffee about a series he was preparing on Slovenian women with particularly unique career paths, asking me to tell my story and hoping to encourage others to look beyond traditional choices. I found the idea both flattering and slightly amusing. I said yes.

The interviewer assigned to me turned out to be a sports journalist. Of course, that choice made perfect sense once I thought about it. My dad had been a national coach for both the Slovenian men's and women's basketball teams, so naturally, the journalist was curious about how growing up in a sports-centric family had shaped my own career.

It was not something I had really reflected on before, but it clicked as I started talking. I told her that Tina Maze—the legendary Slovenian alpine skier and two-time Olympic champion—had actually played a role in how I prepared for my interview at the World Bank. Maze often said that before a race, she would visualise the entire track—every twist and turn—and picture herself crossing the finish line first. For many of us who grew up in a small, newly independent country, her determination was proof that talent and persistence can carry you far beyond geography. Before my World Bank interview, I decided to do the same. I visualised every possible question they might ask, rehearsed my answers, and imagined staying calm and composed. It worked. I got the job.

Before long, I found myself in a world that was fast-paced, demanding, and far more complex than anything I had studied. What helped me navigate it were the people I met along the way. I have been fortunate to work with women who were not only technically brilliant but also generous with their knowledge and time—colleagues and mentors who showed that strength and kindness can go hand in hand.

My academic journey was no different. Each of my thesis supervisors—from my undergraduate to my doctoral studies—was a woman. At the time, some

DOI: 10.4324/9781003732532-6

advised against that, suggesting that male supervisors might offer more 'reliable' guidance. But I trusted my instincts. My undergraduate supervisor, who later became Slovenia's Minister of Defence, indulged my passion for studying ethnic conflicts and encouraged me to continue my studies abroad. She introduced me to the programme at King's College London, where I focused on ethnic groups in the Northern Caucasus—a region that fascinated me.

When I moved to London in 2003, I had the privilege of studying under two leading scholars in post-Soviet security studies. Their work shaped how I understood fragile states and transitions after conflict. Even now, I follow their research closely, especially as my own work at the World Bank focuses on Ukraine—on how institutions can adapt to support recovery and reconstruction in the midst of the invasion.

My fascination with the Caucasus had started even earlier, when, as part of my international-relations degree at the University of Ljubljana, I chose Russian as my second language. It was not a common choice at the time, but I was drawn to the idea of reading Pushkin and Dostoyevsky in the original. One day, my professor handed me an old book filled with stories from the Caucasus, and I was hooked. I could not stop thinking about it. I even started a small blog where I shared reflections about the region. Eventually, I had to pull myself out of that rabbit hole and refocus—this time on understanding how institutions develop and what drives change.

That curiosity led me into the field of international development, where my doctoral supervisor—Maja Bucar, a pioneer in the discipline in Slovenia—helped me connect theory with practice. Before long, I wanted to see how ideas about governance and reform translated into real-world decisions—how post-conflict societies rebuilt themselves, how institutions found their footing again. When the opportunity came to join the Centre of Excellence in Finance (CEF) in Ljubljana in late 2004, it felt like the natural next step.

Building a Foundation

The CEF had been established in the aftermath of the Yugoslav wars to help countries in South-East Europe rebuild and strengthen their public financial management (PFM) systems. When I joined, it was led by two remarkable women who saw potential in me long before I did: Mira Dubovsek and Jana Repansek. They invested in my growth wholeheartedly, sending me to trainings to strengthen both my technical and leadership skills, and trusting me with responsibilities that at the time felt far beyond my reach. Their guidance shaped not only my career but also my understanding of what leadership can look like when it is generous rather than hierarchical.

Finding my footing professionally took time and more than a little trial and error. I discovered that I learn best through experimentation—by testing ideas and seeing how people and institutions respond. That mindset, encouraged early by supportive mentors, helped me later navigate the often formal and male-dominated worlds of finance and development. I began to understand that confidence does not always mean certainty; sometimes it means showing up with curiosity.

While at the CEF, I also learned that confidence and curiosity are not always enough. Shortly after returning from my studies in London, I was nominated to join a working group preparing Slovenia's participation in the European Development Days—a major EU event that brings together global leaders and development professionals. It was a milestone moment for the country: Slovenia's first appearance as a development partner after transitioning from World Bank borrower status to a donor and development partner role. For me, it felt like an enormous privilege to be part of it.

That excitement did not last. During one of the preparatory meetings, a senior official—perhaps thinking himself witty—suggested that instead of presenting our team's ideas, I could dress in a traditional Slovenian costume and perform a folk dance at the country's stand. The room erupted in laughter. I sat there, silent, humiliated. After all our work, that was his contribution: a reminder that, to some, a young woman's value still lay in her appearance.

No one spoke up, and neither did I. But the moment stayed with me. Years later, I ran into the same man while he was out walking with his wife, and I finally told him how belittling that experience had been. He apologised—whether out of sincerity or politeness, I will never know—but saying it out loud mattered.

Looking back, that moment was my first quiet lesson in resilience. It showed me how easily women's contributions can be diminished, even in well-meaning spaces, and how important it is to reclaim your voice, even if it takes years. It also made me realise that professionalism is not only about mastering the technical; it is about knowing when to speak up—and when silence itself is a form of resolve. That lesson stayed with me as I moved from Ljubljana to Washington DC, stepping onto a much larger stage.

A New Chapter at the World Bank

Joining the World Bank in 2015 was both exhilarating and intimidating. We have a saying in Slovenia: *Bolje biti prvi na vasi kot zadnji v mestu* – "It is better to be the best in the village than the last in the city." That is how it felt to move from a small, agile institution like the CEF to a large, global organisation. I wondered whether the curiosity, warmth, and creativity that had guided my work so far would still have a place in such a structured environment.

My first assignment was with the Public Expenditure and Financial Accountability (PEFA) team, which was updating the diagnostic framework used by development partners to assess how countries manage public finances. I was asked to help organise the global launch of the new framework in

Budapest in 2016. It was a huge responsibility, and I wanted to make it different.

Working with two women entrepreneurs from Ireland, we reimagined what a technical event could look like. Instead of a day filled with PowerPoint presentations and formal speeches, we introduced visual storytelling, interactive polling, and elements designed to make the audience active participants rather than passive listeners. At the time, few would have described a public finance event as "fun," but that was precisely what we achieved. Years later, people would still mention that event with a smile.

Not everyone was convinced at first, and interestingly, some of the most sceptical voices were women. I understood their hesitation—it takes courage to try something new in an environment built on procedure and predictability. Yet I also realised that many of the qualities I had once doubted in myself—empathy, humour, intuition—were precisely the ones that helped make technical work more accessible and people more open to learning.

That experience helped me see that gender in public finance is not only about who sits at the table but also about how we work together, how we listen, and how we bring others in. It reminded me that creativity is not the opposite of rigour but one of its most powerful allies.

The Power of Support

During those first years, I was lucky to find two women who modelled that balance of competence and care. One guided me through the Bank's many layers with generosity and honesty; the other brought warmth and steadiness to our team, making even the most stressful days feel manageable. Between them, they taught me what solidarity among women really means—not as a slogan, but as something lived each day. They showed that leadership can take many forms, and that sometimes the most lasting influence comes not from titles or authority, but from how we make others feel seen.

Their support extended well beyond work. When my daughter was born in Washington, DC—a few weeks earlier than expected—they were the first to show up at my door with food, advice, and reassurance. Before my parents could even get on a plane from Slovenia, they became my stand-in family. It was sisterhood in action, and it shaped how I think about leadership: as something that begins with care.

Professional support also opened doors for creativity. During my time at PEFA, I travelled often—from Senegal to Serbia, from Fiji to the Philippines—but one trip stands out. In New York, at UN Women's headquarters, a group of us were discussing how to measure progress on gender equality through the Sustainable Development Goals. It was there that the idea of developing a PEFA gender module first took shape.

At the time, gender responsive budgeting was still seen as an add-on—something optional, even 'soft,' compared to the so-called 'hard' mechanics of fiscal policy. But budgets are never neutral. They shape who benefits from public spending and whose needs remain invisible. I often thought of my hometown, Celje, and its public parks. My mother, who hikes through them almost every day, loves shaded paths and benches where she can sit and talk with friends. My daughter, on the other hand, wants to shoot hoops and run around the playground. Designing a public park that works for both of them requires different priorities and spending choices. Gender responsive budgeting is about that: recognising that people experience public spaces—and public services—differently and ensuring that budgets respond to those differences.

There was resistance, of course. Change rarely comes without it. But I found an ally in my manager, who not only recognised the importance of integrating gender into PFM diagnostics but also trusted me to lead the process. Together with a small, international team, we developed what became the PEFA Gender Framework—the first global tool to assess how PFM systems support gender equality.

That framework remains one of my proudest professional achievements, not only because of its technical contribution but also because of its timing. I finalised it just after my daughter, Anika Orla, was born. In a way, it felt like a quiet dedication to her—and to the many women who balance ambition with care, work with motherhood, and persistence with doubt.

Lessons from Small Island States

To test whether the PEFA Gender Framework worked in practice, we needed real cases. Our first pilots took us to the Caribbean—Antigua and Barbuda and St Lucia—and that was the start of what became a four-year journey working across the region. I fell in love with the Caribbean almost instantly. Public administrators there are not only deeply professional; they are storytellers. Storytelling is how they teach, persuade, and connect. For someone like me—trained to think in data and frameworks—it was both inspiring and, at times, humbling.

That humility came early. I once spoke at a regional event on gender-responsive budgeting to a room full of formidable women—leaders who had built NGOs to support survivors of gender-based violence. When they asked how to better communicate with parliamentarians, I launched into a technical lecture about data and indicators. Within minutes, I realised I had completely misread the room. They needed stories, not spreadsheets. That moment stayed with me. It reminded me that gender budgeting is not just an analytical exercise—it is about empathy, connection, and whose voices are heard in budget decisions, and whose are not.

The Caribbean taught me that preparation can be both a strength and a trap. For years, I over-prepared for every workshop, fine-tuned every slide, and obsessed over every logistical detail—pens, notebooks, coffee breaks.

Meanwhile, my male colleagues often walked in with little more than confidence and charm—and somehow that was enough. They were the rock stars; I was the stage manager. I used to find that infuriating. But over time, I realised that part of the gender dynamic in our field is exactly that: women often carry both the content and the care. We hold the room together, making sure everyone feels seen, while others simply perform.

It has taken me years to loosen my grip on the need to be over-prepared and perfect. I have learned that I do not need to be perfect to be credible. I can be thoughtful and technical, but also light-hearted and human. If a colleague stops by my office to discuss the new Taylor Swift album, I can join in—and then return to public investment methodologies a minute later. It took me a long time to understand that being professional does not mean erasing who I am.

That realisation was reinforced by allies who understood the importance of inclusion. On one assignment in Asia, a male colleague and I shared the stage during a workshop. When questions came, they were all directed to him—even on topics I had presented. Without missing a beat, he redirected them back to me, framing me as the lead expert. It was a small gesture, but it spoke volumes. I have been fortunate to work with men like him—and with managers who not only supported innovation but insisted that women's voices be heard.

Some of my most fulfilling missions were with what I fondly call my "women's squad." On a trip to Grenada, I worked with two colleagues to help the government advance its digital transformation agenda. One had the gift of storytelling—she led powerful interviews with farmers, entrepreneurs, and single parents to capture how digital tools could change their daily lives. The other had an exceptional grasp of operations, understanding how to turn ideas into systems that actually work. Together, we created the space to speak with the Prime Minister, helping him with his vision for reform and encouraging the inclusion of gender budgeting in the broader digital agenda. It was one of those rare trips where everything clicked—where technical discussions, empathy, and purpose came together in a way that made us feel we were building something lasting.

The work then took me further—across the Pacific. In Tonga, I met a colleague from Fiji who had just begun championing gender budgeting in her country. Watching her grow in confidence, and later seeing her lead her own reforms, reminded me of why this work matters. Gender budgeting is not only about policies or indicators—it is about people, about women supporting one another to step into spaces that once seemed closed.

These experiences, from the Caribbean to the Pacific, reshaped how I see leadership. Gender in budgeting is not a technical add-on; it is a way of rethinking power: who speaks, who listens, who decides. It taught me that leadership can be both rigorous and kind, that authority does not have to silence personality, and that laughter and learning belong in the same room.

Speaking Up

After several years working in the Caribbean and the Pacific, I was invited to give a TED-style talk at the World Bank. My manager at the time believed that the story of how small island states were making their public finances more disaster-resilient and responsive deserved to be shared more widely.

Preparing for that talk was both exhilarating and exhausting. I wanted to capture how governments in places such as Grenada, St Lucia, and St Vincent and the Grenadines were strengthening their systems—not through abstract reforms, but by weaving resilience directly into the way budgets are planned and managed. These were countries that faced hurricanes and volcanic eruptions, and yet their public officials were finding ways to make finance systems part of recovery, not an obstacle to it.

I spent weeks shaping the story. My sister designed the slides—striking, full of colour—and my colleagues helped me rehearse until the words felt genuine. I wanted to show that disaster-resilient and responsive PFM was not just about technical fixes; it was about foresight, empathy, and courage. It was about people who refused to let crises erase progress.

When I finally stepped onto the stage, the lights felt impossibly bright. But then I spotted a group of women in the front row—friends, mentors, and colleagues—smiling back at me. In that instant, the fear faded. I spoke about finance ministers learning to plan for uncertainty, about budget officers rewriting procedures after storms, and about the quiet persistence of women who often led these reforms behind the scenes.

It was not the performance that stayed with me, but the connection: the recognition that what we were doing mattered because it made public finance a little more human. When I walked off that stage, I knew this was the kind of work I wanted to keep doing: bridging the technical with the personal, the numbers with the lives they shape.

Finding Balance

When I look back now, I see that much of my career has unfolded in rooms full of men—finance ministers, budget directors, economists. They speak the language of ratios and rules, and I do too, but I have learned to bring something else into those conversations: empathy, curiosity, and a touch of humour. It took me a long time to realise that I could be both technically strong and unapologetically myself.

Maybe that is the lesson I wish I had learned earlier—that strength does not always need to sound loud. It can be patient, steady, and even a little playful. I no longer feel the need to prove I belong by knowing more or working harder. I belong because I care about this work, because I want public finance to reflect the world we actually live in, not the one written in policy manuals.

And when I need perspective, I find it at home. My husband still teases me about how much I prepare for meetings, and he remains my biggest supporter—the person who believes in me even when I start to doubt myself. Our daughter keeps me grounded. I love playing basketball with her and watching her perfect her K-pop moves in the living room. I want her to grow up knowing that she can become whatever she wants to be—that she does not have to choose between being kind and being strong, between being serious and being joyful.

I have come to believe that women in public finance carry a quiet superpower: the ability to connect rigour with empathy, data with people, and institutions with everyday lives. That is what keeps me here—still curious, still learning, still hopeful that a bit of care can make even the most technical reform a little more human.

Chapter 6

Limitless Skies and Endless Dreams

The Story of a Girl from the Mountains

Ayesha Javed

I was only five years old when my aunt warned me "Your dreams are too high. You need to remain on the ground here, where your life is—your life will be confined to this small space where you are." But deep down, even then, I knew, no one would ever draw a border around my dreams. That was the first big life choice I remember making. It's been my choice ever since.

Like many others, I was raised in a society where girls are supposed to do certain things and not others, behave in a certain way, adopt certain appropriate professions—basically, every aspect of our lives was confined to certain expectations. But from the very beginning, I was not certain about all this certain-ness. Maybe my genes had undergone some mutation! I questioned everything about women's presumed role in society and this has been reflected in every choice I've made in life, from that feisty five-year-old girl in a remote village in Pakistan and up until today, as a globally recognised woman leader in public finance management (PFM).

These days, I regularly have the honour of joining large professional and public gatherings, conferences, technical sessions and meetings focusing on the complex challenges of PFM, socio-economic inequalities and other development issues, where I have been generously introduced as a "Public Finance Leader, Public Finance Expert, Guest of Honour or the Honourable Chair." With each of these introductions, I'm always reminded of those professional meetings I headed back in the day—not so very long ago, when people used to enter the meeting room, sit down in front of me and ask "Who's the Chair?" This is the story of my journey from "Who is the Chair" to "*She* is the Honourable Chair!"

Dark Nights, Bright Dreams

I was born in a small village in Pakistan called Barroh, in the state of Azad Kashmir. My remote mountain village was located within the 'line of control,' a region between Pakistan and India, where, since 1947, regional conflicts have escalated into three wars and several other armed skirmishes. These conflicts repeatedly impacted local communities, my own included—

DOI: 10.4324/9781003732532-7

destroying our lives and livelihoods. Our extended family home was on a hilltop just a few steps away from a military post and when we evacuated, the military used to drag a canon right into our house to utilise its vantage point. Growing up, heavy artillery and cannon shelling was a daily routine. We lost people, cattle and cultivated lands. And we often had to flee to other villages when tensions escalated. Electricity was only available for two to four hours a day and often it took many days for power to be restored when we had power-cuts. The men of my village used to bring water from a far-off pond on the backs of donkeys and mules. There was no hospital or health-care centre in any of the neighbouring villages, and we had to rely on 'medicasters' and quacks.[1] Even today, there are still no paved roads in my village. There are still no supply lines for water delivery to households and still no system for sanitation or the drainage of waste.

When I was a child, there was only one primary school for girls at the top of a hill and to go to high school, girls had to walk nearly three hours a day. This was enough to discourage girls' education; their role in economic participation was unimaginable. Girls were expected to have no more than some basic education, if any at all. But the concept of paid and professional work was non-existent, even if you were able to get some higher education. Even in urban areas, the only acceptable occupation for a girl was a teacher or a doctor. Of course, in these circumstances, nobody in my village ever imagined that I could make my way to college or university.

Back in my village, we used to sleep in the open air. On quiet nights, I lay in bed peering out at the magical night skies, wondering what they saw, what the world looked like beyond our small village and the mountains. But our home was located near a military post, so nights were often filled with the boom of canons and buzz of bullets whizzing overhead, and the darkness scared me. I would squeeze my eyes shut and imagine flying to the moon and sleeping peacefully there. My biggest dream was to be able to attend school and study. But where, when and how? I remember clearly how all I could think about was school and books. Maybe I inherited this obsession from my father, who was a schoolteacher. He decided to move my mother and three siblings (two sisters and one brother, me being the eldest) to a town so his daughters could continue their schooling, while he himself stayed in our home village to continue teaching in the public school there. My parents told us that we would have to compromise on many things to afford this education. I was happy to make all sacrifices, as long as I could carry on with my studies.

On the Other Side of the Mountains

I really wonder if someone sitting in an 'advanced' country can ever imagine how burdened my young mind was at that time. I was determined to perform no less than excellent and to be successful—I had no other option. I stood first in my class throughout my school years and was able to secure a merit scholarship from primary school and through my higher education. I completed three Masters degrees: two in Life Sciences (Biochemistry), and later, because of my interest in the social sciences and to prepare myself for the national civil service examination, I earned an MA in Political Science. My academic performance was valued within my family and community and paved the way not only for my sisters but for other girls in my village to pursue their education.

In my girls-only higher secondary school, we were only three students enrolled in science compared to more than a hundred students enrolled in social sciences. I realised that promoting science and technology in remote areas of our country was necessary for development. As a university student, I joined a non-governmental organisation (NGO), the National Academy of Young Scientists (NAYS), and worked with other volunteers to organise awareness campaigns for the promotion of science and technology, particularly focussing on girls' participation in these fields (which were considered boys' subjects in those days). We also promoted young students' engagement in the sciences through local activities, career counselling, awards and scholarships in far-flung areas, such as my hometown. As a result, more students, especially girls, were motivated and enrolment in science subjects improved considerably.

From Lecturer to Civil Service

I started my full-time career in January 2014 as a lecturer in Biochemistry in a medical college. Training young and brilliant minds was an exciting experience. It also offered me an opportunity to closely observe the challenges in the health and education systems in my country. It sparked the desire to improve these systems in the public sector by influencing the public policy process. And so I chose to become a civil servant. I left my well-paid job as a lecturer and joined the public service with the aim of contributing to national-level policy decisions.

On my first day of work, my boss explained all the challenges and opportunities within civil service and ended his conversation "Ayesha, the sky is the limit for you." I had always had a fundamental objection to this phrase because in a way it still tries to limit your possibilities. I silently rephrased it to: "Even the sky is not my limit." That's been my life's motto ever since.

My journey as a civil servant involved two big challenges. First, there are many stigmas attached to civil servants; for example, they are often considered incompetent, corrupt and rigid bureaucrats who rather than being problem-solvers are part of problem. Second, even in the civil service gender stereotypes remained strong. Despite successfully competing for top level, sophisticated policymaking positions, negative stereotypes of women persisted. Historically, women's participation in civil service in my country has been extremely low. So, the government introduced the quota system to encourage women's participation. But the quota system inadvertently fed the prevailing notion that women were less competent. Also, because of socio-cultural burdens of family, domestic responsibilities and cultural norms, women are often not able to give their 100 percent. Women are often not allowed by family to work late hours or travel alone and they remain the primary providers of childcare and homemaking. Because of these responsibilities, they often shy away from challenging roles. As a result, women in civil service were branded as incompetent, weak and unable to handle professional pressures or master technical knowledge.

In response to this pervasive socio-cultural bias in the workplace, I took on the mission of 're-branding' women professionals. I knew from the beginning that I had to work hard to change this image by setting an example of being a competent, skilled and effective public manager and optimising service delivery. I was determined to be living proof that women are more than capable.

Recruiting Allies

A decade ago, strategic planning and development budgeting were heavily male-dominated. Out of 25 officials working in managerial positions, 29 in technical positions and 11 board members, only two were women. I was desperately looking for opportunities to add some value to the existing system through new initiatives. I found that none of the development policy or public sector development programmes was ever viewed with a gender lens. We did not have any national level policy for gender to guide ministries and departments to include gender responsiveness in health, education, climate, etc. This is when I realised that we needed more women at senior levels to make such changes happen.

When I had the chance to be a member (the only woman) in the screening and recruitment committee for the selection of board members for the Planning Commission, I found my chance. I devoted all my efforts to advocating at every administrative level to include at least one woman as a board member—of course only if she duly qualified for the position! We reached a tie situation between two candidates, one of whom was a woman. The Planning Minister, who was chairing the meeting, suddenly turned to me and asked for my opinion, announcing, "Our decision is going to depend on what you say as the last member of committee." I used my voice at that decision-making table on that day and that choice changed a lot of things for me—and for many others.

Fortunately, we hired that female candidate that day, one of the most competent women in the health sector, as a representative on the National Planning Commission of Pakistan for the social sector. After that, much changed, at least for me. Until today, she remains my friend and mentor. We built a two-member team against all odds and the rest is history! We worked on multiple assignments but our focus remained SDGs, particularly SDG-5 (on gender).

Closing the Gap: a National Gender Policy for Pakistan

Our challenge was significant. At the time, Pakistan was ranked amongst the lowest of 146 countries in the World Economic Forum's global gender gap reports, as gender remained the lowest priority in the development programme in the absence of clear policy priority. Pakistan is a country where women account for 50 percent of the population and their equal socio-economic participation is crucial for sustainable development in the country. It was estimated that closing the gender gap completely could boost the country's GDP by 30 percent.[2] Closing this gap would take extraordinary measures. And so, together, the two of us built the most ambitious gender reforms agenda ever seen in the country. It was quite a journey: over four years, we worked tirelessly with meagre resources (both financial and human) and relied solely on our self-motivation.

We developed an Advisory Committee on Gender for the Planning Commission, comprised of a diverse set of sectoral experts and senior key stakeholders to proactively guide the generation of gender statistics for international reporting and to advise on mainstreaming gender in development programmes, policies and institutions. We identified 102 gender focal persons in all the ministries to roll out these gender initiatives and report back on their respective gender monitors. We organised and conducted High Level Consultative Forums on gender in federal government. We piloted a gender study and extended it to all federal ministries and associated departments to identify gaps and make recommendations for making workplaces conducive for women.

Our efforts culminated in the development of Pakistan's first National Gender Policy Framework, unanimously endorsed by all provincial stakeholders and formally launched on March 8, 2022, on International Women's Day; there was no better day to mark the significance of this milestone. The framework was based on extensive consultations with a wide range of stakeholders both in public and private sector, subject experts and national and international development partners. It provided high-impact strategic interventions related to women's education, employable skills, employment and entrepreneurship, engagement, empowerment, and health as well as gender-enabling environments and addressing gender-based violence. We had a plan to mainstream gender across all federal policies and programmes! The year 2022 was declared the "Year of Respecting Women in the Workplace in the Public Sector" by the Planning Commission.

These reforms could not have happened without the leadership of Dr Shabnum Sarfraz, the woman who was nominated to our National Planning

Commission that day long ago when the Minister accepted my recommendation. Until now I think about how entirely different things might look if gender bias had barred us from hiring a woman that day!

From the Ministry of Planning to the Ministry of Finance: Finding a Chair

My experience in public policy and the development sector made me realise that achieving policy objectives and addressing development challenges required the effective management of public resources. Clearly, I needed to develop a better understanding of PFM—yet another area extremely dominated by males. So, in 2021, with the national gender policy set to launch, I joined the Ministry of Finance as the first female Deputy Secretary for Budget, where I continue to serve today. In the Ministry of Finance, I'm involved in strategic financial planning, budget preparation, budget execution, public expenditure management and PFM reforms.

When I embarked on my work in PFM, there were no other female PFM practitioners or experts in Pakistan. As the only female officer among 30 officials in the Budget Department, the environment was quite challenging, and I was often questioned for taking on an extremely difficult technical role. I received comments such as: "Girls are not number persons"; "Female officers cannot work in budgeting, it's too demanding and time consuming"; and "You should look for a softer work position." Initially, it was quite frustrating as I felt the burden to prove myself worthy of handling these technically and administratively difficult tasks. It was often a shock to people when they saw a young female officer leading the management of the Federal Budget and Public Finances. Even though they respected my position, they hardly accepted the fact that a 'girl' might be capable of handling public finances and the resource distribution process, especially those of a big country like Pakistan. It was both funny and sad when I was chairing those budget meetings and negotiations, and senior male officers entered the meeting rooms and looked around and asked: "Where is the Chair?" or "Who is the Chair?" And when I introduced myself, there was that moment of shock or displeasure. At the end of these meetings, people commonly offered their apparent compliments: "We have never seen a young female with this much competence and financial expertise." I only take pleasure in the "young" part of the comment, though!

I worked really hard and strategised carefully to earn the respect I needed to realise my ambitious plans for reform rather than rushing in or aggressively demanding it. I tried first to understand my role, the organisational structure, key players and where the threats and opportunities were. Then I invested my time and energy in building my own capacity-building. During my initial years, I attended twenty training and certification courses strengthen my skill set; I worked up to 18 hours a day. I also built formal and informal networks within my organisation. I started engaging with the different projects of other teams and supported them in implementation. This helped me to build trust amongst my colleagues, and, at the same time, it gave me the opportunity to demonstrate my abilities. Finally, I went beyond my regular duties and functions, identified room for improvements and modifications in the PFM system, and proposed out-of-the-box solutions. It took years of investment proving myself worthy of my position.

And today I can look back proudly on my role not only in planning and implementing the federal budget for five consecutive years but also in reforming the PFM tools and processes to make them responsive to the needs of national policies. It was far from a smooth run—there was resistance, especially at first. Reforms are a painstaking process, especially in the public sector where people are not ready to break with inertia. When I started talking about reforms, I was often mocked for suggesting things outside the box (though not out of context!). But once I was able to show outcomes, acknowledgement of my work and my role in leading change followed.

Landmark Reform for Pakistan's National PFM System: Creating my Own Table

Despite having national polices and agendas to address the multiple development challenges we face, including gender, climate and disaster preparedness, I quickly learned that in Pakistan, as in many if not most countries, there is a clear disconnect between strategic policy frameworks and public funds and expenditures. One of the most challenging but also most significant efforts I've engaged in at the Ministry of Finance has been to address this critical gap by introducing the concept of strategic budgeting and working to cluster the previously undeveloped, scattered and siloed social development programmes into one comprehensive and integrated framework. Over three years, and despite significant pushback, I led the design and implementation of one the most ambitious reform agenda in Pakistan—a unified gender-, climate-, disaster- and SDG-responsive PFM system for the whole country.[3] The adoption and implementation of the "Roadmap and Action Plan for Gender, Climate and SDGs Integration to Public Finance Management System of Pakistan" has transformed the National Public Finance Management System from start to finish (planning, budgeting, approval, implementation, accounting and reporting) and made Pakistan a global leader in advanced PFM practices.[4] All the reforms have now been institutionalised at the national level and constitutional budget documents have also been amended to incorporate climate and gender budgeting. Now, we are working to extend this to all provincial and subnational levels!

Reflections on Success: How Leading from the Front Changed Me as a Person

As a civil servant, I learned that the public sector lacked three things: will, motivation and capacity. So, I developed a strategy to generate support, advocacy and momentum for our reform agenda. I built formal and informal networks by engaging with people at multiple levels.

To build the requisite skills to implement our PFM reforms, I designed a capacity-building programme for the Finance Ministry, and line ministries and departments on PFM systems broadly and on gender, climate, disaster and SDGs budgeting in particular. We have trained over 2,000 government officials from 120 different organisations and departments in federal government and with our proactive efforts, female participation has increased significantly.

To inspire and motivate people, one has to exhibit a consistent pattern of personal values, professional ethics, commitment and dedication, and a vision and a plan to achieve certain goals. A manager with a plan is far more likely to be trusted. I believed that my efforts could make a significant contribution to the public sector and I dedicated myself to this work. I think it was my commitment to these policy initiatives that attracted other people to support and work with me in achieving reform.

Although I started and led these initiatives, it was always a team effort, and it was the support of my colleagues and seniors that led to the successful adoption of these reforms. I've found that a strong anchor in a support system in both personal and professional life is extremely important. We all need a team of people who believe in us, help us in identifying our strengths and weaknesses, and enable us to grow. I was fortunate to have a few amazing friends who believed in me and their guidance played a crucial role in my personal and professional development. My family too, and particularly my younger sister, Bushra, have remained staunch supports for me throughout my professional career. I am lucky to have my sister to take care of me with her love and attention to detail. After my long hours at work, she was always there waiting to make sure I had a warm meal, and everything was ready for the next day. She always offered me a listening ear and wise counsel to help dispel all work-related stress. I am convinced that my achievements in the stress-filled world of PFM were mainly possible because of this support system.

In the early years of my career, I was a star performer as an individual, but along the way, I learnt the significance of building teams and group work. When you engage people, delegate responsibilities, ask for their opinions and involve them in the decision-making process, it motivates them. Everyone feels good about being trusted, being considered worthy of doing something. At the same time, it is challenging as well, as you have to maintain the balance among group differences, conflicts, and your overall goals and objectives. When you are leading, you are also responsible for the performance of others. In my work, I try to apply the philosophy of Peter Kropotkin: "Competition is the law of the jungle, but cooperation is the law of civilisation." Leading is also about continuous learning: I've benefitted immensely from the opportunity to engage with many experts and professionals at national and global levels in my career in PFM.

In addition, being in a leadership position and working on extremely crucial tasks, I have also learnt the art of preserving my mental peace amid chaos. Stress, anxiety and burnout inevitably arise under extreme work pressures. The workload, the associated risks and the burden of responsibility on your shoulders can overwhelm you for sure and can impact the quality of your personal and social life. I learnt to balance these negative impacts with nature. Nature is the least appreciated stress-buster. I interact with nature as frequently as possible. Nature has inspired me since my childhood days in my mountain village. The colours of the sky, moon, clouds, rain, air, water, trees, leaves.... everything acts as an antidote to stress for me, and a reminder of the limitless! I also seek refuge in books and preserve my sanity with good music. Overall, my career in PFM helped me in developing my own brand and turned me into this strong, independent and confident person who is ready to take any challenge without compromising my personal values and professional ethics.

Giving Back: From Inspired to Inspiring

I was both inspired and supported by my family in my unorthodox choices. First, there was my paternal grandmother. I used to call her "Bay Jee." She was the most inspiring and empowering figure in my family. Growing up, I saw her commanding and maintaining her position in decision-making, even in the most conservative family traditions. Then there was my mother—an extraordinary woman with many dreams and ambitions cut short by her early marriage; she poured herself into raising strong and independent daughters, with opportunities to achieve their dreams in her stead. Fortunately, I also have a father who believed that education is a girl's *right* and not a reward or favour. Despite all the pressures of traditions and cultural values, he stood by every choice I made in my life. Without this support system, I would not have been able to continuously challenge a society which was too adamant on a pre-determined role for women!

Today, the little girl who chose not to be confined by the borders of her mountain village is a Deputy Secretary at the Ministry of Finance for Pakistan. I'm presented as a role model for my home community and region. My appointment as Deputy Secretary has also broken stereotypes and opened doors for other women civil servants and policymakers; over five years at the Ministry of Finance, the female to male ratio of officers in the Budget Department has jumped from 1:30 to 1:3!

My work in PFM is now acknowledged by global development partners and financial institutions. I have regular opportunities to present my work as case studies to the global platforms and to share my experience with peer practitioners from other developing countries. It gives me immense pleasure to know that little girls in my village can point to me as an example when they argue for opportunities to study, that young women can look to me as proof that 'finance' does not belong only to the boys and know that they too can lead national policy. And I'm motivated further when I know I can share Pakistan's experiences in PFM to address structural disparities in education, healthcare, economic participation and decision-making, particularly for women, with other countries confronting similar challenges. My struggle for empowering people with the least opportunities continues. And I'm happy I can demonstrate the power of choosing limitless skies—this is exactly what I have strived for throughout my life!

Notes

1 These are people from local communities working as medical professionals without necessary qualifications, skills and formal training in the field of medicine.
2 IMF, 2018. Pursuing Women's Economic Empowerment & National Gender Policy Framework Pakistan, 2022.
3 The PFM tools and processes have been modified to incorporate climate, disaster and gender lenses including strategic planning, budget preparation, climate, disaster, budget tagging in the computerised information system of budgeting and accounting, monitoring, tracking and reporting.
4 This model includes methodologies and frameworks to capture the green component in all public expenditures (including recurrent and development expenditure, grants, subsidies etc.), public revenues (green revenues in tax and non-tax categories), fiscal risks assessment, fiscal risk financing and disaster resilient PFM.

Chapter 7

Resistance through PFM in Ukraine

An Interview

Oksana Tsiupa

Introduction

I met Oksana in December 2013 in Kyiv, just as the Maidan Revolution—the Revolution of Dignity—was beginning. People were gathering on the square, hoping and demanding a European future. Every day the crowds grew larger. Oksana came to interview for a senior position on the Gender Budgeting component of a Swedish-funded project in Ukraine. She arrived after spending the entire day on Maidan, smelling of smoke from the fires people used to keep warm. She was serious, reserved, and preferred speaking Ukrainian, so we used a translator—probably the first and last time we needed one. After that we spoke our own form of Esperanto: a mix of Bosnian, Ukrainian, and my slowly evolving Russian.

Getting to know Oksana, I met one of the most resilient women I have ever encountered in my life—some of her hardships I witnessed myself. Oksana will never tell the part of her story where, nine months pregnant, she fell into a coma, lost her child, and nearly lost her own life—waking up a month later. She will not tell how she later divorced her husband, or how she met Slava five years after that. She will not tell how, after finally becoming pregnant again and giving birth to little Andrej, she lost Slava when the baby was only four months old. How she moved back to Ivano-Frankivsk alone with a newborn, during COVID, only to face the full invasion of Ukraine in 2022—and everything that has followed since.

She will not tell any of this, because she simply keeps going. She works, she parents, she survives. She is a single mother, a fierce patriot, and one of the best gender responsive budgeting (GRB) practitioners I have ever met. Below is my interview with Maja. Maja

Maja Bosnić (MB): *Can you provide a brief overview of your career (in public finance)? What inspired you to pursue a career in this field? How did you get into gender budgeting?*

Oksana Tsiupa (OT): I have always been attracted to the field of finance and deciding to study it was a natural choice. As children, my sister and I

DOI: 10.4324/9781003732532-8

used to play 'bank': we placed imaginary money in deposits, kept some kind of card files, and invented procedures. In addition, my godfather was the director of a bank. He always looked intelligent and dressed in a European style, even though it was still the Soviet Union. Perhaps that was the first time I thought I wanted to look the same way: modern, intelligent, and professional. But most importantly, I have always been drawn to precision and logic. I like it when everything can be calculated, justified, proven, and predicted. I dislike asymmetry, chaos, or uncertainty. That is why finance was a natural choice for me: a field that combines clarity, structure, and the ability to influence important decisions.

In 1991, following my Bachelor's thesis on the "Balance of Financial Resources of the Regions," I was offered a position at the Department of Finance of the Ivano-Frankivsk Regional State Administration. Two other classmates from my programme also joined the department. Naturally, it was challenging at first, as we entered an already well-established team with its own traditions and organisational culture. But the work was interesting. I did well and was appointed to the position of Head of Department (in the department of financing non-productive industries) four years after my hiring, even though there were people who were 15 or more years older than me… It was not easy!

A year later, while still working in the Department of Finance of the Regional State Administration, I enrolled in the Master's programme for "Civil Service," on the recommendation of the department itself, thus also fulfilling my father's dream. The training in a technical university was new to me, and I gained experience in communicating with people of different age groups and positions. Working in the Department of Finance, I gained vast experience in the budget system, and most importantly, I got acquainted with people who formed and implemented financial policy at the regional level, which I had only read about at the university.

I constantly felt the support and mentorship of the head of our department, who tried to introduce me to all the intricacies of the work as fast as possible. She was demanding but fair, and she taught me not to work to just "get through the day," but to work for a meaningful result, one that was clear and important to me. The knowledge and skills I gained during that period have supported me throughout my life, across different fields and in various positions. While working as a chief specialist, I was asked to submit a report on the implementation of the regional budget to the Ministry of Finance of Ukraine. For me, this was a turning point event in my life. I found myself in the corridors of the Cabinet of Ministers of Ukraine and the Ministry of Finance. I was very humbled to be there and could not have guessed that in the future I would feel at home in these institutions!

After my Bachelor's degree, I was offered a place at graduate school with the speciality "Finance and Credit" and got an assistant position at the Department of Finance and Accounting. Professors congratulated me and expected to have me as their future graduate student. But when they found out that I chose to work in the Regional State Administration, they offered the graduate school position to another person, and the head of the department recommended that I start a family instead, and enter graduate school later. However, already in 2001, I was invited to work part-time at the Department of Finance and I began to teach students the "Budget System." I enjoyed meetings with students and the opportunity to teach them the real budget system, as defined by the Budget Code of Ukraine. And so I became a teacher with practical experience, which gave me an advantage. After some time, I left my job at the Department of Finance of the Regional State Administration (though the management did not want to let me go) and moved to the Department of Finance and Accounting of my native university and entered graduate school. Working at the university, I did not break ties with my colleagues in the Regional State Administration and constantly tried to integrate practical aspects into my academic disciplines.

How did I get into gender budgeting? Interesting question! In 2011, my former direct supervisor who was Head of the Department of Finance invited me to join the pilot project "Gender Responsive Budgeting at the Local Level in Ukraine," which was implemented in the Ivano-Frankivsk and Luhansk regions with the support of the Swedish International Development Cooperation Agency (SIDA) and the relevant regional state administrations. It was a new challenge for me. Incidentally, I met two other book contributors on this project: Maja and Catharina Schmitz. Both also relate extensively in their respective chapters their work on that project.

I understood and knew budgeting, but it was the first time I encountered the concepts of 'gender' and 'gender policy.' At the university, at the Faculty of Economics, we did not study anything about the policy of ensuring equal rights and opportunities for women and men. Unfortunately, even today none of the teachers integrates gender policy issues in economic specialties into their educational programmes. Working at the university, I try to use every opportunity across different courses to highlight facts that demonstrate existing inequalities. I continuously advocate for GRB among students, as well as among faculty. (Working with faculty is more challenging—even women professors often do not yet recognise the benefits of this approach, not only for themselves but for all members of their families.) Still, I see progress and real successes.

Currently, fourth-year students who have already completed the course "Budget System" study "Gender Responsive Budgeting." This year (2025), I am supervising a Master's student who is writing her thesis on GRB. My practical experience has also influenced my niece, who will write her bachelor's thesis on applying a gender-sensitive approach to teaching history in schools. In Ukraine, we have a saying: "Water wears away stone." Over the past 11 years, Ukraine has changed a lot, and I sincerely believe that after victory it will continue to grow and improve.

This is how I got familiar with the field of gender policy and how my training began, and I am very grateful that I got such an opportunity.

MB: *Have you observed the changing opportunities for women in public finance over the course of your career? Have you faced any gender challenges in terms of promotion?*

OT: Until the moment I started working in the Department of Finance of Ukraine, I had never felt a specific attitude towards me as a girl. My father and mother never mentioned to me or my sister that we could not do or have something because we were girls. Therefore, for the first time when applying for a job, I faced a prejudiced attitude. Even before the competition began, upon seeing me, the official said, "Girl. And we need guys in the finance department." When they heard that I would also come with a male classmate, they agreed to hire me.

In some instances, when applying for a specific job, I was asked inappropriate questions such as: are you married? do you have a boyfriend? do you plan to have children? do you have a place to live? But no one asked me about the budget and the budget system…

In the Finance Department, where I worked for more than five years, I did not notice such discriminatory signs in the career advancement of middle-aged women (40+), because there were very few men among the staff. But for my cohort, when men's recruitment increased, discrimination was noticeable. Men were promoted to higher positions faster, they were given a higher allowance for intensity in work (optional additional benefit), although they did not work more than women. Management had an explanation: "Boys will not work for such a salary and will leave. We need to keep them." In the Regional State Administration, where I started my career, men have always held leadership positions. During the period I worked there, there was not a single woman among the leaders of the region and their deputies. But there is also another side: many women, having a family, and being single, themselves refuse positions, not being confident in themselves and understanding that working in financial bodies takes a lot of time and effort.

In my situation, it was also so. When I was finally offered the position of Head of Department, I was initially hesitant: would I be able to combine family and professional life (despite the fact that my husband worked with me in the financial body and knew this job); would I be able to work and delegate authority to colleagues who are much older than me? Here, the head of the Finance Department played a big role in dispelling my doubts and supporting me in every possible way in this position. This is why I believe it is very important for management to support more junior staff and mentor them!

MB: *How do you manage leadership roles and make decisions in a male-dominated field?*

OT: I have had leadership instincts since childhood, but I did not understand it then. Probably the example of my parents, around whom people have always rallied, and my genes also manifested themselves. At school, I mainly held the position of an informal leader, whose services were used by teachers to influence the class. Officially, there were 'elders' (elected students) whose parents held positions, but when it was necessary to resolve an issue, they turned to me. Therefore, I already understood the concept of an 'informal leader' at the university. After my first year, I have consistently held leadership positions, including as the chairwoman of the council of elders of the Faculty of Economics and during my Masters programme.

When I became Head of Department in the Department of Finance of the Regional State Administration, it was difficult at first, as older colleagues did not accept my decisions and delegation of powers, but over time they even asked for advice.

My last experience as a Deputy team leader in the "Gender Budgeting in Ukraine" (2014–2020) project was very enlightening. Here, for the first time, I encountered a manager who brought to us a specialist who explained to us that we were all different, and it is a combination of our different characters and qualities that we should use to succeed. For this, I am very grateful to the team leader. As part of the expansion of the project, I became the deputy team leader and was responsible for the implementation of the project at the level of regions and territorial communities, as well as for cooperation in this direction with the Ministry of Finance. There was already a lot of work, but then it increased substantially because the deputy for the implementation of the project at the state level resigned. The team leader moved to another position in the last year of the project, and I was asked to replace her, which was a big honour. I thought for a long time, and considering family circumstances and the situation in Ukraine, I turned it down. But given my experience and institutional memory, I continued to do the work for two. I had to train new people, as there was a turnover of half the project team, and implement the project, cooperate with all the stakeholders of the project, and ensure that we closed the project properly.

After the completion of the world's largest project on the implementation and application of gender budgeting in 2020, I continue to work with UN Women in Ukraine, the National Democratic Institute, UNICEF and other international and national projects and programmes, to apply and popularise this method as an innovative tool for public financial management (PFM), which allows increased efficiency in the use of taxpayers' funds and the quality of public service provision at the state and local level through taking into account the needs, interests and capabilities of girls and boys, women and men.

Working with men is easy, but only after a while… At first, we would face laughter, especially when the topic was about gender and gender budgeting. As project leader, Maja would always respond to men's smiles by pointing out a simple fact: in Ukraine, men live ten years less than women. And their smiles disappeared immediately. In this way, she emphasised that gender-responsive budgeting concerns everyone, not just women. But then, when you pull facts and your experience and skills to your side, you establish cooperation. For example, we had a protracted relationship with the Secretariat of the Verkhovna Rada (Ukrainian Parliament) Budget Committee. We knew we were not in friendly territory regarding gender-sensitivity. When we finally got our meeting, the Chair had questions on every single slide. Everyone else was silent and waiting to see how our dialogue would evolve. Using my experience and the results of the analysis of more than 100 budget programmes at that time came to my rescue. For every question, I had an answer, supported by figures about people, finances, trends and problems. My colleague in the training said that I was just pulling the "winning cards out of my sleeve"… And we have since established cooperation with them.

I believe that a leader (regardless of gender) should be, first and foremost, fair, professional, not always tolerant, and able to delegate authority. One trait that slowed me down a little as a leader is my perfectionism—I was reluctant to delegate tasks unless I was confident in the quality of execution. I always had extremely high expectations primarily of myself—but also of my team. This was not always easy to navigate—especially for my team members.

MB: *What does GRB mean to you?*

OT: GRB is the topic that brought me into the world of gender. It is what taught me the main aspects of gender policy in the world and in Ukraine in particular. Thinking about it today, I believe that if I had not entered this topic through the GRB project, maybe I would not have become an expert on gender equality. Through the prism of financial resources, it familiarised me with the concept of gender gaps and how through finance we can increase or decrease gender inequality. Once we had a dispute in the Gender Budgeting team about who we could make the best specialist in GRB: a financier who understands the budget process but does not yet understand the essence of gender policy, or an expert who understands gender policy but does not understand the intricacies of the budget process. I am glad that my version won: I believe a financier is more likely to be made into a specialist in GRB than a specialist in gender policy.

When I started working on the pilot project in 2011, I was convinced that there was no inequality between women and men in the public sector, because salaries are calculated on the basis of a single tariff scale, budget expenditures per person are calculated equally for all budgets, etc. But in reality these inequalities exist and no one is doing anything to reduce them; no one has ever paid attention to it and will not pay attention to it. And since then, working as a professor, an expert in public finance and gender budgeting, I have been debunking myths about "equality in the public sector." The Gender Budgeting team in the Ukraine Project collected a huge amount of information that convinced the Ministry of Finance of Ukraine and local financial authorities, other central executive bodies, regional state administrations and territorial communities of the importance of considering gender inequalities in the provision of public services to citizens. The results of a gender budget analysis always help to collect this information and convince everyone. After all, during its implementation, we received comprehensive information about the different roles of women and men in different areas and at different levels, the access they have to goods and services, their priorities, needs and responsibilities.

MB: *How do you see the development of the public finance sector in terms of diversity and inclusion? What initiatives or changes do you think are needed to make this area more inclusive for women in the current Ukrainian context?*

OT: There are no limits to improvement. Every year, the inclusiveness of public finances is increasing not only globally, but also in my Ukraine. Today, under war conditions, our country needs to direct limited public financial resources to the growing needs of different groups of women and men, and it is also necessary to take into account our diversity when reforming the tax system, financial control system, etc.

In order for Ukrainian women to realise their full potential in the field of public finances, i.e. to devote more than 12 hours a day to this work, the state needs to facilitate options for care work (for small children, for people with disabilities, for the elderly, etc.), to make it possible for women to devote more time to work and career opportunities, and to ensure a balance between family and professional life. In order for women to make a career in public finance and be more visible every year, special training and the independence of competition commissions are required. Media should also cover more about the role of women in public finance.

MB: *What advice would you give to young women considering a career in public finance? Are there certain skills or qualities that you think are crucial for success in this field?*

OT: Having worked in the field of PFM for about 25 years and reflecting on my professional life, I always wonder, would I be able to work in another field? My answer is "no." Working with public finances provides the satisfaction of trying to make resources, which belong to us taxpayers, work again for the people; it shows how, through financial resources, we can influence girls and boys, women and men of all ages, places of residence, etc. Teaching at the university, I try to convey to students this love and affinity for public finances, for the community budget, for the state budget, to show the relationship between the economic and social spheres and how we can influence them through public finances. It is gratifying that every year two or three of my Master's students go to work for local financial authorities, and that the topic of GRB is increasingly popular every day.

As for advice to girls and women, I recommend being unafraid, to constantly learn and improve, because the field of public finances is changing a lot and you constantly need to be ahead of the curve; be active and try to conduct in-depth research and look for relationships. As for skills and qualities… not only to be able to but also to love to analyse, draw conclusions and, based on them, change the future through financial resources. Today, our partner countries are providing my country with financial resources that enables it to survive. This gives us the opportunity to think and dream about the future. And women in the field of public finance play a huge role in this.

MB: *How do you define success in your career and life? What legacy or impact do you hope to leave in the field of public finance/GRB?*

OT: Honestly, I did not dream of a career in my early twenties. But life each time threw in challenges that I always accepted (my dad and events in my personal life played an important role in this). Every time, I thought "Why do I need this? Something new again. You have to go forward again and learn new things." Success in my career is an opportunity to influence and change *the consciousness of Ukrainians throughout the country.* Unfortunately, the legacy of being part of the Soviet Union for 70 years left a very large mark, including in the remaining echoes of the planned economy both at the central and local levels. Everyone expects someone to come to the community, regional or national leadership and change it with a magic wand. Everyone wants changes, but no one wants it to start with them. And Ukraine needs changes: from elaborating a strategy all the way to its implementation.

During trainings, analytical and expert work, I try to show specialists and students how they can look and do something from a different angle and how it will affect the lives, opportunities of their neighbours, relatives and the country as a whole, how to forecast and estimate costs and benefits, etc. I hope that my lectures and trainings partially change people and the country as a whole. I can already notice these changes: in 2011, few Ukrainians (except for experts) understood the concepts of 'gender' or 'gender budgeting,' and today in 2025 in Ukraine, the use of gender budgeting is the norm of the most important document in the field of budget relations, the Budget Code of Ukraine. And today my task is to make sure that it does not become a formality. Therefore, there is still a lot of work to be done in Ukraine, and every year there are more and more challenges, and gender budgeting must be sensitive to this.

After the advent of a victorious peace, Ukraine needs to be restored, becoming even better and stronger! Glory to Ukraine! Glory to the heroes!

Part II

Finding Ourselves *in* Gender Budgeting

Chapter 8

Gender Budgeting

That Fire in my Belly

Lekha Chakraborty

My mum was abandoned by my dad when I was three years old, just as my younger brother was born. It was while she was in the advanced stage of this pregnancy that my father's decision of '*Talaq*' (divorce) was delivered to her by post in a simple inland letter. From that moment, the way she managed to raise her two children alone is a story of sadness and profound grit that only a few can realise.

Years later, when I began pioneering gender budgeting work in India, every meeting on the subject stirred deep turmoil within me, because every time a gender issue was raised, I felt they were speaking about my mother. Every issue was a personal blow that left me vulnerable within. It has taken a lot of time and work to not take everything personally, to discuss matters related to gender boldly, to move confidently in the policymaking sphere and drive changes in public policies.

In every moment of success, I stood detached to seize that moment, as this abandonment haunts me most in those moments of success; and like a dart, success pierces me with the experiences I have undergone, as a child, and the distance I travelled from a traditional Muslim family raised by a single mother to who I am now. My story is about the power of serendipity, though I have a fire in my belly to 'become someone.' I do not know to articulate how and from where that fire came from. I leave it to you to understand.

Melted Childhood

I was born in my parents' short-lived happy times. My mum was a nurse in a government hospital and my father was a space engineer at the Indian Space Research Organisation (ISRO). In those days, government maternity leave was a mere six weeks. My mum had to return to work, leaving behind a baby not even two months old, with night shifts looming. Initially, my parents hired a maid for a few hours. But, at night, my dad took care of me. Exhausted, he would hand me over to my mum when she returned from her night shift, just before rushing to catch the Vikram Sarabhai Space Centre (VSSC) bus (a 45 minute commute) to the ISRO space centre where he

DOI: 10.4324/9781003732532-10

worked. To ease my mum's journey, they had bought a house within walking distance of the Employees State Insurance (ESI) government hospital where she worked.

As the strain mounted, my mum asked my maternal grandmother to move in and help care for two-month-old me. While my grandmother's presence provided my mum with immense security—she felt safer leaving her baby with her own mother than with a maid—it curtailed my dad's freedom and sense of space. My grandmother also looked after my mum's post-delivery recovery, preparing daily herbal hot water baths, protein-rich seafood, and green leafy vegetables to restore her haemoglobin levels. After a period of exclusive breastfeeding, she also prepared iron-rich grains for the baby's meals.

Despite the support, my dad remained overwhelmed. My grandmother recounted that I was a difficult child who often missed my mum during her night shifts, keeping my dad awake the whole night as he struggled to manage my incessant crying. Exhausted and at his limit, he asked my mum to quit her job.

My mum was shell-shocked. Coming from an extremely poor family, her education had been financed through the strenuous efforts of her mother and my maternal uncle. My maternal uncle actually stopped his own studies to finance my mum's education. She cherished her work and found dignity in pursuing the nursing profession she was educated for. Her response to my dad was a vehement and unequivocal "No." He felt deeply hurt. It snowballed into every aspect of their life and their relationship was strained irreversibly.

This all meant a stark difference in the circumstances of my birth and my brother's. I was born in a public hospital in Trivandrum, the capital city of Kerala, India, where my parents lived. But my mother's second delivery was at her maternal home in the village, unattended by a gynaecologist. There was no prenatal care for my mum. A village accoucheuse with her knife separated the umbilical cord between my mother and younger brother when he was born. Post-delivery haemorrhage was the prime cause for the high maternal mortality rate in those days in India; somehow my mother was spared.

But she was extremely shaken and depressed during the advanced stages of her second pregnancy as my dad never communicated with her nor did he pay her any visits, except to see the face of the baby when he was born. Their relationship was strained beyond reconciliation. The Talaq information arrived in an inland letter. There was no formal divorce proceedings or documents. My mum was abandoned. My dad remarried a few months later. His parents arranged his new marriage to another young lady they had identified.

My mum did not go to court nor claimed alimony from my dad, as she was in too devastated a state of mind to go through any prolonged court dealings, and she did not have any money or family support for paying any lawyers for the prolonged legal proceedings.

My mum felt isolated, even from her own family. Her dad had passed away before she turned one year old. Her maternal family was in a different city, far from where she stayed for work. She did not agree to quit her job and return to her mother's place. She argued for her privacy, as her prime goal was to educate her children when they grew up, staying back in the city where she worked. Among her sisters, she was the only one who pursued studying and took up a job in a different city. Her siblings (except one brother) were lower primary school dropouts.

In the period following, my mum took us with her on her night shifts, where we slept on the floor in the narrow medicine procurement room, near the medicine shelves, while she assumed her duties. Some months later, ESI hospital authorities selected her for joining the physiotherapy training when there was an opening for such in-service training and posted her in the physiotherapy unit of ESI, where there were no night shifts. This arrangement helped her to manage her work and her young children.

At home, one night, when the three of us were alone, my younger brother in a cradle, a thief broke open our kitchen window. Trembling with fear, my mum held me close to keep me from crying out. After that, she started renting out a part of our home so we wouldn't be on our own, and we lived crammed into just two rooms from then on.

The next two decades of my life are ones I still do not want to remember in any detail. One thing I do remember clearly is my mum's insistence that my younger brother and I study well. Without sufficient money or land, my broken mum constantly reminded us that education was the only option available for us to earn a livelihood and reputation. And so I managed somehow to be successful in the government-run girl's high school I attended.

In 1988, I stood in the (parliamentary-style) elections in school and got elected "School Speaker." I studied with students from all walks of life. One image that still haunts me, even today, is the way a few students from ultra-poor families ran towards the government-run van with the midday meals when it stopped at the assembly ground, to have at least a one-time porridge.

Later, in 1990, I enrolled for my Bachelors in Economics with a merit scholarship. I also studied for my Masters with a national merit scholarship. I won the nationwide test for a research fellowship after the completion of my Master's degree in 1995 and I joined a national university for my doctoral studies in Economics.

Leaving Home

I moved to a campus hostel during my research days. I loved the newfound freedom and the power of daylight as I shifted from the dark room of my home where I had sat and studied all those years with untold stories of pain bottled up within me. I found my life partner on this new campus, who was my senior in research. We got married in 1998. In 2000, after finishing my two years of residential requirements for doctoral studies, I moved with him to the capital, New Delhi, where we had each been awarded positions at the research institute of the Indian Ministry of Finance (MoF).

At the MoF institute, when I joined in August 2000, the first project assigned to me was to lead a new project of its kind in public finance titled "gender budgeting," funded by a UN entity. In those days, the concept of gender budgeting was considered by economists as an oxymoron and the MoF had not realised its potential. My senior colleagues were very resistant to this new project. Despite all the good work I was leading. it affected my confidence.

It was a tough task to focus on a pioneering project on gender budgeting and to complete my PhD thesis simultaneously. There were no weekends for me then, as I was deeply involved in my new research on gender, while my doctoral thesis topic was on the macroeconomic impacts of fiscal deficits. Summer and winter passed by, during which I remained completely focussed on my work and thesis. I became very passionate about the 'gender lens' in public finance.

The new city life posed new challenges. It was the first time I had lived in a city other than my hometown. I had no social life. My colleagues often reminded me how aloof I was, sitting in my office with no downtime, not even over a short break for a cup of tea. I was an introvert by nature. While this helped my research, had I been better at sharing the pressure I felt with friends, it might have eased things. I called my mum weekly from the phone booth nearby. Those calls were full of mum's harsh reminders of my unfinished PhD thesis and how lonely she felt without me back home. She was also very concerned about how I would survive the harsh winters and minus-degree temperatures. Till then, I had always lived near her, in a city near the Arabian Sea, a city with no winters. I had nested all my dreams and aspirations in the monsoon rains of home.

I did not have enough money to go home from New Delhi. And no time either, amidst work pressures and project deadlines. The travel home took three nights and two days on a train. It was 3,500 km away. When I did go, those prolonged train journeys in sleeper classes were nightmarish. Still, I was always astonished at the way people connected with each other over the three days of travelling together. Through the train journey, my pain intensified as the landscape changed from my lush green hometown to barren lands. As the heat and dry winds swept past the train window, I remained sad within, thinking of the "lack of recognition for my work" on gender in public finance and about my unfinished thesis.

My mum was determined to see her daughter become "Dr Lekha," but I feared that my dream was slipping out of my hands with all the work pressure. She wanted more phone calls with me, which I avoided as I felt very upset over her questions about my thesis, about my fights with my in-laws and my life in a big metropolis like Delhi with my very long wavy hair that I later shortened to a tomboyish style. Those were terribly huge topics for her, although my "short hair" was the least important for me amidst the burgeoning tensions on personal and professional fronts.

In 2001, my PhD thesis was still pending, and at the same time my thesis chapter-based paper on the empirical link between fiscal deficits and interest rate won the Infosys award for the best thesis paper in the Doctoral Consortium at the Indian Institute of Science, Bangalore in India. I completed my PhD in 2004, while working at MoF institute.

Connecting the Dots

When I began the gender budgeting project two decades ago, no economists had yet visualised a gender budgeting model in public finance. There were no theoretical public finance models to guide us, let alone frameworks for embedding a gender lens into fiscal decision-making. Walking through the corridors of a MoF institute, as a freshly appointed woman economist and working on a gender budgeting project was not easy; no one could connect with the project or understand its possibilities. But as I delved into gender budgeting, it made so much sense to me.

As I began to explore gender budgeting, I learned that, in India, gender discrimination begins even before birth. Empirical analysis had revealed a profound socio-economic asymmetry across the genders. It manifests in the grim calculus of female foeticide (killing the human foetus before birth) and the insidious denial of household resources, nutrition, and healthcare. Amartya Sen's seminal and provocative work published in 1990 about "missing women" (Sen, 1990) in India evidenced the devastating costs of gender discrimination by capturing the female survival disadvantage at a scale exceeding the casualties from twentieth-century famines and WWI and WWII combined. Asia's heterogeneous economies amplify these inequities, from the unpaid care burden that curtails women's labour force participation to persistent gaps in education and health outcomes. The care economy statistics from the first Time Use Survey of India, published in 2000, showed women in the 15–59 age group spent three times as much time on unpaid domestic work as men—fuelling a dual burden that slashes labour participation. Budgets, far from neutral, entrench these asymmetries. Fiscal silence on gender was not benign, and it was a policy failure we could ill afford. I embraced the project and devoted my heart, soul and head to it.

Gender budgeting offered a rigorous framework for fiscal innovation—embedding gender equity into fiscal processes via knowledge-building, designing the institutional mechanisms, and framing accountability mechanisms. I became deeply engrossed in each of the phases of fiscal innovation.

But pushing the frontiers beyond the economic growth paradigm was tough going. I'll never forget the response to my first presentation on gender-budgeting research at the MoF Institute. It was a shocker. The senior colleagues unanimously asked the director of the Institute to roll back the project, arguing that applying a 'gender lens' was not necessary for any budgetary decisions. They accused me of elitist perspectives because I used terms like 'care economy' and of straying from core public finance questions. They maintained that gender could never be a core public finance question. It would be more than a decade before gender would become part of 'normal' discourse. Only today, as gender budgeting and the care economy have become more mainstream ideas in India, and lots of funds are available, do these topics attract many researchers. I remember my lonely days working on these areas and the outright rejection I faced in the public finance world. Yet my research on gender budgeting had become my passion. I ran economic models to substantiate that the coefficients of public policy decisions incorporating gender budgeting have substantially higher impacts on human development than economic growth *per se*. The empirical policy research language of economic models we used was appealing to the MoF. It helped to shift the thinking which viewed budgets as neutral arbiters to understanding budgets as active agents of inclusion (or exclusion). Leading these fundamental shifts in policy thinking was incredibly exciting.

While working on gender budgeting, I quietly battled depression. Outwardly, I was at the peak of my career, travelling across many states in India and around the world, invited to speak on the strength of my work. Yet inwardly, I struggled. The depression was not about wanting to quit; it was about the exhaustion of challenging rigid mindsets, pursuing professional and personal ambitions largely alone, and the deep disappointment of receiving little support from the public finance world. Above all, it stemmed from a profound sense of being unseen. I lived with the bitter irony of widespread recognition and acclaim from the outside world globally, yet not from the institution the way I wanted it to be. When the MoF Institute finally made me a professor, it brought a measure of calm and helped me find stability again.

As a prelude to conduct gender budgeting analysis, dissecting the public finance macro-context was essential. The size of the government matters for gender budgeting. The size proxied by the public expenditure-to-GDP ratios vary starkly across countries, yet human development outlays remain dismal, signalling fiscal neglect of social equity. It was crucial to analyse the fiscal consolidation process and fiscal austerity's toll on gender equity. My 2016 book on fiscal consolidation unpacks deficits' macroeconomic impacts and helped me to set the context for how fiscal rules-bound deficits led to the erosion of gender-sensitive outlays (Chakraborty, 2016).

Institutionalising Gender Budgeting as a Fiscal Innovation

When India's Union Budget 2001–02 was unveiled, the UN commissioned me to analyse it through a gender lens—as a foundational study for advocacy. During Parliament's post-presentation recess, I crafted the "2001 Gender Budgeting Macro Scan Report," disseminating it to Parliamentary Standing Committees to spark informed debates in "Vote on Account" sessions. I presented my study findings to the Rajya Sabha's women Parliamentarians, chaired by the Deputy Speaker, igniting momentum for gender budgeting. Yet formal institutionalisation arrived only in 2004 via the MoF.

With multilateral organisations and UN entities, gender budgeting gained momentum. A pivotal turning point was the UN's inaugural regional meeting on gender budgeting in Kathmandu, in 2001. There, the UN commissioned a South-Asia-wide study, mirroring the methodology I had pioneered. I was tasked by the UN to do my first international assignment: moving to Colombo to lead it, collaborating with Sri Lanka's Ministry of Finance, Finance Commission, Ministry of Women, and sectoral ministries. The framework, far from sector-agnostic, involved crafting analytical matrices and institutional mechanisms with budget officials. Translated into vernacular languages, the research was disseminated provincially for subnational gender budgeting. In the 2002 Budget Speech, Sri Lanka announced its national and subnational rollout—predating India's institutionalisation.

In 2004, India institutionalised gender budgeting. India also rolled out the adoption of fiscal rules capping the fiscal deficit at 3 percent of GDP annually. My expertise in macroeconomics and human development earned recognition; the MoF invited me as a member to the 2003 "Classification of Budgetary Transactions Committee," tasked with institutionalising a template grounded in gender budgeting. Our recommendations led to the Budget Speech announcing that India would launch gender budgeting from 2005–06, enforced rigorously via Budget Call Circulars. Concurrently, the Government of India summoned representatives from 29 states to Delhi for perspectives and training on state-level implementation. Retaining our methodology, I drafted the Methodology Manual and led the sessions. I was thrilled by the earnest deliberations across states—our framework, built from a clean slate, now cascading into tangible policy impacts. It marked a validation and gender budgeting was hailed as fiscal innovation.

Field Level Experiences with Women

With fiscal decentralisation gaining ground, I led a cross-country project in 2003 on fiscal decentralisation and local level gender budgeting, commissioned by UN, in selected countries, including the Philippines, Morocco, Mexico, South Africa and India, and later Vietnam; and the OECD countries including Canada and Sweden. These fiscally decentralised gender budgeting experiments were to move away from 'one-size-fits-all' gender-budgeting models. The inferences underlined that the "principle of subsidiarity"—which states that public service provisioning will be at its best if it is at the level of government closest to people—is crucial for gender budgeting and the feminisation of governance can turn public expenditure decisions favouring women. It was inspiring to me to work at grassroots level across countries and to see how this work fed into public policy and how gender budgeting led to economic empowerment.

These decentralised gender-budgeting experiments were also important to 'decolonise' public financial management (PFM) tools. Dismantling the colonial-era legacy of a top-down fiscal structure inherited from imperial rule and to fight 'elite capture' in gender budgeting also became significant. Gender-disaggregated public expenditure incidence analysis was conducted to understand the distributional impacts and social justice. The access to financial resources across income quintiles and also as an interface between gender and race was studied in my South Africa gender budgeting project. This work emerged as a significant tool to decolonise PFM, infusing fiscal processes of the Global South with gender lenses to reorient public expenditures toward care economies, health, climate change and education—the areas which otherwise can get affected with fiscal hawkism and fiscal austerity.

While the expenditure side of gender budgeting was successfully integrated into the national and subnational levels of government in India, I found the gender lens in intergovernmental fiscal transfers (IGFT) lacking. My research published by the Levy Economics Institute of Bard College, New York, where I am affiliated, substantiates the importance of integrating gender into intergovernmental fiscal transfers to capture the gravity of gender discrimination, and the low 0–6 child sex ratio (that is, the number of girls in the 0–6 age cohort) (Chakraborty, 2010) is a matter of concern in India.

Reaching World Stage

In 2016, the UN Secretary General's high-level panel (HLP) recognised gender budgeting as a PFM tool for women's economic empowerment. It was my honour and privilege to contribute a background paper on "fiscal policies for gender equity" for this UNSG High-Level Panel. The preparatory meetings for the UNSG HLP were held in Geneva. It was equally a proud privilege to lead the IMF 2016 global survey on gender budgeting from the Asia Pacific region, and to contribute to IMF research on gender budgeting (Chakraborty, 2015).

Gender budgeting fora and the network of international scholars I met through them gave me 'tools' to name and analyse what had happened to my mother, what had happened to me, and to deal with those permanent scars. I've learned how to remain undeterred, to take full advantage of the professional space I have earned as a policymaker through my passion and hard work and to advance 'people-matter' policy impacts.

Achieving recognition has also bolstered me. I felt humbled when in an international meeting, my UN peers praised my 2022 book and declared that "Globally no one knows gender budgeting the way she knows…"(Chakraborty, 2022). Getting elected twice—in 2020 and in 2023—to the governing board of management of the International Institute of Public Finance (IIPF), the world forum of public finance economists[1], strengthened my conviction that I am on track.

My approach has always been empirical and policy-oriented. I analyse the data and run econometric models to support the significance of gender budgeting on policy outcomes. But I know it is also important to analyse the compelling stories held by women—like the methodology of "perspectives of poor by poor" adopted by the World Bank. And I know that one such story is my own, which will be of interest to young scholars in gender and public finance and policy. This is why I find this book so important. But it is however only the tip of the iceberg.

And who knows—the untold ocean of stories within me might surface in the near future through a book, if I am destined to write one, which I will write for young girls. As for my contributions to macro-fiscal policies and gender budgeting, I dedicate them to my mum, because her story is my lens for understanding every aspect of my work in this field.

Note

1 https://www.iipf.org/mngmnt.htm

References

Chakraborty, Lekha, 2010. *Determining Gender Equity in Fiscal Federalism: Analytical Issues and Empirical Evidence from India*, Working Paper No. 590, Levy Economics Institute of Bard College.

Chakraborty, Lekha, 2015. *Asia: A Survey of Gender Budgeting Efforts*, IMF Working Paper No: 150, IMF: Washington DC

Chakraborty, Lekha, 2016. *Fiscal Consolidation, Budget Deficits, and the Macro Economy*, Sage Publications.

Chakraborty, Lekha, 2022. *Fiscal Policy for Sustainable Development in Asia-Pacific*, Palgrave Macmillan.

Sen, Amartya, 1990. "More Than 100 Million Women Are Missing," *New York Review*, December 20.

Chapter 9

Gender Budgeting in Me / Me in Gender Budgeting

Maja Bosnić

Introduction

In 2008, I was sitting with my new boss, Martin Bowen, discussing a UK-Government-funded project supporting budget reforms in Bosnia and Herzegovina. He explained that in addition to working with civil society organisations on their budget literacy and participation, I had one more thing to lead on: a thing called gender responsive budgeting (GRB).

It is hard to forget that meeting—and my own thoughts when he started presenting it. And while he was enthusiastically trying to explain the concept to me, I was thinking: "Oh God, what is *this* now? Yet another trendy international concept that will never work… And what does gender have to do with budgets anyway?"

I did not want to work with gender at all. I had never been taught anything about gender equality in my economics studies in the late 1990s/early 2000s. (Actually, I am not sure why I bother mentioning the years here, as gender analysis is still not systematically included in economic studies globally). I also did not want to work with gender because I had a strong feeling that working with gender equality would somehow reduce my reputation as the *Serious Economist* that I aspired to be.

I did not say this out loud, but my attitude was obvious in the following meeting with Priya Alvarez, a Spanish gender-budgeting expert who came to support us in Bosnia. In our first meeting, in our conference room, Priya asked us about the key gender issues in Bosnia. My response was along the lines of: we do not have serious gender issues here; women are empowered and successful; it is all good. A response that reflected my own ignorance but the truth is, I felt somehow personally insulted: who are these people telling me that women in Bosnia do not have the same rights and opportunities? Just look at us, just look at me!

I was wrong, of course. I was wrong on everything I thought about gender equality and gender budgeting at the start of my professional (and it turns out, personal) journey. And in the context of my story with GRB this is important because it tells you exactly what happens when you never let gender analysis enter your education or public discussion space. Nobody (at

DOI: 10.4324/9781003732532-11

least nobody I had access to)—media, educational institutions, government, was talking much about gender equality. As an economist—and an emerging feminist—I became aware how little I knew about human rights and gender equality, as well as the ways in which economics both influences and is influenced by these domains.

The learning that followed that infamous meeting with Priya was steep. I connected with civil society organisations that were working on gender equality. I attended university courses. I read about gender gaps globally and in Bosnia, about violence against women, weak political participation, economic disparities, unpaid work, and our post-war issues related to regulating the status of women suffering sexual violence in the war.

Learning about the early stages of feminism, broader gender issues, and feminist economics expanded my professional world far beyond what I could have imagined. And also my personal world. Because, inevitably, once I started learning about gender equality, I started reflecting on my own life, on the gender norms I grew up with, how they shaped me and how they still continue to do so. I was learning and un-learning at the same time. Much of what I had absorbed through formal training, particularly in economics, all the models and assumptions started to feel incomplete. They overlooked care work, power relations, social norms, and the deeply human dimensions that shape economic outcomes. At the same time, learning about gender equality enabled me to find my own voice and gave me the confidence to challenge norms I began to understand as deeply embedded in patriarchal structures.

Before I Called Myself a Feminist

But let me start from the beginning.

I come from Sarajevo, from a close-knit, middle-class family of intellectuals. I mention this because the achievements of those who came before me have always filled me with pride: my maternal great-grandfather was a doctor and a minister in the former Yugoslavia, my grandfather a doctor, my father an economist.

But it is the women that I admired the most: my grandmother Natalia, a tall, always impeccably dressed woman and a medical doctor. She was a woman far ahead of her time. In our family, there are still stories about how she left my mother—then only five years old—to pursue a master's degree in another city. Of course, she did not truly leave her; she was travelling back and forth. But for a woman of her generation, even that choice was seen as something to be judged.

Then there was my paternal grandmother, Zlata—the shortest woman in the room, and always the strongest and sharpest. With a single look or sentence, she could restore order.

My aunt Neda was different still. She left Yugoslavia in the 1950s, a fiercely progressive, art-loving woman who chose never to have children and moved alone to Paris to lead the life she chose.

And finally, my mother, Tamara. A professor of pharmacy, she defended her PhD when I was ten years old—a moment I remember with pride and awe. A kind and deeply loving woman, yet with a strange ability to sense dishonesty, a skill I came to respect (and somewhat fear) during my rebellious teenage years.

These extraordinary women were important in my life. Through their choices and their presence, they taught me strength and dignity, and the quiet but radical act of being true to oneself. And then I also had a father who encouraged me. He pushed me toward intellectual and athletic challenges alike, especially alongside the boys. He was proud when I showed my physical strength, and just as proud when I outsmarted our friends on the long hikes we took together.

What mattered most was this: no one ever told me there were things I should or should not do because I was a girl. Well—except once. On a hot vacation day on Rab Island in Croatia, I complained about the heat while my father walked shirtless. As I started taking off my shirt too, he said, "Maja, girls can't do that." I was ten. I still remember it because I had never heard it before, and, at least from my father, never thereafter.

I had a good childhood—feeling loved, supported, and protected. I grew up happy, did well in school, spent my time as a gymnast, and was, like many of my generation, considered a 'good girl.' I loved speaking and entertaining—acting in film and on the theatre stage—but I also liked to speak up when something felt wrong. That combination of being able (or at least trying) to entertain while addressing more serious issues would often help me address injustices or negotiate with teachers the things that were non-negotiable. I would often be the one asked to talk to professors to postpone scheduled tests, making all sorts of excuses for all of us in the class. It sometimes worked. This would come in handy later in my work on gender budgeting. When we try to negotiate things that seem non-negotiable, such as thinking who gets public funds, who does not, and why.

What Happens in the War

But my childhood was in the 1980s and 1990s in Bosnia. And, if you know anything about the Balkans, the region I come from, then you know about the wars. The one that marked my life was the 1992–1995 war.[1]

That war shook my happy, loved, protected childhood. Right before the war broke out, I remember people saying "War cannot happen in Bosnia, or Sarajevo: we are so mixed it would be a proper massacre." (Bosnia's population is a mix of Muslims or Bosniaks, Catholics and Orthodox.) But it *did* happen, and with its share of massacres.

In late April 1992, I convinced my family to take me and my nine-year-old brother Marko to Banjaluka, a smaller city in Bosnia, because schools had closed and nobody knew what would happen in the days to come. At the beginning we thought it would only be days. My mum took us by train to Banjaluka and that was a dreamland for me. I had grandparents there, living in a nice, picturesque house and I imagined it would be like an unplanned holiday. But it wasn't. We stayed there for four years. And, for those four years, we were separated from our dad because after we left Sarajevo, the city fell under siege and was closed off. My father stayed, worked and survived. Unlike many others, among them 1,500 children, who were killed in Sarajevo under the siege.[2]

Since then, everything in my life will forever be measured by "before and after the war." I will still remember years in Banjaluka fondly as my friends from that period are still my closest. But I will also remember how it feels when you lose everything that means safety and security overnight, to be forced into independence before you are really ready for it. I will remember how we would watch the boys we liked, 17 and 18 years old, gathering to join the army and thinking we may never see them again.

When the Dayton Peace Accord was signed in 1995, we came back to Sarajevo. I was 18 then. The city that was once mine was not mine anymore, at least not in the same way. I was not there when it was suffering and when it was broken.

It was hard to be gone, and it was hard to be back. And the family that was apart was now together trying to continue as if the abyss had not happened. We managed.

Hello, World of International Development

Two years after returning to Sarajevo, my father, who now worked in the Ministry of Finance (yes, yes, apples do not fall far from the tree), came home one day, looked at me as I was pretending to study in the living room while watching MTV (1990s, remember) and said: "Asja [a colleague of his working at the US Treasury office] told me they were looking for translators and could not find anybody. Can you imagine, it pays 90 dollars per day… 90 dollars per day!?" (The average salary in Bosnia at that time was probably around 400 dollars per month.) What an opportunity for a 20-year-old student studying economics *and* English language. I called Asja to say I was interested and got an interview soon after.

And that is how I landed my first job. I became a translator for a USAID-funded project on bank development and training. My career in international development had been launched, albeit accidentally. In the seven years I would spend working as translator and later as a so-called local expert in Bosnia, I observed and experienced the world of international development first-hand. Clearly, I love the field, since I stayed for some 20 years—but there were also times when I was confused and disappointed.

My first project was led by four international experts—all men (white American men, if you were wondering), all in their late 50s and 60s—with the rest of us, the team of translators, financial assistants, and drivers that supported them. The dynamics of middle-aged white men leading projects and missions continued to follow me for all my professional years to come. Because international development looks a lot like that. And because finance and public finance look even more that way. Over the period I worked in Bosnia, in different positions, I met about 70 international experts, of whom only three were women and only one was a person of colour.

It is hard to forget the uncomfortable feeling at donor meetings when conversations would sometimes feel demeaning for Bosnia. It felt a bit like everybody in the room knew exactly how to run a country (and not just to help reform the chart of the accounts or support the other technical areas they were hired to do). It was then that I promised myself that if I ever worked internationally, I would never be arrogant enough to think I could solve all the problems of the country while I was invited to work on one expert issue. I continue to work hard to keep that promise.

I learned early how the system is designed so local expertise can never really measure up to that of international experts. Somehow, despite the depth and wealth of knowledge of local experts, and the complete absence of contextual knowledge of many if not most international experts, local experts would never get the same respect (let alone comparable pay) as international ones.

At the same time, I met many kind, respectful, and highly knowledgeable people with a genuine desire to help and with expertise that made a difference. Some of them I called mentors and are among my closest associates and friends.

Public Financial Management and Gender Budgeting

After I graduated in Economics, I started working within public financial management (PFM). In the first project, we worked on introducing performance budgeting (ensuring we funded for the results we are trying to achieve), and I immediately found this area fascinating. For me, though, the most compelling part has always been making public finance more inclusive and understandable—ensuring that citizens know how their money is spent and can influence those decisions. Citizen participation in budgeting was also the focus of my master's degree, which I completed alongside my first PFM project.

Budget systems are often rigid, complex, and bureaucratic, making transparency and inclusion a challenge. When budget information isn't published or is hard to understand, it becomes almost impossible to ensure meaningful public participation or to conduct proper gender analysis. After being introduced to the concept of gender budgeting in 2008, the idea of examining the implications of budget decisions on people—women and men alike—seemed perfectly logical to me. I was puzzled that this was not something that PFM had always done; how could we not bother to look at who was actually receiving the public funds? (Spoiler: usually not women.) Out of roughly 190 countries in the world, 140 enshrine gender equality in their constitutions—so shouldn't public spending reflect that commitment? In reality, it was far from easy. While knowing who benefits from public funds sounds obvious and necessary, it is deeply entangled with the politics of gender equality, the technical complexity of PFM systems, and the persistent disconnect between budgets and real policy outcomes.

The resistance to gender budgeting I have experienced over the years has been matched only by my passion for it.

Becoming a mother is that moment when your feminist self awakens, at least this is what many of my friends experienced, and how I experienced it too. And you feel exactly how much a system is supporting or not supporting you. With my first boy, Andrej, who was born in 2008, I had just two months of paid leave from the USAID project I was working on and then two months unpaid before I had to return to work. So, after four months, I ended up giving most of my salary to a nanny who was babysitting while I was at work.

When I joined UN Women in Bosnia in 2010, they asked me to go to Bratislava to meet with the Regional Director just five days after newly joining the team. My second son, Jan, was just four months old. I remember asking if we could postpone the meeting by a week because I was nursing a baby who was allergic to any milk other than my own. But they insisted the trip could not be delayed. When I came home two days later, my infant son was red and swollen because of the allergic reaction. Following that, I got a daily break for two hours to go and nurse him during lunchtime. This was something UN Women would enable new mothers to do, and it was a true lifesaver.

That period of having small children with such limited maternity leave was one of the hardest periods in my life. I remember wanting to scream as it was almost impossible to leave a four-month-old at home—and even more impossible to focus on progressing in my career even if it was speeding up. I was exhausted but determined to make it work. As we women do, especially when the system we live in is not supportive of us.

Hard Lessons: GRB in Ukraine

In late 2013, just as I started calling myself a GRB 'expert,' I became the team leader for the largest global gender-budgeting project: Gender Budgeting in Ukraine, funded by Sweden. If GRB had changed my life, working in Ukraine deepened that change. The project was a huge five-year project (later extended by two more), with 12 full-time and 20 short-term experts, plus international consultants.

I arrived in Kyiv alone to set up the project and prepare for the family's arrival, leaving my three- and five-year-old boys with my husband back in

Bosnia. On our kick-off day at the Ministry of Finance on February 20, 2014, I found myself in a large, intimidating room on the top floor of the ministry. I was just introducing the project approach when an urgent call came in. We were evacuated mid-meeting: 100 people were killed nearby that day. I was attempting to flee the city and get back home, but our driver Pavel indicated that the city was sieged and the road to the airport was likely to be blocked. Sitting in that car, separated from my family, I remember thinking: *I will walk if I have to; just get us to the airport.* The siege of Sarajevo was too vivid in my memory and I was really afraid. I was desperate to avoid being separated from my family again, terrified that the same scenes we once experienced were happening again. I remember taking a cigarette from my colleague Rimantas who was sitting next to me and both of us smoking in panic. The ride felt like it was taking forever but we managed to fly out of Kyiv that day. Fifteen days later, the situation stabilised and I came back—ready to work, with my family joining soon after.

Ukraine was the most challenging job I could imagine. It took nearly two years to fully understand the institutional culture and procedures, and to align finance and gender expertise into a single approach, as gender budgeting was new for my team as well.

As a young woman in a senior position, I tried hard to be a serious, reserved version of myself for the first years. But soon I realised that that version does not exist: I needed to be me, and as soon as I realised that, things got better. Things also got better thanks to the Project Director, Catharina Schmitz, a gender budgeting expert, who supported me at every step and acted as a true mentor (see her story in Chapter 15). Our team, mostly women, was dedicated and professional, and working together on GRB brought us closer. One of my closest colleagues was Oksana Tsuipa (see Chapter 7) who led the work with the regions.

Over the next seven years, 4,000 civil servants learned about GRB through a training programme we designed and ran. I loved those trainings— those moments when a participant discovered gender equality as something that actually impacts their daily work.

I will always remember Victor Kvyat, the Deputy Head of the Budget Department in the Villnica Oblast (region), who at our first meeting admitted he wasn't sure how gender related to his work. After he participated in the gender budget analysis of the health programme focused on tuberculosis that showed people (especially men) in the rural areas have limited healthcare access, he included funding for a mobile tuberculosis testing lab to reach rural communities. Later, he submitted a proposal to the Ministry of Finance to include GRB in Ukraine's Budget Law. Seeing this change in finance officers—their a-ha moments—was the best part of the job. That, and the tangible results we would see. Like when Lviv Oblast changed its diabetes financing after gender analysis showed insulin procurement wasn't planned properly. Or when the city of Kyiv started engaging more girls in sports thanks to the gender analysis we did together—work that later influenced sports funding at the state level.

I also vividly remember often being the only woman, or one of very few, in donor meetings on PFM. After a roundtable at the Ministry of Finance where I presented on gender budgeting, a 'colleague' from a Western bilateral agency remarked, "OK, now that we have gender budgeting, what's next—animal rights budgeting?" It was a reminder of how entrenched biases can be, even among senior professionals who should know better.

Despite all challenges, together, with our committed colleagues, we achieved something that seemed nearly impossible at the beginning: Ukraine truly started introducing GRB systematically. Gender budgeting is now part of the budget circular, and the GRB Methodology became the first official decree in 2019 recommending all the ministries in Ukraine to do gender analysis as part of their regular budget work.

Ukraine also taught me some hard truths: some people will never embrace gender equality, which makes legislation essential—gender analysis cannot be optional or left to the goodwill of civil servants.

I went back to Ukraine in 2023, as part of the team UN Women engaged to analyse the state of GRB several years after our project ended. Ukraine was then in the middle of war, a full-blown invasion. Most of the Ukrainian budget is now funded externally because of the war. We found the need for GRB to be integrated into this external funding glaringly obvious: donors should be supporting gender analysis including new needs created by the war within a gender budgeting framework that is already established. The Ukrainian government has provisions for gender budgeting, but donors and international partners are not using this framework to make sure gender analysis is done and funds allocated based on the needs of all. The multi-million donor funds coming to Ukraine are not gender-responsive. What a missed opportunity.

International Finance Institutions, TED and Sweden

Somewhere around 2016, GRB was really becoming a thing in the global scene (see Chapters 1 and 19). Finally international finance institutions (IFIs) were starting to pick it up. And I was lucky to be in the right place at the right time, because I had an opportunity to collaborate with the International Monetary Fund (IMF), the Public Expenditure and Financial Accountability (PEFA) Secretariat and the World Bank when some of the GRB frameworks and approaches were just being developed.

On the US election day in November 2016, I was in Washington DC with my colleague Catharina Schmitz to attend the Gender and Macroeconomics Conference organised by the IMF. Christine Lagarde was to open the conference and all we would be talking about was how to bring gender issues into the macroeconomic agenda as well. Bliss!

This was the first time I heard the IMF talk about GRB. I stood up and asked Christine Lagarde a question: "What do you think of the approach Ukraine is taking on gender budgeting to integrate gender throughout budget process?" Her response: "I take my hat off to Ukraine for their work on GRB." From then on, I used this quote in all our project communications!

I will also always remember a presentation I was invited to do for the PFM divisions of the Fiscal Affairs Department of the IMF. I was asked to do an impromptu presentation on GRB and our Ukraine project. I knew this would be one of the first presentations on GRB that some of the colleagues would hear and I really wanted to be an impactful advocate. This was my chance to convince PFM people that GRB made sense and should be integrated more fully into their work. I spent a lot of time thinking about how to engage them. Do I need to be more 'IMFy' (I imagined this to be serious, using lots of charts and research examples and well, a bit dry…)? The meeting was scheduled at 12 noon. I came ten minutes early to already a full room; everybody was in a suit, serious, and, honestly, quite intimidating. I started with my favourite examples and let the presentation flow.

I know in stories like this you expect the writer to tell you how magnificent it all went (or was disastrous), but my presentation was neither. It was a good presentation, but what was most intriguing for me was the marked differences in opinion about GRB expressed by colleagues from the same organisation. Some questions indicated gender equality was really not discussed within PFM reforms, even in institutions such as the IMF. Others relied on personal reflections about gender relations in their countries, pointing both to limited engagement with theoretical frameworks and to the fact that some timid work on gender was often more driven by a specific country (or personal) interest rather than a clear mandate on PFM reforms. That experience underscored the importance of raising awareness when introducing gender perspectives in the mainstream work of IFIs taking a new interest in this direction.

In the years that followed, I was honoured and humbled to collaborate with many great colleagues across institutions and organisations. In these years I have learned that gender budgeting is possible but still very slow and politically coloured (for example, "Oh, now we have a new government they will not support gender and therefore gender budgeting is no longer on the agenda").

I also met colleagues from all over the world (some contributing to this book) and was amazed at how quickly friendships formed, especially with the women I met through this work. Conversations would often shift rapidly from the technical to the personal, and it felt like this had much to do with the nature of gender budgeting itself. By pushing us to talk about real gender issues, the work naturally led to more open, human exchanges.

I was also getting invitations to speak at various events and conferences, an experience I truly enjoyed. One of the most transformative experiences happened in 2021, when I spoke at a major TED conference: *TED Woman* in Palm Springs. I arrived in Palm Springs accustomed to speaking at technical financial gatherings and unprepared for the scale and nature of a TED event. The experience was certainly overwhelming—especially speaking right after Lilly Singh, the brilliant Indian-Canadian comedian. (I was not exactly used to speaking after brilliant entertainers, with all due respect to my public finance colleagues.) Yet it was also deeply humbling to speak about GRB in front of such a large and diverse audience and to focus on one message: public money should serve everyone, not just some of us. The talk—*How to Share Public Money Fairly*—has since reached nearly two million viewers and been translated into eleven languages.

TED opened my world to new sectors and conversations: I met people from the private sector, banking, publishing, and entertainment. That broadened my sense of what collaboration in the nexus of gender and finance might be possible.

Since 2019, our family is living in Sweden as I was invited to continue working for the consultancy firm that implemented the GRB in Ukraine Project (Niras). After years in countries that are shaped by tension and war, my husband and I felt it would be good to live in a place where people can simply live in peace. I am still struck by how naturally gender equality shows in everyday life in Sweden—from girls playing football to fathers walking alone with babies—small scenes that are rare in the countries where I've lived and worked.

As for my family, my husband and our two sons… for years, it bothered me that every successful woman always felt the need to speak about her family one way or another, almost as if she was excusing herself for being successful ("It is all good, all the people are taken care of, my family did not pay the price of my success"). I always resented this patriarchal approach, so I decided that this was never going to be my way. But the truth is: my story would not be mine without them. My husband, Dino, left the civil service in Bosnia to follow my work in Ukraine and later to Sweden, where he rebuilt his own career. Having him as a partner and steadfast supporter through these moves and our life meant more to me than I can fully capture (and more than he would ever like to read!).

Today, I still work with GRB and will probably work with it for all my active years to come. In my mid-forties I am pursuing a PhD focused on, well, gender budgeting. But I am also exploring other areas that have emerged from my work on gender finance. Most recently, I've taken the deep dive into the private sector—my friend Meri Causevic Podzic and I have founded a company that is scaling up the work on GRB to support companies, banks, and yes, governments, in doing better to provide services that will be equitable, sustainable and impactful, especially for future generations. With my colleague and friend Kris Kauffmann, we are working to harness advances in AI to strengthen PFM and deliver broader policy outcomes. Our goal is to ensure that AI is used thoughtfully—to support gender, green, and other priority objectives, and to make better policy delivery possible.

Working on GRB brought together everything I believed in, ensuring that human rights and gender equality are part of the finance conversations. I am hoping that this book will also contribute to this conversation.

Now

It is late 2024, I am sitting somewhere in a Caribbean country on a work assignment. Colleagues from two other PFM missions have joined our team dinner and now six of us are around the table. I am sitting with five men, all of them English speakers, all of them white. Thirty years on from my entry into international development, this world looks just the same as when I was starting.

It is my world, the one I grew up in, but it feels unsettling that we are leaving this kind of inequitable field to new generations who come after us. It feels unsettling knowing that inequalities in our PFM world are insufficiently named, confronted, or acted upon. I hope, I really do, that we won't have to wait thirty years from now to look back and see collective recognition finally gave way to meaningful change.

Meanwhile, I will continue to forge ahead with cherished colleagues, including many contributors to this book, toward a more inclusive world of finance because I plan to be here to witness real change in the way we imagine and re-imagine public and corporate finance.

Notes

1 The Bosnian War (1992–1995) followed the breakup of Yugoslavia. It ended with the Dayton Agreement, establishing Bosnia and Herzegovina's current political structure.

2 UN, 1994, Final Report of the United Nations Commission of Experts Established Pursuant to Security Council Resolution 780 (1992). https://dpu-p-001.sitecorecontenthub.cloud/api/public/content/9984b8ea94b941bf9412da7c078566ed?v=57c7fc17.

Chapter 10

Public Finance Made Me a Feminist!

Hajar Ben Ameur

Back to the Roots: Between Tradition, Ambition and Modernity

Friday, December 24, 2010: I land at Fez-Saïss Airport, returning from Montpellier, the city that hosted me while I was pursuing my Master of Science in Strategic Management, thereby supplementing my degree in economics with management skills. While I studied in France, returning home before December 24 each year had never really been my choice; it was always decided for me. It was an injunction from my mother, who was worried after the wave of attacks that had struck the old continent earlier. She categorically refused to allow her daughter to stay in Europe during Christmas, arguing that these attacks followed a very specific agenda... Of course, we can't blame the terrorists for the lack of transparency regarding their intentions. Yet behind this 'security' argument lay another truth, a much deeper concern and a more intimate fear, rooted in social and cultural codes.

Returning to Morocco each year gave my dear mother the assurance that her daughter, then 24 years old, was not living 'the French way,' with the kind of romantic adventures that the collective imagination associated with the holiday season. So I spent New Year's Eve under her kind, benevolent but vigilant supervision in my hometown, Meknes, one of the four imperial cities of Morocco, where festive life is almost non-existent, while she repeated her familiar monologue about what distinguishes a 'girl from a good family' from others.

Like many Moroccan mothers, mine had very clear expectations: her daughter was meant to study, of course, but above all to respect traditions and conform to social norms, namely, to 'preserve' herself to be considered 'good to marry.' This involved being a devoted wife, a talented cook and an irreproachable mother. In short, a perfection codified by culture. My mother reproduced these traditional patterns, even though she had herself the opportunity to pursue higher education and work as a teacher. She rebelled, yes, but in her own way, with the tools and limitations of her generation. She insisted on being financially independent, on taking decisions at home, on doing things people called 'men's tasks': driving, managing construction

DOI: 10.4324/9781003732532-12

works... But she never crossed the deeper boundaries set by tradition, the ones that weighed most heavily on women.

In fact, in our society, women, and mothers in particular, are cast as the guardians of the temple of traditions, responsible for the education of children and the transmission of cultural values, while ensuring that family honour is preserved. And this 'honour' rests above all on the girls, since the slightest deviation, the faintest rumour can be enough to 'sully' the family's reputation. This notion of honour runs across all social classes, even if it shows up with different forms and different levels of intensity from one context to another. Under this overwhelming pressure, mothers are forced to exercise extreme and permanent control, as if their vigilance alone could contain society's judgments. This imposed role transforms motherhood into a battlefield where daughters' freedom clashes with norms and where mothers become both the protectors and the police of dictated social conformity, intending to avoid any harmful outcomes. I grew up within this framework without fully questioning it.

Then came December 24, 2010. Like every year, I returned home, though I didn't yet know that this time would be different. At the airport, my late father was waiting for me with a radiant smile and told me the unexpected news: I had a job interview scheduled two days later at the Ministry of Finance in Rabat. Surprised by this timing, an avalanche of questions fell on me: how am I going to prepare for an interview in just two days? I don't know anything about public finance, apart from a few basic concepts learned in class... And what about my life in France? My projects? My friends? My belongings? My parents reassured me, "You won't lose anything by trying. In any case, there is little chance that you will be selected."

That night, something in me resisted the idea of walking into the interview unprepared. Maybe it was pride, or simply curiosity, the quiet need to understand what I was getting into. I spent hours scrolling through articles about Morocco's budgetary system and the mission of the Ministry, trying to make sense of a world I barely knew. In my head, I told myself it was a chance to serve my country, to challenge myself in a field I had not yet mastered, and to join a prestigious institution. Even today, I'm still not sure whether that was a genuine conviction or a quiet defence mechanism, a way to make peace with a path I hadn't chosen... yet.

Five months later, on May 3, 2011, I officially took up my duties at the Ministry of Finance. I will skip the months leading up to that date, filled with doubts, uncertainties and conflicting emotions. I felt torn between the desire to rebel against every social injunction and the need to please my mother who after all, only wanted, according to her frame of reference, "the best for her daughter"; this involved a return to the country to remain under her gaze as well as her protective affection and vigilant control.

As a docile girl, who had always followed instructions to the letter, I resigned myself to becoming what society and its norms expected of me: to be independent but not too much, to be ambitious but not too much, and above all to respect (a little too much) traditions.

At that time, I would have liked to understand the dynamics of gender, to lighten the weight of guilt that society inflicts on us, to gain free will and to understand earlier why my ambition had to be conditional and why the word 'choice' sounded more like a privilege and not a right… But this awareness would come ten years later.

Landing in the Corridors of the Budget Machine: Whirlwind and Attachment

This is how I was propelled into the fascinating, yet confusing, world of public finance and budget management, a career that I would not have imagined embracing, as I saw myself rather destined for research and economic models.

At that time, everything looked like a scene from the movie *Inception*: nested dreams, landmarks that bend without a fuss, and the spinning top of a stubborn doubt that never stopped turning. I was moving in this fluid setting, alone with my questions, aware that something inside me was moving forward, without yet knowing where to.

The first years were thus marked by a feeling of being lost, fuelled by several factors. First, I found myself immersed in a world that I did not know, a complex and rigorous field where numbers, laws and procedures seemed to have their own language. Secondly, the weight of expectations, both personal and professional, accentuated this feeling of loss. I was fighting to find my place, to prove my competence in an environment mostly run by men, where I felt like an outsider, navigating a system with codes and subtleties that I was just beginning to master. At the same time, I struggled with doubts and uncertainties about the choices imposed by the circumstances, and the expectations of my own family, who saw this position as an assured success.

Yet, like those suspended moments in *Inception*, where everything wobbles without collapsing, I had a glimmer of light in me, small but tenacious. A discreet hope, a still timid but persistent conviction that, despite the challenges, I would eventually find my own path in this unfamiliar universe.

The first years were also marked by a continuous learning process both technically and interpersonally. It must be said that I was lucky enough to be assigned to a unit that was being established to oversee the new budgetary reforms. I was the first to join this unit, which often earns me the joke of the 'dinosaur' of the team.

Little by little, the team grew, driven by a work dynamic based on respect, solidarity and true kindness. This atmosphere was due in large part to the human qualities of our manager. But the balance shifted with the arrival of a member in a middle management position, which gradually plunged the team into an atmosphere of adversity, tension and misunderstanding.

As soon as this new member arrived, harmony within the team broke: tensions arose, misunderstandings multiplied, and trust between colleagues eroded. Managing this situation was challenging for everyone, as it influenced not only the work environment, but also the collective morale.

What made the situation more disconcerting was the tendency of this person to lash out, particularly at the women on the team, condescendingly questioning our skills under the guise of professional demand. Her remarks, often laced with gender stereotypes, revealed deeply internalised sexism, more troubling because it came from a woman.

There is often a tendency to associate workplace harassment, in all its forms, with men's actions. However, some women can, consciously or not, reproduce the same mechanisms of domination as those exercised by some men. This is what makes such situations of abuse particularly confusing and difficult to address, even taboo. But whatever their origin, these behaviours must be named, confronted and denounced, which was done in this case.

After several months of unease and unspoken tensions, a few of us, men and women collectively, finally found the courage to speak up, softly at first, then with growing certainty. This was not easy; there was hesitation and the quiet fear of being misunderstood. But once the words were out, something shifted. The issue eventually reached top management, who decided to reassign her to another department, not as a sanction, but to give her space to reflect on her management style. That decision brought a sense of relief, not triumph. It was about restoring balance, about proving that solidarity, when grounded in truth, can protect more than disrupt.

From a personal point of view, it opened my eyes to the complexities of workplace relationships. Having evolved from the very beginning in an environment that was generally supportive, at least on the surface, this was my first direct confrontation with open conflict. Beyond the daily tensions with this person, it was the apprehension that weighed on us the most: the fear of the next clash, the misunderstanding that might arise with a colleague, or the falsehood that would be reported without any basis. This constant vigilance exhausted us much more than the disagreements themselves.

I, who had always believed that discipline and competence were enough to guarantee balance at work, discovered that some interactions escaped the logic of reciprocity. They rest on fragile balances, where power, authority, ego, fears and prejudices quietly intertwine.

I also came to understand another reality, more insidious and often passed over in silence: in some professional settings, the simple fact of having a somewhat assertive presence, or a certain ease of interpersonal skills can be enough to disturb and arouse jealousy. We do not always measure how destabilising appearance and confidence, even subtle ones, can be, especially when they come from a woman in a context still marked by implied power relations.

This realisation was not easy, because it shook up my vision of the professional world. But it also helped me shape my professional character and the management style I wanted to adopt. It must be said that we often prepare for professional life by developing our technical skills, but we often neglect preparation for the complexities of human interactions.

The world of work is not only about the accomplishment of tasks or the processing of files. It is, above all, a question of navigating relationships, with colleagues, hierarchy, and sometimes oneself, while learning to read the invisible dynamics that shape every exchange. And among these dynamics, those related to gender are often the most insidious because they are pervasive, influence perceptions and draw unconscious power relations that need to be perceived and addressed.

With hindsight, I realise that we don't really set foot in the world of work. We land there, often tiptoeing our way, seeking a fragile balance between what we thought we knew and what we discover about ourselves. At the beginning, everything was a matter of hesitation. Nothing had the clarity of an arrival, nor the sharpness of a point of departure. As if suspended between two states, it took precisely this vertigo to find a point of support, where something was beginning to take shape.

It may not have been the path I had imagined, but it is the one that built me.

Becoming a Chief: a Combination of Circumstances

When I joined the Ministry, climbing the ladder of responsibility seemed like a distant goal, almost unthinkable. My ambition at that time was simple: to do my job as well as possible and fulfil the missions entrusted to me, while devoting my evenings to academic research and dreaming of a quieter, more introspective future.

I imagined myself in a withdrawn profession, shaped by models, equations and far from human interactions. I had never thought of running for a position of responsibility. But, as is often the case, life took care of changing the script. What I imagined as a straight line turned into a side road.

The first opening toward leadership arrived in 2015, through a confluence of circumstances since fate, or what resembles it, led me to a unit in the process of being established. With a search for a managerial role, I faced a dilemma: should the opportunity be seized? Should I manifest interest? Above all, the question I couldn't silence: was I truly legitimate?

Four years had already passed since I joined my first unit. By then, I had built solid skills and developed a surprising and growing interest in fields as varied as budgeting, performance monitoring, training and communications. Despite this, the question of legitimacy remained omnipresent, like a sword of Damocles hanging between what I did and what I thought I was worth.

This constant self-questioning was not trivial. As a young woman, I continually faced biases that challenged my competence and my ability to assume leadership roles. Sceptical looks, subtle but persistent comments about my age or experience, and smiles tinged with surprise when I spoke in meetings, were relatively common. Nothing overtly hostile, just a few micro-aggressions, hard to name yet enough to shake my self-confidence little by little.

And then there are those scenes, almost banal, yet unforgettable. Who among us women have never heard the famous "I'd like to speak to your boss…." Implicitly, a man of course, as soon as a problem arises or a decision displeases. As if our word was just a draft or an insignificant version before the final statement. As if authority, the real authority, always belonged a notch higher. A masculine notch of course. And in my head, the response is scathing and sharp: "He's in a meeting with the patriarchy, can I help you in the meantime?"

These moments are not ideal. They accumulate, and they shape a posture by force: that of having to constantly prove, legitimise and explain. Not just doing but justifying doing. In such an environment, it was hard to feel fully legitimate, which fed my imposter syndrome. A nagging feeling of having to constantly earn one's place, especially when climbing the ladder of responsibilities, promised to be strewn with pitfalls. Indeed, the process of accessing to a managerial position, involving a formal application and high-level interviews, is a real test of endurance. It carries an emotional weight, a mix of hope, doubt, and, at times, disappointment. Success brings joy, but rejection often leaves a silent wound.

My own path to leadership was no exception. I eventually got the positions I applied for, usually on my second try, but each time felt like a marathon that tested far more than just technical skills. Behind the calm smiles and polite exchanges, there were quiet rivalries, unspoken games, and moments that left invisible bruises.

And I cannot forget the times when I was not selected after working so hard. I remember it with painful clarity. Failure, in those moments, was not just professional, it was intimate. It stepped into the fragile space between who I was and who I thought I could become, leaving me haunted by a single question: why? Why hadn't I been judged up to the task? I later understood that the answer was not always straightforward. It was not necessarily about being a woman, or about an intentional bias, but often a complex mix of criteria and circumstances I could not control. Eventually, I stopped trying to understand every detail; only the feeling stayed.

And yet, as painful as this ordeal was, it ultimately strengthened me, giving me the perseverance and confidence to follow my own path. What had seemed like an irreversible failure turned out to be a disguised opportunity, a chance to redefine myself.

And with years of experience, I came to realise that sometimes it is you who must say no. I remember having to turn down a position within an international organisation, a role that matched everything I had worked for, simply because I was not able to move abroad. It was a very difficult decision, that left a lingering trace of regret.

Through those experiences, and many others, I came to understand then that a career path would not be reduced to positions won or missed, but to this ability, patiently forged, to transform adversity into momentum. For that, I can only be grateful.

Then came a new challenge, one that would shake my accustomed life and transform the way I see the world. In 2019, I was entrusted with managing the deployment of Gender Responsive Budgeting (GRB) in Morocco. This is how my professional trajectory would come across, even though I had never really claimed it, feminism.

Gender Responsive Budgeting: the Project That Led Me to Feminism

I still remember the day my superior came to inform me that our unit would take charge of the GRB file, and that I would be given its operational management. At that moment, I was far from enthusiastic. My schedule was already full, and the idea of taking on another project seemed overwhelming. To be completely honest, this subject, which I barely knew, did not spark any excitement. It aroused neither curiosity nor enthusiasm, just an inner sigh. But I accepted. Without realising it, I had just stepped into a professional and personal journey that would gradually unsettle certain obvious facts and offer me a new way of reading reality.

There was no sudden revelation, but rather a slow, methodical, and almost insidious deconstruction. Through readings, training workshop and above all the people I met, a veil was gradually lifted. As I immersed myself in the realities of gender inequalities, I understood how deeply systemic they were. Gender inequality is a mechanism, embedded in laws, public policies, budgets and even in institutional silences.

To address these structural gaps, Morocco, like many countries at the time, turned to GRB as a concrete tool, using the budget not only to finance policies but also to address inequities.

Over the past two decades, the country has built one of the most advanced and institutionalised GRB models in the region. What began in the early 2000s as a small pilot gradually evolved into a national approach anchored in the Organic Finance Law. The creation of the Centre of Excellence for GRB in 2014 consolidated this progress, providing technical support, training and analytical tools to line ministries and agencies. These combined achievements, legal anchorings, instruments, institutional structures, and international recognition, form a solid foundation that few countries have yet achieved.

Yet this progress came with challenges: misconceptions about GRB, subtle forms of resistance, and deeper structural obstacles that touched core dimensions: data, actors and process. The lack of reliable sex-disaggregated data made it difficult to measure impact, the level of engagement among actors varied widely, and embedding gender across all budget phases, including procurement policies and public investment, remained difficult. Overcoming these obstacles required patience, evidence, and continuous dialogue to show that GRB strengthens not only equality, but also efficiency and accountability.

Within this evolving landscape, my main role was to ensure a pragmatic approach to GRB deployment, closely aligned with the logic of performance-based budgeting. I wanted gender to be more than a social ambition; it had to become a measurable policy outcome. Guided by this conviction, I contributed to the development of several key instruments, including the gender budget tagging system, sectoral gender analyses, and the setting of gender-sensitive objectives and indicators.

So, through Morocco's experience with GRB, I learned to read between the lines of budgets, to spot what is not counted, to see those who are made invisible and who end up being ignored. This nourished in me a deep conviction: that of contributing, even modestly, to a change in outlook and practices.

GRB also allowed me to open up to the world. I met remarkable, committed experts (yes almost exclusively women) from all over the world. With some of them, bonds have been forged naturally driven by a common energy. A rare and precious form of sisterhood, difficult to find in other fields. We shared our doubts, difficulties and small victories. Often, it was the small details, tricks, and bold ideas that rekindled our hope that, sometimes, the lines can move. Over time, I became part of a real community of practitioners, nothing formal, just familiar faces encountered from one mission or workshop to another, united by the same convictions and the same drive to advance equality.

Being part of such a global community pushed me beyond my linguistic comfort zone. I spoke my broken English with experts whose French was just as imperfect, but our discussions were always filled with humour. The bursts of laughter, especially when Maja Bosnić confused '*marquage*' ('tagging' in French) with '*maquillage*' ('make-up' in French), during a workshop with 20 people, still resonate in my memories. These moments of lightness hid a deep strength: the feeling that, despite our different languages, we were ultimately speaking the same one, the language of change.

And then, this project opened the world to me in a different way, through the travels it made possible... Abidjan, Libreville, Yaoundé, Abu Dhabi, Istanbul... and so many others. These are not just names of the cities where I landed, they are fragments of my path. I remember the faces I met, those who reached out to me, offered me an opportunity to collaborate, shared knowledge or confided a moving story. I think back to the country experiences, the collective commitments and the passion of the actors who campaign, often with few resources, to advance the equality agenda.

And there were also the places that carry within them a painful memory, such as Kigali, whose poignant history continues to haunt and inspire.

Rwanda, a country that, despite tragic hardships, has risen to become a model of gender equality. These countries have transformed me as much as the missions I have carried out there.

But on the ground, there was a lot of resistance. On several occasions in meetings, I was told that "these women's stories" were an unnecessary constraint, a kind of fad imported from abroad that supposedly had no connection to local realities. I was often told that equality was already achieved: "There are women in meetings, aren't there?," as if their mere presence was enough.

The most frustrating thing was the refusal to listen, the disguised contempt. Of course, when a topic was considered 'serious' or 'technical,' everyone paid attention. Still, as soon as it was a question of gender equality, many feel exempt from learning, convinced that they already knew. This showed how marginalised the issue is still being seen, a mere 'bonus.' This is why mastering the technical aspects of the budget process and gender equality issues is not enough. You also have to know how to convince and defend the cause in spaces that are often hostile or indifferent. Expertise alone does not make change, it must also be translated into a powerful plea, capable of shaking up certainties.

This path, demanding and sometimes confusing, has made me, today, a feminist, both by choice and through experience. A feminism grounded in one simple truth: women and men belong equally to humanity and must therefore enjoy the same rights and deserve the same dignity. And because rights only become real when institutions make them real, my feminism is institutional and pragmatic, born not in the streets or through slogans, but from the perseverant and persistent work of reforming systems, questioning what is called 'neutral' and turning equality into a measurable commitment rather than an abstract ideal.

All thanks to the GRB project that I had agreed to lead, at the beginning, out of nothing more than simple duty, unaware of how deeply it would reshape me.

A Journey Made Possible: the Key Role of Support

If I have been able to move forward on this path, it is largely thanks to the precious support I have received, first and foremost from my husband. He was, and remains, a constant anchor, a partner on the road who understood very early on that my ambitions were not opposed to our family balance, but that they were fully part of it. He never asked me to choose between being a woman, a mother, or professionally accomplished. He simply supported me without ever dramatising his support, as if it were the most natural thing in the world.

And yet, even with a 'deconstructed' partner, the mental load sticks to the skin. My days are dense, sometimes overflowing; I often exceed normal hours at work, attending back-to-back meetings, giving presentations and urgent reports before running home so as not to miss my son's bedtime ritual. Meanwhile, my mind remains alert: I think at the same time about the fridge, my husband's vegan meal to prepare, homework to check, my mother's medical appointment and birthdays not to forget… Even when tasks are shared, planning, anticipating, coordinating and everything that wears without seeing each other, continues to be assumed, almost naturally, by women. So yes, I have a deconstructed man by my side, but I live in a world that is not.

Along this journey, I also had the chance to meet inspiring people, some with more experience who not only passed on their technical know-how to me but also opened my eyes to perspectives I would not necessarily have considered on my own.

There are also those rare but valuable colleagues who taught me that success is not only about our individual efforts, but also about the relationships and alliances that nurture our progress. And that in the often-hostile corridors of the administration, a well-placed word, a knowing look, a network can change a destiny. Thanks to this support, I learned to face failures, to be reborn after each setback, big or small. I consider myself fortunate to have these essential mentors and supports. In turn, I try to reciprocate by accompanying the youngest, especially women, by reaching out to those who still have doubts, and by reminding every woman that she carries within her a strength much greater than she imagines.

GRB was an essential part of this journey and brought me exactly where I needed to be. It acted as a breach and was a mirror through which I learnt to see, to think and to exist differently. It is also through this project that I met luminous, brilliant women, free in their posture, who made me want to be like them, by revisiting my own frameworks, my own certainties and by broadening my perception of what is possible.

Today, I no longer define myself solely as a practitioner engaged in a budget reform aimed at gender equality. I am, in my own way, a feminist convinced that the public budget is a real lever for equality. On my bedside table, Simone de Beauvoir's *The Second Sex* does not sit as a rigid manifesto, but as a complicit voice that guides my reflection and accompanies my questions. This book obviously taught me that you are not born a woman, you become one.

And, beyond that, something even more intimate: one is not born a feminist: one becomes one. Sometimes at the turn of a budget that renders people invisible, sometimes through a fight that we thought neutral, sometimes through a silence that has been tolerated far too long. It is in this passage from silence to voice, from conformity to gentle yet determined and thoughtful rebellion, that the true power of feminism emerges: the one that liberates, transforms and illuminates, both those who embody it and those who cross its path.

My story is not inspiring in the classic sense of the word. It is the story of a woman who has long been a conformist, not out of weakness but out of prudence, for fear of disappointing the expectations placed on her. A girl who followed the lines, ticked the boxes, learned to do well, to speak well, to please well. And yet… it is precisely in this fragile balance, in this balance between what she was supposed to be and what she sensed deep inside, that an inner shift took place. From a slow, almost imperceptible, but irreversible awakening, was born a passionate woman, who puts all her heart into what she undertakes and who learns to welcome what life offers her.

And perhaps this, after all, is what deserves to be told.

Chapter 11

Beyond the Numbers

Making Budgets Work for Women and Girls

Ermira Lubani

Introduction

When I got the call for the job interview in 2009, I wasn't quite sure what I had applied for. Terms such as 'gender responsive budgeting' and 'public financial management' were new to me, and government budgets were neither my strength nor my area of expertise. Yet at that point in my life, I was aware of gender inequalities, deeply committed to human rights, and eager to work in a field where I could make a real difference in the lives of women and girls. I went to the interview, and that moment changed the course of my professional life. Gender responsive budgeting (GRB) soon became a central part of it.

My Foundations

Growing up in Albania at the end of communism in the 1980s meant living between two worlds: one where equality was loudly proclaimed, and another where inequality shaped daily reality. The propaganda celebrated the young women driving tractors and machines, creating an illusion of liberation, while expectations at home stayed the same. Women were placed in so-called 'neutral' jobs in name only, without any support for their double burden: earning a wage outside while caring for the family and community inside. Looking after children and the home was seen as a woman's 'natural' duty; something that never belonged to the world of men.

In the public sphere, equality was measured in numbers; in the private sphere, patriarchal hierarchies remained untouched. Men held positions of elite party power, while women were steered into 'feminine' fields such as education, health, and welfare. Domestic violence remained invisible, women were unprotected, and official mechanisms were absent. The state controlled the narrative: rights were 'granted' from above and any demand for more was stigmatised. A feminist movement was unthinkable; gratitude was expected, and activism discouraged. Professed equality was a façade; the reality was discipline and silence.

DOI: 10.4324/9781003732532-13

Even when women were 'included,' the power to reshape their roles was never theirs to claim. The promotion of working-class women served as the ideological decorum of a 'classless' society, yet in practice it created another layer of exclusion. Women from other social classes, especially those with no direct ties to the communist system, were left aside. This focus on formal equality was most evident in public life and institutions, where women's visibility in prominent roles was presented as proof of the state's success in achieving gender equality. Thus, the system produced formal equality for show, but substantial inequality for real life.

A New World of Freedom

When communism collapsed in Albania in the early 1990s, I was a student, immersed in the spirit of change and eager to join the movement for a new democratic system. It was an extremely intense and transformative period in my life and, looking back, I realise how deeply those experiences shaped who I am and the path I ultimately chose. The transition from a strict authoritarian regime to an open democratic system was not just a shift in government or policies. It was a completely new vision of what life could look like, especially for those of us who had spent our youth under the constraints of communism.

I remember the energy in the streets, the whispering conversations that suddenly turned into open calls for change. For the first time, people started talking about things they had previously only dared to think about, as Albania opened its doors to new ideas and opportunities. For me, joining this movement was like entering a new world where freedom and self-expression were no longer taboo ideals, but realities you could achieve. I became quite confident that change was possible and that each of us had a role to play.

As a student, I joined marches, discussions and protests, driven by a passion for freedom and the idea that every individual had rights worth fighting for. Those first days of transition built within me a spirit of steadfastness and an unwavering belief that freedom and human rights are worth every effort. At the time, I realised that it could even take one person alone to make a difference, contribute to change, which was completely opposite to what communism had taught us: be silent and obey the orders and ideology of the party.

During that period, my father was the president of trade unions in Albania, leading numerous protests across the country. Watching him fight so passionately for change, I saw him as a hero, a man who brought hope and transformation to our country. He was an inspiration and guide to my later career ideals.

The transition from communism to democracy gave me new lenses to see the world. For so long, my understanding had been shaped by the state's carefully crafted narrative, but now I could explore different perspectives, read about events in other countries, and hear voices that had previously been silenced. The more I learned, the more I realised that the struggle for freedom and equality was not unique to Albania; it was part of a broader global effort. This was particularly illuminating in the field of gender equality. I was eager to learn what was happening beyond our borders, especially in terms of human rights and gender equality. I read articles, listened to debates, and absorbed everything I could about how other societies approached these issues. The more I learned, the more I felt compelled to be a part of this great movement for change.

Now, with the freedom to discuss, question and learn, I realised that true gender equality was much more complex than a simple declaration of equality by the state. It required systemic change, a shift in attitudes, behaviour, and opportunity.

In the years that followed, this commitment to gender equality became central to my work and identity. I wanted to channel that energy and passion into helping other women experience the freedoms and rights that I had learned to value so much. I saw gender equality as a fundamental human right, and I knew that achieving it required not only political change, but also a profound cultural shift in the way we see and appreciate each other.

Looking back, I realise that my experiences during this transition from communism to democracy didn't just change my perspective; they gave me a purpose. I had seen firsthand what it meant to live under a system that restricted freedoms and controlled narratives, and I never wanted to go back there. I became determined to work towards a world where everyone, regardless of gender, had a voice and a seat at the table. This journey from a student protester on the streets of Albania to an advocate for gender equality on the global stage was not just about changing systems: it was about wanting to help women and girls harness their potential and power to shape the world around them.

In order to turn that commitment into practical impact, I knew that I needed to have not only the tools to realise a real change, not only the language of human rights, but I needed the skills to build programmes and manage the results. So I decided to study further and received a postgraduate degree in 2002 in International Project Management in Canada, where gender, international development, and economic growth were addressed in depth.

Finding My Path

When I was selected as coordinator of the GRB programme at UNIFEM in 2009 in Albania, I was excited but also worried. Then, my biggest question was: "How can a national budget support women's rights and equality?" The link between budgets and policies was not yet clear to me, and I had to learn how public finances relate to the real-life outcomes we see in society. It was an overwhelming concept at first, but I was determined to understand and bring gender considerations into discussions on public finance.

At first, discussions were often unpleasant or difficult. I had to convince others that budgets were not just about numbers, they were about people's lives and affected women and men in different ways. Raising the topic of gender in discussions on finance, though, met resistance, scepticism, and sometimes outright rejection. I remember one of my first meetings in the Ministry of Finance. I was surrounded by senior officials and felt the weight of their scepticism as I began to talk about the importance of GRB. As I introduced the concept of gender, a senior official interrupted me and said, in front of everyone, that "numbers don't have sex." According to him, finances and policies were gender neutral, and it made no sense to try to approach budgeting from a gender perspective. He suggested that I focus on "real issues of gender equality," which, according to him, meant going and meeting representatives of the Ministry of Labour and Social Policy. I realised that I was not only facing resistance to my ideas but also a deeply ingrained mindset that saw gender issues as separate from the heart of government and, above all, from money!

The official went further, adding that the budget was an essential government policy, too important to be 'complicated' by gender issues. He advised me to talk to women working in the Ministry of Finance if I wanted to talk about 'women's issues.' The subtext was clear: gender issues were minor, 'women's work,' and had no place in high-level financial planning. At that moment, I felt disbelief and disappointment, but even more determination than ever to keep working.

I left that meeting knowing that changing mindsets would require not just passion but evidence, economic arguments, and strategic patience. I realised that if I could convince even one or two decision-makers of the importance of GRB, it could have a spiralling effect. I started digging deeper, learning everything I could about budgets and public finances. I studied how budgets were designed, how they reflected policy priorities, and how they could produce tangible and measurable results. Slowly, I began to realise that the budget is not just a financial document; it is a blueprint of a country's priorities and values. It's a map that shows what a government cares about and who it believes is worth investing in.

Over time, I learned how to build bridges between gender issues and financial policy, formulating arguments that spoke to the concerns of officials in the Ministry of Finance. I began to point out examples of how investments in health, education, and economic opportunities for women and girls could bring tangible economic benefits, pointing out that GRB was both a social and economic necessity. I started to frame GRB as a way to make public spending more effective, more efficient and more responsive to the needs of women and men, girls and boys.

It seemed like a pioneering effort, and I was navigating unknown waters, testing strategies, and figuring out what might work in our context. It was a difficult undertaking, but the more I worked, the more I felt the sense of purpose and calling. This was the right thing to do! How can we manage public funds without knowing the basics?

Building Regional Alliances

I wasn't alone, though. Colleagues at UN Women (formerly UNIFEM) across the Western Balkans were doing the same, each in their own country, trying to pave a path for the GRB in environments where it was largely unknown. Our regular team meetings became invaluable, as they provided a space where we could gather, discuss experiences, share frustrations and discuss new solutions. We talked about what worked, what didn't, and how we could adapt and reproduce the best practices we found.

Little by little, GRB began to take shape as a regional approach. It was no longer an isolated initiative in one country; it was becoming a recognised strategy across the Balkans, with the potential to have a real impact on gender equality in every state. We knew that our efforts could influence policies that affect the lives of women and men, and the sense of purpose and responsibility was both exciting and challenging.

An essential part of our work was to draw inspiration from countries where GRB had already proved successful. We studied the Austrian, Spanish, Icelandic and Swedish experiences, countries that had already established the GRB framework, and used their successes to build credibility in the eyes of our governments. We wanted our governments to see that GRB was not a complex or impossible concept. By presenting case studies and examples from these advanced countries, we demonstrated that the GRB was not 'hard science'; it was an accessible and effective approach that could be adapted to our context. Showing our government counterparts these practical examples helped break some of the initial scepticism and resistance.

From the beginning, we understood that making GRB sustainable required more than just government engagement. We were clear about the role that civil society, parliaments, supreme audit institutions and gender equality activists should play.

From Concept to Impact

The GRB is not just about allocating funds; it is about creating accountability, transparency and ensuring that budgets reflect the real needs of everyone in society. We needed social actors who could continue to push for these changes, monitor progress and hold governments accountable. With this in mind, we worked to create the first 'GRB watchdog' network across the Western Balkans and Moldova. I remember the emotion in the first meetings, the energy in the hall as we discussed how we could together shape the future of GRB in our region. We knew this network would take time to grow and strengthen, but we also knew its potential power. We envisioned a future where this group would have a strong and unified voice, advocating for gender equality and holding our governments accountable.

Looking back, I realise that what we achieved was not just about implementing a budget framework. We were planting seeds for a cultural shift, showing that budgets can be used as tools for social change. It was an effort rooted in collaboration, resilience, and the belief that meaningful change is possible when people come together around a common goal. The journey was challenging, but the progress we made and the network we created with government officials continues to inspire and remind me of the power of perseverance and partnership.

Global Momentum for GRB

The GRB is no longer a new or experimental approach; in fact, it has gained a huge scope globally. Today, 110 governments report on the implementation of the Sustainable Development Goals 5.c.1 indicator.[1] This indicator measures the extent to which countries implement GRB as part of their commitment to the SDGs. By tracking the GRB within the framework of this indicator, countries not only show commitment to gender equality but also create tangible systems to ensure that gender considerations are integrated into their budget planning and processes.

Furthermore, GRB has become an integral part of the "Public Expenditure and Financial Accountability (PEFA) framework." PEFA has incorporated gender considerations directly into public financial management (PFM) reforms, which means that gender is increasingly seen as central to effective and fair management of public finances. This integration is a powerful step forward because it puts gender considerations at the centre of how public funds are allocated, spent and valued. Rather than being seen as an add-on or secondary concern, gender equality is now recognised as essential to achieving transparent, accountable and efficient public financial systems.

Through these frameworks and indicators, the GRB is gaining recognition not only as a tool for gender equality, but as a vital component of sustainable development and good governance. Countries are increasingly recognising that GRB helps them address gender inequalities, meet the needs of all citizens more effectively, and build more sustainable economies. By institutionalising the GRB within PFM reforms, governments are creating sustainable structures that prioritise gender equality, while ensuring that resources are allocated in ways that support women, men and marginalised groups fairly.

Today, I feel a sincere sense of pride and hope as I look back at the impact of our work. We set out on a journey to make GRB a reality, and now we're looking at the ways it's really changing lives. Every step we have taken has brought us closer to a vision of equality that is not only theoretical but visible in the everyday realities of women, men, girls and boys.

I remember the emotion I felt when the 'budget law amendment' was adopted in Albania in 2016, when gender considerations became mandatory in the Budget Circular, programmes and budget processes. What was once simply an idea is now a legal requirement, GRB directly involved in the budget-making structure. Then came the moments when we saw changes in 'specific subsidy programmes' that directly benefited women living in rural areas, such as those in the Ministry of Agriculture and the Ministry of Economy. Suddenly, women who had been neglected were receiving direct support.

One of the most significant achievements was the reform of the 'economic aid law.' Previously, cash transfers were administered almost exclusively by men, leaving aside many women in need. But now, thousands of women have direct access to these funds, giving them not only financial support but also autonomy. And I can't help but feel immensely proud to see supreme audit institutions in the Western Balkan countries produce reports that hold governments accountable, urging them to meet commitments on gender equality and demanding transparency about how budgets are allocated and spent.

I also see an increasing number of civil society organisations involved in budget oversight and participatory processes, amplifying community voices and adding accountability requirements. Seeing the rise of women advocating for their needs at local budget meetings is inspiring. These are women who, not so long ago, might not have thought that their voices would have weight in such processes. Then there's investing in the 'care economy'—a once-neglected area now recognised as essential to reducing gender inequality.

We understood the importance of 'gender-segregated data' to assess how resources are used and what impact they have on gender equality. We've included 'gender impact assessments' for the new revenue and spending proposals, and we're seeing IT systems evolve to correctly identify gender-related spending. This also includes tracking gender-specific spending within plans, spending and keeping sex-disaggregated data in procurement databases.

Gender budgeting thrives when there is an enabling environment that supports it, and that environment does not happen by itself, it is built. We have worked to create this through a strong legal framework, a coordinated GRB implementation structure and a support network involving civil society and the public. We have prioritised capacity-building for civil servants and have invested in data management practices so that information collected and published by national statistical agencies reflects the realities of gender dynamics.

The Other Side of the Story

This chapter helped me reflect on my journey, in which working for GRB has been an essential part of the past two decades. Twenty years is a long time to devote to a concept. However, for me, GRB has never been just a concept. It is a whole-of-government approach that recognises that governments exist to serve people, and that people's lives, needs, and realities are not the same.

As I wrote this story of my life, I hesitated to talk about my family, beyond GRB's 'working family.' Perhaps because, somehow, it annoys me how often women are expected to express gratitude for understanding husbands and supportive bosses, or for anyone who 'allows' us to be ourselves. Sometimes it makes me feel like we're almost apologising for being successful and constantly surrendering our power. But here I am, and it would be impossible to write my story about GRB, or any story of my own, without talking about my family... my reality. Without it, history would be incomplete. My husband, Arben, an Albanian like me, non-traditional, feminist, has been my unwavering support. It's thanks to Ben that I was able to work long hours, travel 200 days a year and still come home to love, root, and belonging. His quiet strength and shared values supported me to follow my path with all the demand and intensity that was required. My two daughters, who didn't fully understand the impetus and sometimes my 'crazy' passion for work, are now two strong, wise and loving women, with their voices and stories to share. They understand now, in ways they couldn't as children, why this work mattered. My mother has been my quiet anchor, her strength, resilience and unconditional love have kept me going through every challenge. Even from afar, her presence reminded me of where I come from and why this work matters.

The Road Ahead: Equality as a Goal

Looking back on this journey, I realise that it has not been an easy path, neither personally nor professionally, but each challenge has strengthened my belief in the power of equality and the power of fighting and working for what I believe is right. I have been fortunate to meet brave feminist women and men along the way who have been my friends on this journey. They touched my life so deeply, making it richer and more meaningful. Now, as I advance in my career, overseeing GRB initiatives across the Europe and Central Asia region, I feel more inspired than ever to continue this work. The journey is far from over, but with every step, I see the transformative impact we are creating, and it renews my commitment to advancing gender equality.

Every step forward is proof that budgets are not just numbers on a page, they are tools for equality, instruments that can shape a fairer future. Knowing that I have had a role in bringing these changes to life gives me a great sense of purpose and optimism.

It challenged me, inspired me, and gave me purpose to continue in the future.

Note

1 Goal 5 | Department of Economic and Social Affairs, https://sdgs.un.org/goals/goal5.

Part III

From Margin to Mainstream: Gender *in* Budgeting

Chapter 12

Pioneering Gender Budgeting in Indonesia

An Interview

Maya Rostanty

Introduction

I have had the privilege of working with Maya Rostanty for six years. She is widely recognised as one of Indonesia's foremost experts in gender responsive budgeting (GRB) and a rare example of someone who has been working both within the non-governmental organisation (NGO) and government sectors, earning deep respect across the board.

Tanty, as we call her—partly to avoid the confusion of having two 'Maj(y) as' in our circle—is soft-spoken, measured, and exceptionally sharp. She doesn't speak often, but when she does, her insights cut straight to the heart of the matter. As we talk, I am reminded that she has been instrumental in reshaping Indonesia's entire GRB system, ensuring that gender analysis is an integral part of strategic planning and budgeting in Indonesia.

When I first approached Tanty about sharing her story, I wasn't sure she'd agree. She prefers action over talking about herself. But I was wrong—she had plenty to say. Her journey spans over two decades, from working inside one of Indonesia's leading NGOs (PATTIRO) to spearheading reforms within government and international development projects. She has consistently championed budget transparency, participatory decision-making, and gender inclusion. And above all, she cares deeply about real results—the kind that transform lives, especially for women. Those were the examples she shared with the strongest passion.

I expected our conversation to be brief. It wasn't. We talked late into the night, right up until she had to leave for the airport, where she would spend the night waiting for an early-morning flight to Bali. I urged her to stay at my hotel until morning. She refused. "It's easier this way," she said, with quiet determination, before walking off into yet another budget-reform-related trip—I am really honoured to know Tanty! Maja

Maja Bosnic (MB): *Maya, you are considered one of the leading experts in GRB in Indonesia. Can you tell us about how you got involved in this field?*

Maya Rostanty (MR): My journey started at the end of 2001 when I joined PATTIRO, Indonesia's first governance-focused civil society

DOI: 10.4324/9781003732532-15

organisation. This was a transformative period—Suharto had just fallen, decentralisation was starting, and there was a newly-found freedom for civil society organisations (CSOs) to work on transparency and public financial management (PFM).

Honestly, I never imagined that my chance interaction with PATTIRO would influence my life's journey: I've spent almost half of my life with the organisation. I heard about PATTIRO through a college friend. In 2000, my little family decided to move from Yogyakarta to Jakarta. Yogyakarta is a nice city where my husband and I studied at Gadjah Mada University, and Jakarta is the capital of Indonesia. When I moved, I told my college friend (Dati Fatimah) that I was moving to Jakarta and asked her to let me know if there were any job opportunities. One day, Dati called me and said that a relatively new NGO needed an accounting staff member. It is then that I started working at PATTIRO. Working in an NGO was not something I had ever planned. I started learning from the beginning how NGOs work and gradually discovered my passion in the area of PFM, particularly gender budgeting.

I initially joined as an accounting staff member, but since the organisation was small, I had the chance to learn about budget reforms, advocacy, and participatory budgeting. My senior colleagues in PATTIRO also urged me to learn about it. So, I am grateful to have been in an environment that supported me in developing my expertise in the PFM area.

In my first year, I came across GRB through a workshop with Debbie Budlender. It was eye-opening to realise that budgets are not neutral—they can impact men and women differently. That set me on a lifelong journey to integrate gender perspectives into financial planning.

MB: *What was the state of gender budgeting in Indonesia when you started?*

MR: Back then, the government was transitioning to performance-based budgeting, and gender analysis was almost unheard of. There was no structured framework for addressing how public funds impacted women and men differently. It was a time of learning and experimentation. We were fortunate to have insights from international experts such as Diane Elson and Rhonda Sharp, which helped shape our approach.

MB: *You emphasise the importance of adapting gender budgeting to Indonesia's context. What does that mean in practice?*

MR: Every country has a unique social, cultural, political, and economic structure. Indonesia is an archipelago country that has around 17,000 islands. This geographical feature results in inequality in the provision of infrastructure and basic services between rural and urban areas as well as between inland and coastal areas, which contributes to gender inequality.

In Indonesia, one of the most critical issues is unpaid care work, which disproportionately affects women. If we don't account for that in budget planning, we risk reinforcing gender inequalities. For the remote areas, the road to the health facilities and schools is very important to reduce inequalities, in particular, to reduce the maternal mortality rate and increase the school enrolment rate of boys and girls.

Another key principle is working from the ground up. At PATTIRO, we always engaged with grassroots communities. It's easy for gender advocacy to become elitist and detached from the real struggles women face daily. Our goal was to connect their needs to budget decisions, rather than just focusing on high-level policies.

MB: *Can you share a specific example where GRB made a tangible impact?*

MR: In 2005, we worked on a GRB initiative in a city in Java. The community was dealing with severe flooding due to rising sea levels, which was increasing their economic hardship as well as doubling the burden on women who were in charge of cleaning their houses after the flood. We conducted a needs assessment with local women and the broader community, then translated their concerns into a concrete budget proposal for flood protection. The local government accepted it, demonstrating the power of participatory and gender budgeting working together.

MB: *You have worked closely with both civil society and government. What has that collaboration been like?*

MR: Collaboration is essential. PATTIRO played a bridging role, connecting NGOs, communities, and government to ensure policies were truly inclusive. One of our major successes was in 2012 when we helped integrate GRB into the national budget circular for four ministries. That was a milestone moment, as it institutionalised GRB at a higher level. And from 2020, we continued our work to support the government in drafting the National Strategy for Strengthening Gender Mainstreaming Implementation. Currently, the draft is still being discussed among ministries. With collaboration, we believe that the huge amount of work can be shared to improve burden-sharing with a high ownership of stakeholder to make the result more impactful.

MB: *Were there moments of frustration in this work?*

MR: Not frustration, but I've always been mindful that GRB shouldn't become overly technical. It's easy to focus on frameworks and indicators and forget the core question—why are we doing this? So, I always reminded myself that the ultimate goal is to improve the lives of people, especially those who are marginalised.

I was born in a village in Banyumas Regency (Central Java Province) and we had neighbours with low income and a lack of access to public services. This life experience motivated me to work towards helping improve quality of life for disadvantaged people. I also learned from my mother who is a teacher in a secondary school that as a woman we should have endurance in life.

When I feel tired, I imagine the faces of village women who work hard in the fields as agricultural labourers who have not been impacted by government programmes. I also envision the dream of no more pregnant women dying on the way to health clinics due to inadequate infrastructure. Our intention to help Indonesian women get better public services makes us continue to be enthusiastic in facing various challenges in advocacy.

MB: *What do you see as the biggest challenges for gender budgeting in Indonesia today?*

MR: One challenge is that a large portion of the government budget still goes to salaries and administrative costs rather than direct public services. If we compare the advocacy we do at the local level working with the community with the conditions when we work with the government, we find large differences. We work in the same area, namely gender budgets, but there is still a disconnect for the government because their GRB process is still focused on a technocratic process and is less concerned with fulfilling the needs of final beneficiaries at the community level. So, we work to overcome this disconnect problem to ensure the GRB will improve the quality of life of women and men across Indonesia. We need to continue pushing for a more equitable distribution of funds. Also, we need stronger gender-disaggregated data to inform policy decisions more effectively.

MB: *What is your dream for the future of GRB in Indonesia?*

MR: I want to see GRB making a direct impact on final beneficiaries—ordinary women and communities. It took me 12 years to fully grasp gender analysis, and I believe the real transformation happens when we work from the bottom up.

We currently have 56 percent of women participating in the workforce. My dream is to see that number rise to 70 percent. That would mean we are not just talking about gender budgeting in institutional terms but in a way that truly changes people's lives. GRB is not just about institutions—it's about humans.

Fortunately, the government strengthened its commitment to gender equality. It is now stated in the new Long Term National Development Plan 2025–2045 and derived in National Medium Term Development Plan 2025–2029. Government has also been improving the governance of GRB to ensure implementation in the full budget cycle, including procurement, both at ministries/agencies level and at local governments level. We have 38 provinces and 514 districts that are ready to implement GRB. With our collaborative approach, I am optimistic that we will produce good results.

MB: *That's a powerful vision. Thank you for sharing your insights, Maya.*

MR: Thank you—it has been a pleasure to reflect on this journey.

Chapter 13

Making the Personal Political

Activism, Academia, and Beyond

Angela O'Hagan

Introduction

My life in gender budgeting began 26 years ago and the start of a new era—or so we hoped—for political life in Scotland, with devolution of powers from the UK government through the creation of the Scottish Parliament. In that time, gender budgeting has been at the core of my professional, academic, and personal life thanks to the enduring friendships that have been forged with sister activists and advocates for gender budgeting—as a transformative feminist mechanism for advancing women's economic status and eliminating entrenched gendered inequalities. Later in this chapter, I will come back to the other ways in which this work has been part of my personal life.

My professional progression is closely interwoven with the development of gender, equality, and human rights in Scottish public policy, and includes an extended interlude working in a university where I was as much an 'academic activist'[1] as an active researcher and committed teacher. I am now in a different role, with a light foothold in academia as an emeritus professor continuing to support PhD students and early career researchers, on the outside of direct activism, and instead in a leadership role in the national human rights institution in Scotland. All my reflections and commentary in this chapter are from a personal perspective.

The Promise of a 'New Politics'

We start in 2000 as the Scottish Parliament was coming into being following the creation of a new institutional framework in the UK, with devolved governments established in Scotland and Wales, and reset in Northern Ireland. These multi-level governance arrangements have shaped UK politics and political relationships over the last almost 30 years and have presented significant opportunities for policy innovation for women's rights and gender equality, and policy divergence across the constituent territories of the UK. Arguably we have seen that potential for advancement weakened as

DOI: 10.4324/9781003732532-16

governments have rolled back on their commitments and political activism on gender equality has become more fragmented.

My story introduces the early days of devolution and the opportunity for a 'new politics' in Scotland. Devolution is the term we use in the UK to describe the allocation of competences and resources to sub-national legislatures, such as the Scottish Parliament. Aspirations were high for a new politics of collaboration, less confrontational and more discursive in character, and focused on the context and needs of people in Scotland with the opportunity to legislate directly on those issues in the country, rather than from the distance of the UK Parliament which increasingly and for some time had not reflected the voter preferences of Scotland. This democratic deficit fuelled the long-standing and evolving calls for greater 'home rule' and further into proposals for independence.

The dynamism of feminist activists and what the academic literature would characterise as 'policy entrepreneurs' acting to seize that opportunity for change was bolstered by impetus of the Beijing Platform for Action. It then moved into the process of attempting to embed, dare I say 'mainstream' gender budgeting in the Scottish budget process, fuelled by inspirational feminist women and the potential of institutional engagement.

At the end of this chapter, I focus on the personal and my decision to step from activism into academic life as a PhD student and then continuing in university life as a research fellow and lecturer, and ultimately as Professor of Equality and Public Policy. Throughout these different professional roles which were exciting and fulfilling—and paid the bills—I remained committed to and heavily engaged in both the feminist activism and advocacy, and in the more formal/institutional processes seeing to advise and engage government.

Activism: Gender Budgeting and the Opportunities of Political Change

Following the 1998 Scotland Act, the devolution of powers from the UK government at Westminster to the Scottish Parliament created an ongoing process of policy development and structural change. This domestic context of the development of a small nation, growing its autonomous (devolved) competences was significant in building a distinctive discursive narrative around equality and human rights, and many of us felt and hoped it reflected ambitions of transformational and alternative policymaking.

This was a time of political excitement, anticipating the new institutions. It was a moment full of promise of increased women's representation and a 'women-friendly parliament' with gender-aware practices including more accessible sitting times and even nursery provision. In 2000, the then Scottish Executive (now Scottish Government) produced the first (and only) Equality Strategy.

In this window of opportunity, feminist activists, boosted in part by the campaigns for a gender-equal parliament and the heady discourse on equality and opportunity, spotted the opening for new approaches to managing Scotland's finances. Thanks to the engagement with international processes, namely the Beijing Fourth World Conference on Women in 1995, and eagle-eyed activists keeping up with developments elsewhere, the concept of gender budgeting was flagged, firstly by local feminist campaigner Fiona Forsyth to a number of feminist activists, including myself (employed at the time as a development officer with the then statutory gender equality body, the Equal Opportunities Commission) and significantly Ailsa McKay increasingly known at the time as that exotic creature, a feminist economist!

In keeping with many of the typical origin stories of feminist organisations, the Scottish Women's Budget Group (SWBG) was brought to life round a kitchen table. We were forming as a group to advocate for and build competence in integrating gender analysis into the budget processes of the new institutions of the Scottish Government as scrutinised by the Scottish Parliament. Building our knowledge and networks, our core group grew. We were having to work quickly to bring this new idea into the new institutions. I remember early appearances with the Finance or Local Government Committees of the new parliament where we were presenting the potential of gender budgeting—having just been reading up on the ideas and experiences from elsewhere the night before!

International experiences and learning were central to developing our knowledge, formulating strategies to inform and influence the new budget process. Building our knowledge from government officials in countries where gender budgeting was also being introduced and reaching out to feminist organisations with similar styles and at various stages of development was a big part of our early period. We organised seminars with colleagues visiting from Canada, contacted officials and activists in the Basque Country, read up on the developments in the 1980s in Australia and 1990s in South Africa, and crucially met with and cemented relations with the UK Women's Budget Group (WBG). Our 'big sister' of the WBG had been established a few years before with the leadership of visionary feminist economists Diane Elson, Sue Himmelweit, Ruth Pearson, and others. What better mentorship could we have had?! I admit to being seriously in awe of these leading thinkers and nervous at meeting these women who have turned out to be among the most important personal mentors I have had, as well as of course among the pioneers in gender budgeting. I am personally very grateful for their support, and for the many years of solidarity from the UK WBG to the SWBG, a relationship which continues to thrive.

When the Political Becomes the Personal

The political is personal and the personal is political. This became an immediate reality when aged 40 and in a full-time job as Campaigns and Communications Manager and, having been Acting Head of Oxfam

Scotland and chaired the Coalition for Make Poverty History in 2005, I became pregnant with my first child. Clearly, no better time to give up a full-time salary in a permanent post and take up a postgraduate stipend to pursue doctoral research on… gender budgeting! Heavily pregnant with my second child, I began the PhD in earnest, acting in good faith on the advice from my dear friend and mentor, Professor Ailsa McKay who was cheerfully adamant that combining early PhD study and early parenthood was a great move. And you think your friends always have your best interests at heart! In fairness, it was good advice as it opened up a new pathway in my life that I would not have otherwise considered and has allowed me to gain a huge range of skills in research and teaching, as well as drawing me into the dynamic world of gender budgeting and the many wonderful women—and some men—that inhabit and create it. Talking of Ailsa and wonderful women, I want to acknowledge Ailsa as a friend and mentor, her work as a feminist thinker and leader, and the pain and loss I feel across my professional and personal life since her passing aged only 50 in 2014.

My PhD focused on charting the approaches to the adoption and implementation of gender budgeting in three sub-national government contexts which were embarking on this approach to public finance and gender equality at the same time and where learning from one another was a central part of the feminist learning that underpinned the advocacy to government.

I had the privilege and immense pleasure of conducting my research on Scotland, the Basque Country (Euskadi) and Andalucía in Spain—all similar in budget size, experiencing the political opportunity of regime and institutional change, and at that time with a strong commitment to advancing gender equality. While the framing of gender equality policy varied to some extent, with different emphases on economic growth and development, gender justice, and societal development, there were multiple learning points across the structures of government and the size and structure of the budget, with a mix of locally and centrally generated revenue and limited controls on revenue-raising and policy competences.

The Adoption and Implementation of Gender Budgeting: a Framework of Favourable Conditions

One of the core findings and contributions of my doctoral thesis was the production of a 'Framework of Favourable Conditions' (FFC) for the adoption and implementation of gender budgeting (O'Hagan, 2015). The framework examined the important conditions that need to exist for gender budgeting to be adopted and then implemented. A starting point for this framework was an early analysis by Sharp and Broomhill (2002) on adoption and implementation and the combination of relevant variables including actors, institutions, policy, and policy-framing that have been successful in achieving a gender-aware budget. Guided by conceptualising gender budgeting as a form of feminist policy change, drawing on public policy and policy analysis literature alongside the conceptual literature on gender budgeting and feminist policy analysis, I presented the analysis of my findings as a framework of variables—some prerequisite structural conditions that support the introduction and practice of gender budgeting.

These variables include elements at the advocacy and agenda-setting phase where the policy and political discourse, institutional attitude and character require the combination of a 'pro-equality climate' with a commitment to gender mainstreaming, open to external drivers for policy change, such as direction from the EU or UN, etc. The opportunity of political change and windows of opportunity for constitutional or other institutional change (political opportunity structures) offer entry points for different ways of thinking, such as gender budgeting. Institutional infrastructure needs to exist or be created, such as the 'gender equality architecture' of women's rights organisations or governmental departments, with a positive disposition from government to greater openness and participation from civil society and more cross-departmental working and engagement with women's/feminist organisations external to government.

Of course, favourable economic conditions help support the institutional disposition to think differently, but the adoption of gender equality policy should not only be a 'nice-to-do' when, all things being equal, the economy is going well. Quite the contrary, greater attention to economic disparities and gendered inequalities are even more important at times of greater economic constraint or crisis.

A key element in supporting the move from engaging conceptually in gender budgeting, supported by a commitment to gender equality, is the need for policymakers—elected members and officials—to understand the budget process. It should not be overlooked, or taken as read, that this is knowledge that government officials or parliamentarians (or local councillors) will have, especially at the start of a new parliamentary cycle. Without understanding the technical and procedural dimensions of the budget process, beyond the political cut and thrust, policymakers will (continue to) miss the opportunities—and necessary places—for gender analysis.

Moving into the second phase, formal adoption, the required conditions are a clear conceptual framework for gender budgeting as promoted by advocates and understood by those charged with implementing it. These must include engaged actors, including finance officials, politicians and parliamentarians, and civil society organisations. Without political will—visible, strong and sustained commitment to gender budgeting that will support the necessary positive institutional arrangements—gender budgeting will not be able to break through the established institutional norms.

And to support implementation, the third phase is a gender-aware budget which requires, evidence in practice, political leadership, and of course a strategy for continuity. This implementation plan has the aim of delivering what Sharp and Broomhill (2002) define as measured by changes in budgetary allocations and policies in a way that promotes gender equality and is evidenced in a gender-aware process that results in a differently formulated output, that is: a gender-aware budget process and related documentation.

The framework can be used in multiple ways for policymakers and feminist advocates in identifying the structural or conceptual gaps, the entry points for advocacy, e.g. through robust gender equality architecture, or for analysis through a clear and shared understanding of the budget process.

Institutionalising Gender Budgeting or Setting a Narrative?

The FFC, which I am pleased to see has been widely cited, encourages activists and officials to consider the political environment, institutional capacity and preparedness, as well as focus on the conceptual basis of the adopted/adapted approach to introducing gender budgeting and the significance of the policy framing.

The thesis and findings highlighted the importance of the political and electoral context, in what has proven to be a salient variable in the three case study areas. Andalucía at that time was leading the pack, in my three case study areas, and in Europe. However, the rise of the populist right in Spain in recent years, has resulted in the Partido Popular gaining majority and Vox breaking through into the Andalucian Parliament and securing power in Junta de Andalucía in the 2022 elections, with the subsequent dismantling of the most procedurally developed gender budgeting mechanisms and the dilution of the legislative underpinning. This is an important warning for us all that even the 'protection' of legislation integrating gender budget analysis in the budget process has now been proved not to be sufficient to secure and protect this approach from ideological disagreement and a denial of the fundamental necessity and right of equality for women and the realisation of women's rights.

In Euskadi, the drive for gender budgeting was closely associated with the statutory gender equality institution, EMAKUNDE, the Basque Institute for Women, and led with varying levels of vigour by the Government of the Basque Country. Like many countries and territories, there have been fluctuations in the political support for gender budgeting and the advancement of practices. Currently the 2030 Strategy for Gender Equality includes a focus on funding for gender equality policies, which while welcome is not the integration of gender analysis and allocation processes across the government and public authority budget process. While the public finance actions in the strategy appear to take more of a tagging approach to identifying spending for specific gender equality actions, there is also a requirement in the Basque Equality Law for public authorities to integrate a gender perspective into budget design with the aim of identifying the different realities of women and men and promoting equality across all policy domains.

Gender budgeting in Scotland has also had varied and limited success. Important early actions included an exercise in the tracing the budget process, meaning simply plotting through the steps in the budget process which was new to many of the officials inside as well as external advocates for gender budgeting when the Scottish Parliament was created. There then followed two pilot studies—on smoking cessation and on women and girls' participation in sport. These pilots were conducted over 20 years ago and have been followed by multiple studies and reports on approaches to integrating gender analysis in the Scottish budget process including most recently a review by the OECD. Principal among the recommendations from the OECD was the need for a set of clear gender equality objectives and a comprehensive gender equality strategy. This is a proposal echoed by the current First Minister's Advisory Council on Women and Girls.

Arguably what we are seeing in Scotland has been some important structural developments with the introduction from 2002 of a focused advisory group on integrating 'equality' analysis in the budget process. Currently framed as the Equality and Human Rights Budget Advisory Group (EHRBAG), this entity comprises external advisors and government officials, including Exchequer, policy, and the Human Rights Directorate. The push for a human-rights framing for budget analysis is welcome and offers a clear framework for budget design and policy formulation. However, it is being overlaid on a less secure, shallow basis of gender analysis of resource allocation, spending, and revenue-raising decisions which makes for limited gender-aware policymaking and budget setting. This is disappointing given two other significant developments with real potential for transformation. One is the Equality and Fairer Scotland Budget Statement (EFSBS), first introduced in 2009, which has the real potential to work through a gender (but usually characterised as a broader 'equality') analysis of policy and related resourcing decisions and publish that analysis in a way that demonstrates decisions taken and outcomes achieved. Despite many iterations and a substantial amount of work from officials over the years which is to be commended, the EFSBS has still not attained the shape and function of providing that diagnostic and analytical resource as intended.

From the Outside in: the Influence of Feminist Advocacy

The second positive development, and another in which I have had a longstanding involvement and commitment, is the growth of the SWBG. For years we struggled on with the goodwill and voluntary time of committed and energised members producing briefings ahead of the Draft Budget and analysis of Scottish Government budgets. Unfunded and not formally constituted, the first 20 years of the SWBG were archetypal feminist activism—voluntary, relying on the good will of individuals and sister organisations, and resources begged and borrowed. In 2020, a grant from the Open Society

Foundation via the UK WBG had a transformational effect on the SWBG. It is now a registered charitable organisation, employs three amazing staff members, has produced multiple reports and analysis, and has engaged with other women's organisations to co-produce intersectional analysis on the economic status of disabled women, racialised women, and women marginalised by their income status and other protected characteristics. Not only as members of EHRBAG, but as a constant presence in public policy discourse, SWBG is making an impact in policy deliberations and surfacing evidence of women's economic status and injustice in Scotland, with a new generation of feminist leaders steering it on to its next successes.

It is clear that in the Scottish experience, the favourable conditions of a strong feminist movement, a clear understanding of the budget process, and some institutional gender architecture have been in abundant evidence before, during and since devolution (including multiple national and issue specific feminist organisations including Engender, Close the Gap, and the Scottish Women's Convention, and the creation of the First Minister's National Advisory Council for Women and Girls in recent years, and others). There has also been a chilling effect on all of this as funding has become more fragile, and as discourse on gender equality has become increasingly fractious and fragmented along gender-critical, inclusive feminism, and pro-transgender schisms. Throughout devolution there has also been strong political narrative and evidence of political will. Disappointingly, that has not turned into gender-aware budgets and budget documentation, so the struggle continues.

Life's Work or Work of a Lifetime

Gender budgeting has been a central part of my professional and activist life for the last 25 years. That has meant a lot of sacrifice of family time and has always been characterised by unstinting support from my husband and daughter. As I said earlier, I was pregnant when I started my PhD. I was pregnant twice. The first time in 2005 when applying for the PhD, but the start was delayed as my son was stillborn at full term. In 2006, having re-started the PhD process, our daughter arrived—prematurely and dramatically, but thankfully has thrived. She was a constant companion in the early days of the PhD research and happily (for me at least) has attended a good number of SWBG meetings and international events too and was well known as a baby to colleagues in the European Gender Budgeting Network. Along the way, and in common with others in this volume, managing gender budgeting advocacy and breast-feeding was an additional challenge. I vividly remember clanking around with my expressing kit and bottles!

As my daughter grew, she became very familiar with the repeated questions about the progress of my PhD. While my supervisors Ailsa McKay and Fiona Mackay were commanding me to "Put away the placards, stop the campaigning and get on with the PhD!," my daughter was asking me with the same cadence and phrasing that every adult she ever met with me, "So, how's that PhD coming along?" As many readers and contributors in this volume will know, children—and family—keep us grounded. Not just in the everyday, but also in keeping our work in context. A memory I cherish is having been invited to participate in a government seminar in Mallorca, a dear friend from Barcelona offered to come over as babysitter while I was at the seminar. Arriving just as I was finishing my presentation, my friend was very impressed that I was delivering it in Spanish. Her enthusiasm was shattered when my daughter responded to her excited "Listen! That's your mummy speaking," with a dismissive "Yeah. More blah, blah, blah." From the mouths of babes...

At a difficult moment in the PhD—and there were a few—Fiona Mackay reminded me that a PhD may be the work of a lifetime if not a life's work. I understand that advice more and more as the years pass. Gender budgeting, women's economic status, and the realisation of rights for all are indeed my life's work. Throughout all this work I have had the immense good fortune to meet, be supported by, and become friends with many women across the formidable gender budgeting community. I cannot name them all, but friends in Spain G A-G, YJB, PdV, PC, and AdO, and elsewhere, you know who you are. Through the women in the European Gender Budgeting Network, which is being given a new lease of life with the energy of colleagues across Europe including Elisabeth Klatzer (as always), the incomparable Mary Pyrgos in Cyprus, and the warm energy of WBG colleagues, I have learnt and been enriched as a scholar and practitioner. Diane Elson, an internationally acclaimed feminist scholar and activist, and thankfully part of this book project (see Chapter 17), has been a constant support and mentor. If friendships and collaborations are part of what characterise a life well-lived, then I am having a very good life!

Snowball Effect or Sisyphean Labour?

In conclusion, I will reflect on the nature of progress. As the sub-heading suggests, has there been contagion and a joining on and gathering of momentum in gender budgeting, or has it been a constant rolling of boulders up the same mountain? Honestly, it is a bit of both.

What we have seen globally, and is testified in this volume, is an explosion in approaches to gender budgeting, a significant expansion in the engagement of international finance institutions including the development of the gender PEFA framework (see Chapter 5), and the constancy of feminist action. This is all, however, in the context of a rolling back of political commitment to gender equality and a weakening and deconstructing of feminist and gender equality institutions in Europe and globally. This disestablishing of institutions to drive gender equality and the rise of an anti-gender politics, from the populist right across the world as well as from within feminist movements creating internal schisms which have not spilled over accidentally into public debate but have been deliberately funded and constructed to create division and diminish nuance and respect for the rights of all.

The persistent advocacy for gender budgeting is just that, persistent. The advocates in this volume and the countless others across the world maintain the effort of rolling the boulder up the hill on a daily basis making and remaking the arguments, engaging in the research to build the evidence base, and repeating as the electoral cycle turns.

Our future is challenging on a number of levels. The political context and the turn away from the international order of human rights and human rights institutions are a threat to progression. The dilution and under-funding of feminist organisations dedicated to advancing gender equality are undermining feminist activism externally and limiting discourse inside institutions. However, while the burgeoning of multiple approaches to budgeting—children's rights, human rights, environmental rights and climate change responsiveness, and so on—can put at risk the focus on gender equality, they is also evidence of a wider movement challenging established orthodoxies in public finance management and budgeting. All that is one of our central challenges, but also a significant opportunity. Given the tenacity and collective intellectual capacity of the movement, as evidenced in this volume, I have to be hopeful that the 'project' of gender budgeting is in good hands.

Note

1 A term coined by feminist political scientist Fiona Mackay and which I first heard at her professorial inaugural lecture in 2014.

References

O'Hagan, A., 2015. "Favourable conditions for the adoption and implementation of gender budgeting: Insights from comparative analysis." *Politica economica*, 31 (2), 233–252.

Sharp, R. and Broomhill, R. (2002), "Budgeting for equality: The Australian experience." *Feminist Economics*, 8 (1), 25–47.

Chapter 14

Roots, Resilience, and Reform

My Life in PFM

Nordia Campbell

Early Beginnings: The Seeds of Determination

My life began in the vibrant yet challenging inner-city community of Charles Town (often called Marley), Jamaica. A prevailing sentiment in the area was encapsulated in the phrase, "*Nutten gud nah come from yah,*" a colloquial expression that suggested nothing good would come from the community.

And so, it seems, my life was destined to be an uphill battle. My parents embraced the Rastafarian faith. In the 1970s, it was a frequently ridiculed, ostracised and misunderstood religious belief. Rastafarians were often prosecuted and persecuted for the use of marijuana, which is part of their religious sacrament.

Despite these stumbling blocks, I was treated differently from a young age. The expectation was that I had a special spark and could rise from the shackles of poverty. This belief was reinforced not only by my family but by my community. Neighbours and elders gave me considerable responsibilities long before I could fully grasp their significance in preparing me for the future.

My paternal grandparents owned and operated a bar, where I assisted my grandfather every Sunday, selling beverages. The community quickly took note of my aptitude for calculating drink prices and providing the correct change. This recognition led to more responsibilities. I was frequently called upon to read letters for the elders who were illiterate or write letters to their family members overseas. These small but important tasks solidified my emerging leadership role.

My maternal grandmother, Jane Christie, was a powerful influence in my life. Though deaf and illiterate, she consistently impressed upon me the enduring importance of education, which shaped my values and aspirations from an early age. I recall that during the summer months, Grandma Jane would save her income from being a domestic helper to purchase second-hand textbooks and reading materials for me and my siblings. She would also pay for my summer classes. Her unwavering support planted the seed for my lifelong dedication to learning and personal growth.

The role models in national life were mostly men. Women were typically homemakers and in rare cases, if they had paid jobs, it was most often as a

DOI: 10.4324/9781003732532-17

teacher, secretary or clerk. Still, there were some remarkable role models who had prominent positions within our community. Joan Barnaby was an extraordinary teacher. She devoted 40 years of her life to teaching and leading the elementary school as its beloved principal. Her influence on me was undeniable. She fostered a sense of discipline and ignited my desire to give back to the community. And so, in 2023, I had the honour to nominate her for a national award for her dedication to our community in education.

The 1970s and 1980s in Jamaica were economically challenging years. Life in my rural community was particularly difficult, as families struggled to provide for their households while navigating the uncertainties of daily life. During this period of political tension, the Rastafarian community faced additional hardship. My father, whose unorthodox philosophies limited his access to traditional employment, was unable to secure steady work. I still recall the day in 1983 that he decided to cut his locs, in the hope that doing so would allow him to secure employment and provide for our family.

Limited resources forced me to take an unconventional path toward my educational goals; a trajectory that may have been inadvertent but laid the foundation for my future career in public finance. Twenty years ago, the Common Entrance Examination was still a rite of passage for primary school students in Jamaica. A high score provided the opportunity to attend a prestigious grammar school. My family's financial circumstances often limited my ability to attend school, and as a result, I failed the exam. I therefore enrolled at Marcus Garvey Technical High School, a trade institution named after Jamaica's first national hero and renowned Pan-Africanist.

By the end of my secondary education, I had surpassed expectations, emerging as a top performer in my school and successfully matriculating for college. Despite my academic success, my family's financial situation made attending college an unattainable dream. At the age of 17, I entered the workforce, beginning a career that would later see me break barriers in public financial management (PFM).

Laying the Foundation: PFM Chose Me

PFM was not a career I actively pursued. Straight from secondary education, I spent 12 years in local government at the St Ann Municipal Corporation (formerly St Ann Parish Council). These early years gave me hands-on experience in all facets of PFM, including budget formulation, accounting and reporting, payroll and treasury management, internal audit and the preparation of financial statements. The experience solidified my commitment to the principles of accountability and transparency—values that had guided me throughout my unorthodox upbringing.

My introduction to PFM reforms came during the early 2000s, when the first module of the Integrated Financial Management Information System (TurboPay Payroll) was piloted in the public sector in Jamaica to replace the manual payroll systems. I led the implementation of the system at our municipal corporation, marking my first step toward digital financial management reforms. At the same time, Jamaica had embarked on a local government reform programme, which remains a work in progress today. The reform required all finance and accounting departments to be staffed with college educated personnel. This presented a barrier to my advancement, as I lacked formal college education.

Recognising the need for higher education, I enrolled in evening classes in pursuit of a bachelor's degree in accounting. For four years, after work, I attended classes four days weekly, commuting 45 minutes from work to school.

At age 27, during my second year in the part-time undergraduate programme, I faced one of the most challenging periods of my life. I was pregnant with my son, Jelani. I attended a Christian institution, operated by the Seventh Day Adventist Church that had strict codes of conduct that prohibited unmarried mothers from continuing their education. I found myself at a crossroads. Disclosing my pregnancy would trigger immediate expulsion, effectively closing the door to higher education and the career path I had worked so hard to carve out. Faced with this grim reality, I made the difficult decision to hide my pregnancy for the duration of the academic year.

With the support of my classmates, I managed to keep my condition hidden, wearing loose-fitting clothing and staying mostly within the classroom. This was not just a challenge of physical endurance but a deeply emotional one. Six weeks after giving birth to my son, Jelani, I returned to school, juggling the demanding responsibilities of motherhood and academia. I chose to exclusively breastfeed for the first six months of his life while continuing my education and being on extended maternity leave. I even had to resort to bringing my son with me to classes on some days. I have often joked with Jelani in later years that he had already 'attended' college as I was pregnant while in school.

Mine is not a unique story; so many women have to juggle the responsibility of family and home with the pressure of work. This is even more prevalent in fields such as PFM. In an industry where women are often underrepresented and face heightened scrutiny, we sometimes must work twice as hard to maintain our footing and advance. This can mean spending extra hours preparing for meetings or reports, taking on challenging assignments to prove our competence, and advocating for ourselves in promotion or leadership opportunities. Even something such as arriving late because of attending to a sick child can attract disproportionate criticism. The pressure can be overwhelming and, at times, discouraging, especially when balancing the demands of visibility, perception, and the responsibility of paving the way for other women. My experience at university is an example of the societal expectations placed on women and how these expectations can shape or even limit our access to opportunities. On the other hand, it underscores how determination to break barriers and shatter the glass ceiling can create opportunities and successes, and how support from other women can play a crucial role in overcoming obstacles.

PFM—No Looking Back!

I received my undergraduate degree at age 30. This propelled me into senior roles in PFM. The Caribbean enjoys a relatively high prevalence of women in management roles. According to the International Labour Organization (ILO), my home country Jamaica has the highest proportion of female managers globally, accounting for nearly 60 percent of the management force. However, while Jamaica leads in the proportion of top female managers, the study found that women are still underrepresented in representational politics. As women strive to reach top management positions, they continue to juggle and navigate the demands of family life with their professional pursuits. Sometimes this delicate balance can become chaotic.

Armed with my degree, I was promoted to the role of Chief Internal Auditor in the public health sector. This period marked a significant evolution for internal auditors, as the profession was shifting from traditional compliance-focused roles to a risk-based, value-added approach. We were now expected to operate with greater independence and transparency, particularly through audit committees. In previous years, our primary focus had been on verifying payment vouchers to ensure adherence to national standards. My new responsibilities, however, required me not only to ensure compliance with broader financial laws and regulations but also to identify and address systemic issues within the organisation.

This shift presented new challenges, especially as, occasionally, some operational officers attempted to conceal discrepancies from me. My relentless pursuit of accountability and transparency often led to misunderstandings, earning me the nickname 'bulldog,' which was meant to be a slur. Rather than being recognised as a dedicated advocate for integrity, I was alienated.

My pursuit of transparency and accountability led to a few officers being arrested for embezzling public funds. One was a well-known member of a community, and I soon learned that fighting for accountability and transparency had consequences, especially for women. Your sense of security can be shattered by bullying and pressure to back off. I still recall how difficult it was to re-enter the facility to give a statement to the police, the solitary drive back from the workstation where the arrests were made, the pleas from senior staff within the organisations to not proceed with the matter and the loneliness when you stand up for what is right. This experience shaped my belief that workers in the public sector who put themselves at risk to protect the public purse should be provided with some level of security.

While that period in my professional career in internal audit was perhaps the most difficult, professionally, it was the most rewarding and the body of work I am most proud of. I learned to stay grounded by my values and to remind myself often why integrity matters, even when it comes at a personal cost. Prayer and quiet reflection helped me stay calm when the pressure became unbearable. I leaned on a few trusted people outside the workplace for advice and emotional support. Over time, I got the senior managers to understand the importance of the role. That period taught me that resilience in public service is not just about strength—it is about courage, faith, and knowing that standing for what is right sometimes means standing alone, values that were instilled by my community and parents.

As my career developed at age 34, I took on a more senior executive role within the public health system, overseeing one of the 14 parishes. This was my only departure from PFM—a shift that, at first, felt like an exciting new challenge. However, I quickly realised that the health sector had little space for those of us without a core background in healthcare. More than that, as a woman in leadership, I encountered additional layers of resistance. The entrenched hierarchies within the health system were not only rigid but also deeply influenced by gendered expectations. But I was determined to make an impact. I championed a customer-centred approach, shifting the focus to patient experience and service delivery. Under my leadership, the staff, including doctors, were held accountable. They were held responsible for arriving on time, delivering quality care, and upholding professional standards. Patients were no longer seen as passive recipients but as valuable human beings deserving respect and efficiency. Value for money became a guiding principle and ensuring resources were used effectively to enhance care was prioritised.

Navigating the space required toughness, but also compassion for patients and for staff, many of whom had unique personal challenges. Holding professionals accountable, particularly in a male-dominated structure, often invited scrutiny and pushback. Yet, the results spoke for themselves. My tenure proved that strong leadership regardless of gender could drive meaningful change, even in institutions that had been accustomed to doing things a certain way for decades.

While serving in the health sector, I successfully completed my postgraduate education in Banking and Finance, providing me with a springboard for further career advancements. I had ambitions of leading the organisations one day, but despite being qualified, I was hit with the stark reality that while hard work and dedication were essential, they were not always enough to secure a promotion or further career advancement. Progress depended far more on political influence than on merit, a sobering realisation. I learned the hard way about the intersection of politics, family background, and professional development—there was little opportunity for advancement without the right connections. My Rastafarian background and humble beginnings did not provide me with the social networks or status necessary to secure these connections.

This setback hastened my return to PFM. However, reintegrating into PFM was not as straightforward as I had hoped. By this time, being the Parish Manager for St Ann Health Services, I was at a grade level above most PFM peers, and further vertical movements would require that I relocate to the capital, Kingston—a move that demanded careful thought.

By now, I had primary custody of my son, who was nine years old, and every professional decision had to strike a balance between career advancement and his well-being. There were at least two job offers, but I had to weigh several considerations before making a decision. Kingston was expensive, and without family support there, managing both work and childcare would be challenging. The city's relentless traffic posed the main difficulty—how would I navigate long commutes while ensuring stability for my child? More importantly, moving to Kingston would mean taking him away from his father, disrupting the structure and routine he had always known.

As my son's primary caretaker, I valued effective co-parenting. I believed my son should have a strong relationship with both parents, and I was not willing to make a decision that would jeopardise his bond with his father. My appreciation for the strength and unity of family was deeply rooted in the values instilled in me by my Rastafarian parents, who shared an admirable devotion to family. My father, in particular, demonstrated an unwavering love for his family, always willing to go above and beyond to ensure our well-being.

The cost of living in Kingston, coupled with additional expenses such as housing, childcare, and transportation, would have significantly diminished the financial benefits of taking a higher-level job there. I was unwilling to make a move that would leave me in a worse financial position.

Turks and Caicos, Here I Come

Career choices for women, especially mothers, are rarely just about ambition. They involve a complex web of practical, financial, and emotional considerations, requiring sacrifices on both personal and professional fronts.

Never satisfied with the status quo in the health sector and wanting to return to PFM—which matched both my core experience and my recent qualifications—I began searching for a way to move forward without jeopardising my financial stability or the well-being of my only child. An opportunity came for me to leave Jamaica, and it felt like the right move.

After careful talks with my family, friends, and Jelani's father, I decided it was time to spread my wings. My journey took me to the Turks and Caicos Islands (TCI), a British Overseas Territory in the Caribbean. I was determined not to disrupt Jelani's life in a major way, so, his dad and I agreed that Jelani would live with him, at least until I had a chance to assess the lie of the land. In the end, I decided that the best option was for Jelani to remain in Jamaica, and I would visit as often as I could and use technology to stay in constant touch. This new chapter promised financial stability and professional growth.

My new assignment as Budget Director in the Ministry of Finance, Trade, and Investment (MoFIT), was a very senior role that required a deep immersion into PFM. After careful assessment, I determined that some reforms and upscaling were required. In my corner was a Permanent Secretary open to reasonable reforms that could improve processes and make the department more efficient.

My team and I spearheaded several key reforms including the introduction of the medium-term fiscal framework, the transition of the budget from line items to programme performance, and the introduction of fiscal risk management practices including enacting a section of the PFM Ordinance that required state-owned enterprises to report to the Ministry of Finance on a quarterly basis to manage state-owned enterprises risk profiles. We consolidated the budgets of the central government and all other statutory authorities, aligned the national budget with the Sustainable Development Goals, and introduced the Citizens' Guide to the Budget to promote transparency and public engagement.

I spent 11 years in TCI; I have focused on ensuring fiscal sustainability and strengthening medium-term fiscal planning, which helped facilitate several notable achievements in PFM. The territory recorded 11 consecutive years of budget surplus, except for 2020 due to COVID-19. Core government debt was reduced from USD 170 million (2014) to less than USD 0.5 million (2025). I feel a deep sense of pride in having contributed to the strong fiscal performance that enabled the economy to withstand significant economic shocks, including the COVID-19 pandemic and two major hurricanes without resorting to additional borrowing and cash reserves equating to about 25 percent of GDP.

In TCI I encountered new dynamics. For the first time, I found myself in an environment where women were not only present but also dominant in leadership. A female deputy governor, a female attorney general, and a female chief justice were all occupying key positions, and later, I witnessed the swearing-in ceremony of the country's first female premier. Her bold declaration that she was the "best man for the job" resonated deeply. I have always believed that leadership should be defined by competence and determination rather than by gender. It was a moment of inspiration—one that reflected the progress women had made in breaking barriers.

Gender Balance Matters

While the presence of women in top government positions had signalled progress, the lack of participation in leadership and public service by more young men raised important questions about societal expectations and support systems. This reality prompted me to reflect often on the broader implications of gender representation in leadership. Are there systemic factors discouraging young men from pursuing these roles? Do traditional gender norms play a part in shaping career aspirations?

I could not ignore the noticeable gender inequality in top public sector roles. The deputy governor acknowledged that women had long held prominent positions in the country, which has a population of just 35,000 people, particularly in education, medicine, politics, and government. She stated that there were no formal barriers to entry or upward mobility. Yet, as a mother raising a son, she admitted to wanting to see more done to motivate young men to excel and assume leadership positions. Her words resonated with me because they highlighted a reality that I have often grappled with, and I wondered how, across these Caribbean islands, we could do more to bring marginalised young men to the table so they can fully participate and help shape our society.

For so long, the focus has been on ensuring women have a seat at the table—a necessary fight. But now, I find myself reflecting on the implications of a leadership structure where men, particularly young men, seem to be disengaging. If the goal was a gender-balanced society, then it should not be just about supporting women in leadership but must also be about ensuring that young men saw viable pathways to success. There is no question that we must preserve the progress that women have made, but we must also understand why young men are not stepping up in greater numbers. Is it a lack of role models? Is it shifting societal expectations? Or an unintended consequence of the push for gender equity that has left our young men without the same structured support?

On the other hand, as I reflect more deeply, my experience in PFM highlighted a glaring contradiction. In the Caribbean region, while women are well-represented in senior positions, they are often technically not the ultimate decision-makers in shaping financial and economic policies. Therefore, leadership visibility does not always translate into full participation in strategic decision-making. The question is whether or not women in these roles have the same level of influence as their male counterparts or whether structural limitations still exist beneath the surface. True progress is not just about the number of women in leadership but about ensuring that leadership regardless of gender is meaningful and impactful.

Gender equality in leadership should not be framed as a zero-sum game but as a shared responsibility, one that requires a collective effort to create pathways for all individuals to contribute meaningfully to governance and development. Witnessing the strides women have made is inspiring, but it also reinforces my belief that progress must be inclusive. Leadership should not be a space in which one gender rises while the other falls behind. The leadership space should provide opportunities accessible to all, where competence, dedication, and vision define who leads.

It is a positive development that PFM discussions are increasingly centred on gender considerations in budget planning and formulation. Given the evolving leadership landscape and the broader global emphasis on gender responsive policies, it is a natural progression to place greater focus on gender budgeting. In 2022, through my leadership, TCI took a significant step in this direction by initiating training in gender budgeting. By the 2023–2024 budget cycle, the country had formally adopted gender responsive budgeting principles, marking an important shift towards ensuring that fiscal policies and resource allocations are made based on the different needs of and impacts on men and women.

This development reinforced my belief that leadership and policy formulation must go beyond representation and visibility. True gender equity requires structural mechanisms that integrate inclusivity into decision-making processes. Gender budgeting is not merely about allocating funds to women-focused initiatives but about embedding gender analysis into the entire budgetary process, ensuring that national priorities reflect the realities of all citizens. Witnessing this shift firsthand underscored for me the importance of aligning fiscal strategies with broader societal goals, fostering a governance model that values equity in both leadership and resource distribution.

Balancing the Personal and the Professional

A year after I went to the TCI, the impact of my absence on Jelani's schoolwork became evident. As he prepared to enter sixth grade, the pivotal year to sit the primary school exit test, his performance had dropped to an average of about 50 percent. I had not recognised that he was struggling; I was so focused on my professional responsibilities that I didn't see how much he was affected by my absence. Jamaica's education system is highly competitive and the pressure on Jelani was immense, and I had not fully grasped the challenges he was facing.

This situation left me feeling conflicted. I cried myself to sleep many nights, unsure of what to do. While I wanted professional growth, Jelani's academic and professional success was also a major priority. I realised that I had to find a way to balance both, so I decided to bring him to TCI during the summer break. I bought two sets of textbooks—one for him and one for me—covering both the fifth- and sixth-grade curricula. I also retrieved past exam papers and the fifth-grade curriculum from his teachers and became his teacher for the holidays.

By the time the sixth-grade term started, I felt confident that Jelani was back on track. I stayed involved throughout the year and we used Skype to study together after school and complete assignments. This intervention allowed us to grow even closer. I recognised also that boys learned differently and that he craved one-on-one teaching environments.

Jelani became better aware of why I had to pursue my career in a foreign country and how important his success was to me. His success became a shared victory. After the national examination, he was awarded the "Most All-Round Boy" top-performing male student trophy, which was not just a testament to his hard work but to the bond between us that we had strengthened throughout that year. Jelani's success in the examination for the prestigious Munro College was more than just the fulfilment of his own dream—it was the realisation of a lifelong dream of mine to have attended a traditional educational institution. Watching him achieve what I once aspired to filled me with immense pride and gratitude. I am now the mother of a "*Bobo-Ski-Watten*" (a colloquial term used for Munro College) graduate. I am immensely proud to know that his success in attending and graduating from Munro College reflects the values of discipline, perseverance, and faith that have guided our family's journey. And that he is well on his way to completing university education.

The journey has revealed the delicate balance I've had to maintain between my unorthodox upbringing, professional ambitions, and the responsibilities of motherhood. It has not always been easy, but it has taught me that with dedication, resilience, support from others, and love, it is possible to grow as both a leader and a parent, shaping a future for Jelani as bright as my own. Every challenge faced has been a lesson, every success a reminder of what determination can achieve.

The next chapter of my journey is yet to unfold… *Jah Rastafari*!

Chapter 15

"Are you the Secretary?" "No, I'm the Boss"

Catharina Schmitz

Introduction

This was a common assumption when I began working in international development cooperation in the 1990s. Naturally, I was expected to be the secretary, while my male colleague was assumed to be the boss. I quickly learned to introduce myself right away to set the record straight.

If this had happened only once, I might have laughed it off. But it was a recurring issue during my early working years, leaving both of us uneasy and forcing me to reassert my authority—a start that felt like being an underdog.

I have over 30 years of experience working in development cooperation and public management. When I began, there were, of course, other women in international cooperation, and some in public financial management (PFM), but they were far fewer than men. Gender issues were not a priority and were rarely included in projects outside targeted support to gender specific stakeholders.

Over the years, the approach to gender issues has evolved. What once prompted a good laugh, a crude comment such as "I love women," or even a dismissive statement such as "We have no gender inequality in this country—just look at how many women work in the ministry!" has slowly become a topic taken (almost) seriously.

Shaping My Feminism

I grew up in Sweden, a high-income country where the women's movement began early, and many progressive policies were already in place during my childhood in the 1960s and 1970s.

Key reforms such as inheritance rights were established already in 1845 and ensured that both sons and daughters had equal inheritance rights. Childcare services were already state-supported in the 1930s and 1940s, targeted to low-income families, and the first daycare centre was established in 1948. Accessible and affordable childcare became part of a broader social welfare reform agenda in the 1960s, enabling both parents—especially

DOI: 10.4324/9781003732532-18

women—to enter the workforce. In 1975, the Daycare Act expanded daycare services for children aged 1–6, ensuring that all children had the right to attend daycare if their parents were working or studying.

By 1971, joint tax filing had been abolished; in 1974 parental leave was introduced, making it possible for both parents to take time off work to care for their children, which further supported the idea of shared child-rearing responsibilities. The Sex Discrimination Act, passed in 1979, prohibited sex-based discrimination in employment and set the stage for gender equality across all aspects of society, including education, healthcare, and work.

So, in the 1970s, when I was a teenager, women were entering the workforce in large numbers, with 74 percent of women in paid employment by 1980. All of this was the result of a strong feminist movement, which had been active since the late 19th and early 20th centuries, combined with the long dominance of the Social Democratic Party and its welfare state vision from the 1920s, as well as factors such as economic necessity, cultural shifts, international influences, political will, and legal and institutional frameworks.

The shift in societal perceptions over time is exemplified by changes in the uptake of paternity leave. In the 1970s, only 2–3 percent of men took parental leave, as societal expectations and gender roles at the time still heavily favoured women as the primary caregivers. The idea of fathers taking parental leave was not yet normalised. However, this has drastically shifted and by 2024, 90 percent of fathers are taking parental leave. Key reforms played a pivotal role in this transformation. Notably, the introduction of the 'daddy month' in the 1990s incentivised fathers to take a larger share of the leave, along with providing additional parental leave for families in which both parents took time off to care for their children.

Growing up with these fundamentals in place, the society had already lost some of the most obvious gender stereotypes and I came to believe that gender equality was the norm. I did not initially see the structural inequalities. However, as I grew older, I became increasingly aware of the inequalities that exist and still persist in Swedish society, such as labour market segregation, the 'glass ceiling,' women predominating in the care and education sectors and men in the private sector, men holding most managerial positions, sexist attitudes in certain sectors and men's violence against women.

Looking back, I realise that growing up in a relatively gender-equal society has been an advantage in my international work. Over time, I have come to realise how crucial these reforms have been for achieving the level of gender equality we have—a realisation that has been invaluable. In contrast to many people, I have worked with colleagues from countries with very low gender equality, where they often struggle to grasp the key components needed to foster a gender-equal society and do not understand the importance of specific reforms. While I do not claim to have perfect answers—since context always plays a significant role—there are certain foundational elements that must be in place for gender equality to flourish. Key reforms such as childcare and parental leave are essential. Without such measures, it is incredibly difficult to reduce women's high levels of unpaid care work, increase their participation in the workforce and society at large, and shift societal attitudes towards gender norms.

Starting My Career

I did not know much about international cooperation growing up, as I was raised in a rural area where people mostly had traditional jobs. In high school, I happened to attend a boarding school where several of my classmates had lived in Africa because their parents were missionaries or worked in international cooperation. This exposure gave me a new perspective, which I believe influenced me later in life. However, the path to a career in development cooperation was not clear to me when I finished university. Although I had taken courses in political science and economic history as part of my degree, I did not know anyone in the field, had no one to guide me, and for that matter lacked relevant experience.

With my degree in public administration, I started my career at the county board. This was in the late 1980s, when new public management was being introduced in many countries, including Sweden, and I worked on implementing that change process. This gave me the experience I needed and six years later I secured a Bilateral Expert position with the Swedish Development Agency (SIDA) to work in a major budget and accounting reform project at the Ministry of Finance in Lesotho.

The project involved introducing a new computerised accounting system across the national and district levels of the public sector. I joined during the final two years, when the focus had shifted to training the accounting staff in PFM and in the computerised system. My role included setting up training courses, recruiting local trainers, and overseeing the rollout of the training programme. I travelled extensively throughout Lesotho—often to remote areas with limited road access—sometimes flying in small four-seater planes, carrying an overhead projector in my luggage.

This was during the end of apartheid, and Lesotho, along with other frontline states in the region, supported the regional push for a democratic South Africa, advocating for a smooth transition and standing in solidarity with the African National Congress (ANC). Lesotho had hosted a number of strategic meetings throughout the 1980s, provided shelters and logistical support to the ANC. Being in Lesotho during 1993–1994 gave me the chance to follow the process and election that led to Nelson Mandela becoming president. Such a historic moment. At that time, many countries were boycotting the South Africa apartheid regime and Lesotho was a key location for anti-apartheid activity and solidarity. Also, the internal political situation in Lesotho was at a crossroad and in 1993, after years of military rule, Lesotho restored democratic governance through a fair election. This resulted in a time of political tension and unease among opposition groups and culminated in an attempted coup by King Letsie III, supported by the military in 1994.

One Sunday morning I woke up to the sound of gunfire, unsure of what was happening. The radio stations were only broadcasting in Sesotho, so we could not understand the announcements. I called the embassy, and they informed me that a coup was underway. They advised that it was unsafe to leave the house, as checkpoints had been set up all over town. The safest option was to stay inside and hide in the corridor. It was frightening not knowing what would happen next, and my first thought was, of course, to try to leave the country—but the borders were closed. We spent the entire day in the corridor, only venturing into the kitchen briefly to prepare some food, all while hearing gunfire and shelling above the house and people yelling outside.

Apparently, our house was situated between central Maseru and the military barracks that served as the command centre. By evening, the gunfire subsided, and the embassy called to advise us to grab our most essential belongings, leave the house immediately, and drive to a colleague's on the other side of the city, further away from strategic locations. We drove through the rain, passing groups of soldiers and armoured vehicles on the streets, but fortunately, we were not stopped. Many embassies evacuated their citizens to South Africa during the first week of the conflict, but not the Swedish Embassy. We stayed inside and waited. After a week, we were able to return to the government office, though I cannot recall what we did there, as troops were positioned to prevent the government from functioning effectively. The fourth week of the conflict, the Basotho went into a two-day strike in demand of the reinstatement of the democratically elected government, and diplomatic interventions by South Africa, Botswana, and Zimbabwe helped to restore the government. After the government was restored, a curfew was imposed, soldiers patrolled the streets and checkpoints were set up across the country. Random checking happened frequently, which was quite intimidating, especially since Lesotho was a major producer and transit country for marijuana. Soldiers also used marijuana heavily while on duty.

Although the conflict was difficult to live through, it was such an interesting period. Combined with Lesotho's beautiful landscape and the warmth of the Basotho people, it strengthened my desire to pursue a career in development work.

How I Became Interested in GRB

Gender studies were not a mainstream topic in universities in the 1980s, nor were they a focus in development cooperation. The first Beijing Conference on women's rights did not take place until 1995. I first encountered the concept of gender in development when the South African government created its first development strategy and the South African feminist movement successfully lobbied for gender budgeting to be introduced into the budget process. At that time, I was the team leader for a PFM project involving 13 ministries of finance in Southern and Eastern Africa. We included the topic of gender responsive budgeting (GRB) on the agenda at a regional conference by Lake Malawi in 1997. This eventually led the Tanzanian and later the Kenyan governments to initiate GRB work, and it was during this time that I developed my passion for GRB. I had always been more interested in social development than in purely economic topics and GRB brought these interests together for me. Feminist theories helped me make sense of the gender differences I was observing, showing how they are socially constructed rather than natural or inevitable. While working on health reform, I realised that decisions about which services are publicly financed reflect political priorities. Women's specific needs—such as access to maternal healthcare and the presence of a doctor during delivery—were not treated as high priorities. Through this work, I began to understand structural inequality and its disproportionate impact on women.

In my first ten years in development cooperation, I worked on PFM reform, accounting, budget and financial management information systems implementation in Southern and Eastern Africa and the Baltics. The international advisors were all men—I cannot remember a single woman, although there were many women among the local staff, mostly in middle and lower-level positions. I was also one of the youngest advisors. Being a young woman sometimes worked to my advantage, but it also led to me being overlooked. Like many women, I had to prove myself more than my male colleagues. While I would not say I experienced overt discrimination, I did encounter frequent misunderstandings, probably due to my communication style, which differed from the male norm. I cannot count the number of times a man has repeated exactly what I just said and received acknowledgement for it. In such a context, it was of course even more challenging to introduce and argue for including gender equality perspectives in the PFM work.

So I was met with a lot of doubt when I started raising awareness on GRB in southern Africa in the early 2000s; there was little support and often open scepticism and resistance from established PFM experts, both male and female. Comments such as "Gender has nothing to do with PFM" and "PFM is neutral" were very common and still are. The PFM community is, unfortunately, often hindering the uptake of innovative approaches.

The idea that PFM systems are neutral could not be more misguided. All PFM systems are, of course, shaped and influenced by the specific context in which they are being implemented. While they might be designed with neutrality in mind, they often unintentionally reinforce existing societal inequalities and discrimination unless active countermeasures are put in place. Therefore, understanding gendered structures and existing gender gaps within society is essential to prevent the system from reinforcing inequalities already present in the society or a sector.

Consider the example of women's subordinate position in rural communities. In agriculture, for instance, female family members who work on farms are often not recognised as 'farmers' and therefore are not the primary contacts for field officers, nor targeted for training or receiving other support. As a result, much of the agricultural budget—whether for training, fertilisers, seeds, or other support—is accessed mainly by men. Without active programme goals to include, reach, and deliver results for women in farming, these resources often fail to benefit them.

A second example is fiscal strategies. Budget priorities are influenced by societal norms and may not support transformative change towards greater gender equality, such as prioritising funding for care services.

I often recall being the only woman at the management level and sometimes facing stereotypical expectations. For example, when I had my son in 1999, many people assumed I would stop travelling. A common question was "Who is taking care of your son?" The idea that he might be at home with his father did not occur to most people.

However, I also received great support from some of my male colleagues. When my employer asked me to lead an international conference in 2000, just six months after my son was born, I was still breastfeeding and on parental leave. It was difficult to hand over the responsibility for the conference, so I agreed to go to Swaziland on the condition that my husband and son could come along, as I needed to continue to breastfeed.

The conference, attended by accountant generals and managers, a majority of men, from 13 countries in Southern and Eastern Africa, was held at the Royal Swaziland Hotel. My husband would come and knock on the door when it was time for me to breastfeed, which the participants found hilarious. While the conference was ongoing, my husband stayed by the pool with our son, but the attendees quickly warmed to the baby and even started carrying him around. Perhaps more moments like this are needed to challenge traditional expectations. I worked with this project for eight years and got to know some of the accountant generals very well, especially those from South Africa, Botswana, and Zimbabwe, who became close friends; they were great colleagues and also became supporters of GRB.

GRB Work in Practice

In my experience with GRB initiatives, one thing is clear: change takes time. Systems, people, and institutions all need to adjust, and this process cannot be rushed. While this is true for gender-related work, it applies to other reform work as well. However, development assistance often overlooks this reality. Many projects are too short and overly ambitious in scope. For instance, terms of reference that aim to implement GRB within two years or cover all central government agencies in the same period demonstrate a lack of understanding of how change processes work.

Successfully implementing GRB involves several key steps. First, there is a need to build a shared understanding of the goals, such as identifying gender priorities and gaps. Second, new methods need to be established and integrated into regular working processes. This also requires significant effort in changing institutional mindsets and improving staff capacity through training and awareness-raising activities. Third, sufficient time must be allowed for learning and adaptation, recognising that a single budget cycle spans at least eighteen months and permits only one full learning cycle. To establish a more comprehensive GRB process, I believe it is essential to cover at least three full budget cycles, which will require four to five years. This timeframe provides sufficient time for learning, adaptation, and meaningful change to take root.

I can say that I have been part of rolling out GRB on a large scale, starting with my first awareness initiatives in the late 1990s up until now. My involvement in the pioneering work in Southern Africa led me to a team leader position for the Nordic Council of Ministers on a three-year project. This project aimed to test and develop a GRB methodology suited to the Nordic context. The groundbreaking work in Southern Africa inspired the Nordic countries, which, in turn, contributed to shaping the GRB methodology. At that time, all five Nordic countries had strong gender policies and established gender machineries. The GRB project was a collaboration between the ministries of finance and the ministries responsible for gender equality in Sweden, Finland, Denmark, Norway and Iceland. Of these, Sweden was the only country with prior experience in piloting a GRB project, known as "Follow the Money," while GRB was new to the others. Although we did not receive overwhelming interest from the ministries of finance, the assigned project staff were dedicated and pushed the pilot work forward. Our team consisted of eleven women and one man.

Although this was a government project, the feminist movement played a significant role in integrating gender perspectives into the discussions. This was greatly facilitated by the project coordinator at the Nordic Council of Ministers, who had strong connections within the Nordic feminist movement and regional gender research institutions. We organised joint workshops and seminars in countries and regions, where gender researchers, gender experts, civil society organisations (CSO), and broad groups of government staff—fiscal and gender policymakers and public finance managers—would meet.

One of the best pieces of advice I ever received came from a gender expert in the Swedish government. She told me: "When working on gender equality, be context-specific and use evidence-based information." This advice has been invaluable. Arguing the relevance of gender equality with people who have little understanding of the issue can be challenging, as these discussions often become personal or emotional. However, using sex-disaggregated statistics to make your point is far more effective. This approach usually helps the person understand and accept the point we are making.

The project seminars were often highly effective in visualising gender inequalities. I recall Iceland presenting a photo book featuring images of board members from state institutions and government-owned enterprises. The photos were almost exclusively of men, which powerfully illustrated the glass ceiling in these organisations.

I also remember a Finnish CSO who worked to criminalise the purchase of sex, countering the notion that women were voluntarily choosing to be sex workers by conducting an exhibit showing photographs of the same women over a two-year period, illustrating the negative effects that their work conditions had on their health.

These meetings in which gender researchers, activists, and CSO representatives provided insights on policy effects to the policymakers and PFM staff helped in bridging their understanding on how GRB approaches would help in increasing gender equality.

Through the Nordic Council of Ministers, the insights gained from the project were shared with the European Commission and other ministries of finance across Europe. I believe this project played a crucial role in advancing GRB in Europe. After the project ended, I engaged in numerous GRB training sessions in various European countries and the Balkans.

Another significant GRB project I had the opportunity to work with in the early 2010s was in Ukraine. I was contracted by SIDA after they decided to specifically support gender equality work in all their bilateral aid countries. In Ukraine, SIDA had a PFM project within the Ministry of Finance and wanted to explore how a GRB component could be integrated. This became my longest GRB project by far, spanning ten years.

The start, however, was challenging. The international team leader for the ongoing Swedish funded PFM project did not believe in GRB and was unwilling to cooperate. Even though the project was Swedish-funded, it didn't help. He thought that "Gender is not the first priority." First the budget cycle needed to be reformed, and adding a component of gender analysis would be too complicated. We could not convince him. Fortunately, a female manager in the Ukrainian Ministry of Finance suggested piloting GRB in two regions (Ivano-Frankivsk and Luhansk) and SIDA then opted for a parallel project, a stand-alone GRB reform project. Together with the SIDA Head of Office, a woman at that time, we embarked on the journey of convincing the regional Ministries of Finance to let us conduct pilot work. Official presentations were useful, but bonding over food and good stories proved even more effective, and we eventually got the green light. This project would last over ten years, cover all regions, involve all ministries, and include a large number of local administrations. Several of the Ukrainian PFM experts assigned to the project are now leading GRB experts in Ukraine (see Chapter 7). The pilot work was very hands-on, involving gender analysis in selected areas, conducted by local working groups made up of regular administrative staff.

The Ukraine project stands out for its long-term engagement and excellent results. Ukraine is special to me for many reasons—we began the work in the month of the Maidan protests, and the Russian occupation was always looming, yet the Ukrainian team continued working with colleagues in the occupied territories. When the project ended in 2020, GRB was established in all regions. Today, GRB is a regulated key aspect of the budget process in Ukraine, contributing to critical equality measures, even in times of war.

Was it easy? No! It was hard. Throughout the process, high-level managers in the finance sector, while not openly opposing GRB, did not facilitate its implementation, even up to the very end. What made it possible was undoubtedly the female middle managers in the Ministry of Finance and the progressive regional leaders, many of them men. They were open to new approaches, eager to contribute to change, and engaged with GRB with genuine interest. Without the support of these progressive managers, a strong team leader, and a local project team that 'knew the context,' we would not have succeeded.

The lengthy and comprehensive process in Ukraine also provided us with the opportunity to collaborate with those working on forming a common GRB methodology. The practical experience gained in Ukraine was later used to inform Sustainable Development Goal (SDG) 5 monitoring, the PEFA Gender, and the OECD approach.[1]

Progress of GRB and Its Future

Looking back, GRB has progressed slowly, but there has been a noticeable shift toward positive support, particularly since the mid-2010s. Suddenly, many international organisations and countries embraced GRB. The Asian Development Bank is one of the more 'recent' financiers and is now supporting GRB introduction across Asia and Pacific.

What does the future of GRB look like?

I believe two key aspects could significantly advance its impact:

1 The PEFA Supplementary Framework for Assessing Gender Responsive Public Financial Management supplementary framework has significantly contributed to demystifying GRB, and many countries are actively conducting assessments using it. While the indicators effectively measure the existence of specific measures, they fall short in assessing the quality of their implementation. This is a critical gap, as a country may achieve high scores on certain indicators despite the fact that the measures fail to address key gender gaps.
2 Building on the issue highlighted above, while most countries have gender equality strategies in place, they often lack a dedicated fiscal

framework to finance gender equality effectively. As a result, gender-relevant financing typically relies on reallocations within existing programmes. Unfortunately, this approach often fails to secure funding for critical reforms, such as affordable childcare.

I deeply appreciate the impactful discussions and the opportunities GRB has created for me to build relationships, embrace new challenges, and work in so many exciting settings.

Note

1 Downes, R. (2020), "Designing and Implementing Gender Budgeting—A Path to Action," OECD Journal on Budgeting, Vol. 20/2 https://www.oecd.org/en/publications/oecd-journal-on-budgeting/volume-20/issue-2_59ff7e16-en.html.

Chapter 16

Demystifying Budgeting in and for Lebanon

Lamia Moubayed

How to Run a Country Without a Budget

The chilling words of then Lebanon's Foreign Minister spoken on January 23, 2019 on the sidelines of the World Economic Forum in Davos still reverberate in my mind with an unsettling resonance: "We should maybe teach them how to run the country without a budget." By 'them,' the minister was referring to the international community, particularly institutions and agencies in Washington and London, that were scrutinising Lebanon's fiscal health and rating the country. At that time, Lebanon grappled with the world's third-highest debt-to-GDP ratio, a stark indicator of its economic fragility.

The statement, delivered with an air of nonchalance, lingered like an echo in a canyon, challenging my long-time academic and practitioner's construction of the fundamentals of governance and fiscal responsibility, at a time when I was dedicating my work to budget transparency, public procurement reform, and capacity-building in Lebanon. The minister was defaulting on the foundational principles of financial management with a casual shrug, oblivious to the dire consequences of such an inconceivable theory, the outcome of which did not take long to bowl Lebanon into a spiral of dire predicaments.

The disbelief I felt was no less than that of CNN's anchor Becky Anderson, who was visibly taken aback, her usual composure momentarily shattered, her eloquence faltering in response to such a perplexing assertion. It was not an unconventional opinion she was receiving, nor an abstract conjecture. It was a statement by a high-ranking official. It is one thing to debate views or ideas; it is another to hear a high-ranking official casually dismiss the necessity of budgeting at a prized international forum.

How can a state function effectively without a clear plan for income and expenses? Without a budget, how can a government prioritise spending without risking inefficiencies, overspending in some areas, or neglecting critical needs in others? How can it plan for the future, respond to emergencies, or invest in essential projects? Moreover, without a budget, how can citizens

DOI: 10.4324/9781003732532-19

understand how public funds are being used, and how can accountability and transparency in fund management be ensured? More importantly, how could anyone involved in politics and policy proclaim with assurance that a country could thrive—or even just survive—without a formal budget?

This deviation from conventional wisdom was not merely a technical misstep; it was a serious disregard for the fundamentals of public financial management (PFM). It struck at the core of the work of my colleagues and I who have devoted our careers to restoring integrity and order to Lebanon's finances, a painful affront to our tireless dedication. To witness that labour dismissed so casually was not just disheartening; it was deeply unsettling, undermining the collective hope we'd placed in the future of our country.

At the Heart of Lebanon's Financial Machinery

As I recall this trail of misfortune, I reflect on my own journey to modernise Lebanon's fiscal management, advocating for key practices vital to transforming the country's archaic budgeting system and building the capacities of public servants to better manage public money. My career as a development specialist has been a winding path. It spanned private sector consulting and roles at United Nations agencies, ultimately bringing me to the very heart of Lebanon's financial machinery—the Ministry of Finance. In 2000, as Lebanon was experiencing the benefits of major reconstruction efforts and regional improvements, I was tasked by the French Ministry of Finance to lead a bilateral cooperation project –originally launched in partnership with Lebanon in 1996– focused on building capacity in PFM. My mission was to transform the project into a legally established public agency serving Lebanon with a regional portfolio; a mission that I took with much enthusiasm oblivious of what was coming.

What began as an optimistic assignment quickly confronted the harsh realities of post-conflict landscapes. Immersed in a world of unadorned realities and grim statistics, I witnessed firsthand the devastating impact of enduring conflicts on both institutions and human capital. I observed how erosion of human talent and political capture cripple institutions' ability to implement effective financial strategies. I saw up close how the misallocation of resources combined with widespread corruption, damages trust in fiscal institutions.

The contrast between idealistic narratives I often heard, and the grim realities of Lebanon's financial mismanagement was stark. The gap between international support being offered and the actual on-the-ground realities was even more glaring. In many cases, external interventions aimed at assisting Lebanon failed to align with local needs as they overlooked the complexities of the political landscape.

My experience stripped away any remaining illusions of optimism. It became painfully clear that recovery would require much more than external assistance—it would demand a full restoration of institutional capacity, alongside a profound overhaul of entrenched practices. I understood that a dual approach was necessary: the immediate stabilisation of basic government functions to bring relief combined with comprehensive reforms to address the root causes of financial mismanagement. I also understood that to advance progress sustainably we need a new generation of fiscally savvy 'in-house groomed' reform-minded men and women and concerted efforts to demystify budget and budgeting.

Fighting for a Seat at the Table

When I assumed my role as the President of the Institute of Finance Basil Fuleihan[1] in 2003, the mission was clear, though narrow: to build essential capacity in revenue generation and train the new recruits at the Ministry of Finance. However, I quickly recognised that this limited focus would not be enough to address the broader needs. I therefore worked to widen the Institute's scope, extending its services to all public entities and broadening its beneficiary base. At the same time, I sought to modernise the ministry's recruitment processes. I understood that weak financial management capabilities were a source of significant fiduciary risk, directly undermining government performance. In a country constantly at risk of crises, I believed that every manager of public funds—whether at a strategic or technical level—had to be equipped with the right skills and selected on merit, not only to mitigate those risks but to ensure the sound stewardship of Lebanon's resources. This expansion was met with significant resistance.

As a woman in a male-dominated environment, I faced constant questioning—not only of my vision but also of my legitimacy. Many felt threatened by the breadth of change I was advocating for, especially regarding bringing in more diversity to top positions. Sectarian governance, where appointments were based more on political and religious affiliations than on merit, had become a defining feature of Lebanon's post-war civil service, clearly favouring men in top positions. The costs were staggering—this system was siphoning off roughly 9 percent of the country's GDP annually,[2] while stifling the potential of its institutions. But the true injustice lay in its impact on qualified women who were often locked out of opportunities for advancement and leadership. It was a system that, by its very nature, excluded those who didn't fit the narrow mould of political or religious affiliations, effectively silencing voices that could bring fresh perspectives and much-needed change.

Despite the pushback, I remained unwavering, focused on two key objectives: establishing the Institute with a foundation of substance and excellence, ensuring it became an indispensable force in the public sphere, and seizing every opportunity to influence the recruitment processes at the Ministry of Finance and the civil service at large. For this, I leveraged my experience in international development cooperation and my professional network. Slowly but surely, the Institute's work and legitimacy gained grounds. It evolved from a modest training centre into a leading knowledge hub, offering policy advice, training, and capacity-building services. Over time, and together with an exceptionally talented team—many of whom were women—we cultivated a distinguished portfolio of partnerships and collaborations that spanned the Mediterranean and reached far beyond.

The opportunity to push for a merit-based recruitment system—one that prioritised competence over connections—finally emerged, and I was entrusted by the Minister of Finance and then the Prime Minister to lead the charge. My task was clear: chart the process, pilot it, and eventually transform the experiment into a legal framework. However, despite the promising results, the proposed changes to the legislation were never put to a vote. The four-year pilot was a defining moment. It demonstrated that Lebanon could unlock its full potential by creating a more inclusive, effective public service. At the heart of the reform promise was its capacity to open doors to equal opportunities, giving women a chance to have their voices heard in shaping institutions.

As Maya Angelou famously said, "Diversity makes for a rich tapestry, and we must understand that all the threads of the tapestry are equal in value."[3] In Lebanon's male-dominated political and institutional structures, Angelou's belief in the inherent value of all voices was not widely accepted. Power remained concentrated in the hands of men, and women's contributions were often undervalued. While I was fortunate to earn the trust of visionary male leaders who believed in the power of women, diversity and equality were not widely embraced; instead, power and decision-making remained largely the domain of men. It wasn't easy. I often found myself having to fight for my place at the table, challenging not only the status quo but also the deeply entrenched gender biases that sought to keep women sidelined. Yet, my resolve was set. This mindset helped me to persevere in the face of resistance and bias, whether it was based on gender or institutional inertia.

As Lebanon's financial landscape evolved, I focused my work on two key areas: budgeting and public procurement.

Budget: the Myth of a Legal Instrument

Lebanon's budgeting system is outdated, relying on a 'line-item' format from 1963 that fails to connect spending to broader policy goals. Moreover, it tells only part of the country's financial story. Imagine a grand tapestry where many threads are missing—this is how Lebanon's fiscal picture appears.[4]

Furthermore, Lebanon consistently missed constitutional deadlines for budget approvals, relying on temporary measures such as the 'one-twelfth rule.'[5] Attempts to pass budgets were often delayed, outdated, or rushed. Despite efforts, the Finance Ministry's ability to produce accurate accounts dwindled as the crisis deepened. Persistent deviations from sound PFM principles eroded fiscal discipline. This situation was further exacerbated with years of regional tensions and refugee influx, contributing to a severe financial collapse that struck the country in late 2019, described by the IMF and World Bank in 2021 as Lebanon's worst in decades.

My exploration into Lebanon's budgetary practices revealed another sobering reality. Transparency, accountability, and public participation were markedly lacking. The International Budget Partnership painted a stark picture: Lebanon was among the world's 10 percent least transparent countries in 2019 when it came to budgetary practices, with a system fixated on spending inputs rather than aligning expenditures with broader policy objectives. This was mirrored in the outdated legal framework that offered scant room for effective planning or budgetary information. Accountability suffered from weak oversight mechanisms and incomplete reporting. Public participation in the budgeting process was minimal, with scant opportunities for citizen engagement or input.[6]

The Lebanese budgeting system was a relic from another era, ill-equipped to address contemporary fiscal management needs. Yet both policymakers and civil society were unconcerned. Where global budgeting had advanced—linking expenditures to performance indicators, strategic outcomes, and measurable results—Lebanon remained far behind.

As for gender budgeting, it was nowhere to be found in Lebanon's policy conversations—an absence that stood out like a glaring oversight in an era when inclusivity and equity were becoming central to financial planning worldwide. Despite its critical role in ensuring that public resources were allocated to address gender disparities and promote equality, the issue seemed to have been relegated to the periphery. In a world that was increasingly recognising the need for diverse perspectives in decision-making, the omission of gender considerations in budgeting was not just an oversight—it was a missed opportunity to drive meaningful change.

Worldwide, men predominantly control the narrative on PFM with their voices and perspectives significantly outnumbering those of women. Historically, Lebanon's Ministry of Finance has been led exclusively by men, with only one woman ever appointed to this pivotal role. Similarly, the head of the Budget and Finance Committee in the Lebanese Parliament, a key position influencing fiscal decisions, has consistently been occupied by men. This male dominance extended to the broader financial sector, where women's participation remained restricted.

The male-dominated leadership reflected a broader challenge in achieving gender equity in Lebanon's governance structures, highlighting the urgent need for reforms that foster greater inclusion and representation of women in financial decision-making roles. The lack of gender diversity in high-level financial positions not only skewed policy priorities but also perpetuated a narrow viewpoint, often overlooking the diverse needs and contributions that women bring to PFM.

Learning to Budget: an Uphill Battle

When I began my work at the Institute of Finance, Lebanon's focus on capacity-building was largely centred on revenue generation, leaving a significant gap in budgeting. The challenge of transforming this landscape felt like planting seeds in barren soil. Together with my team, we envisioned a comprehensive capacity-building programme that would reach across all sectors—civil, military, state-owned enterprises, and municipalities. The real challenge was not only in introducing new principles but in reconciling them with an entrenched system resistant to change.

I was determined to change this by introducing modern, results-driven budgeting practices, such as programme budgeting, performance budgeting, and gender budgeting. But the difficulty in reconciling these progressive principles with an archaic legal framework made it impossible to apply concepts such as multiyear expenditure planning or performance-based budgeting, both of which were essential for effective fiscal management. The disconnect between the old system and the new approaches we were trying to implement was stark. In our workshops, we introduced innovative budgeting principles, yet we were working with a system that was increasingly disconnected from modern governance practices.

Imagine the frustration of trainees as they struggled to apply modern concepts to a budget process that still adhered to rigid, outdated practices. We faced an uphill battle as we attempted to bridge the chasm between cutting-edge principles and a traditional, almost anachronistic system. Each training session was a delicate dance, balancing the aspiration for modernity with the stubborn realities. It was not just about teaching new methods but about instilling a mindset shift in a context where the old ways were deeply ingrained. Building champions of change within the system—individuals who understood the need for a more transparent and effective budgetary process—was key.

Despite these obstacles, both my commitment and that of the Institute team remained steadfast. We understood that our journey would be fraught with challenges. Our reform champions, however, faced significant hurdles: they were positioned between a political class often indifferent to sound budgeting practices and a citizenry largely unaware of the intricacies of the budget process. To bridge this gap, we prioritised budget literacy as a vital tool for building support. By educating both policymakers and the public about the importance of transparent budgeting and active participation, we aimed to foster a more engaged and informed constituency. This approach aligned the necessity of both institutional and public engagement in driving meaningful fiscal reform.

Empowering Financial Literacy Through Budget Awareness

Budget documents are a fortress of complexity—dense, impenetrable, and often indecipherable to the very citizens and policymakers who needed them most. They leave even the most determined souls struggling to understand how fiscal policies affect their daily lives, and even more so, how they could have a say in the process. The result is a profound disconnect—where those most affected by government decisions are excluded from the conversation.

Determined to change this, I set out to demystify the public budget driven by a simple, yet profound belief: that understanding the budget is not just for experts, but for everyone. By simplifying fiscal data and making it relatable, we empower people to move from passive observers to active participants in the budgetary process. When citizens understand how their government spends their money, they gain the confidence to question, challenge, and ultimately shape the policies that affect their future.

Partnering with a civil society organisation, we produced Lebanon's first manuals, launched a campaign to debunk myths, and collaborated with the Ministry of Education to create a capacity-building programme for economics schoolteachers. Inspired by the success of this programme, I prompted the development of educational and gamification tools to combat 'budget illiteracy' including a cartoon book: *Leich Mnedfah Darayeb* ("Why Do We Pay Taxes?") that explained public finance in an engaging way, and *The Game of Flouss* ("The Game of Money"), an interactive game that helped youth understand through playing the budget process and the role of the Minister of Finance. These tools became central to our outreach programmes, engaging youth from schools and universities through annual flagship initiatives.

The introduction of the Citizen Budget marked a pivotal moment in my quest to fight budget illiteracy. Conceived as a tool to demystify the complexities of government budgeting, it evolved through numerous iterations into a visually compelling and accessible resource, tested on family, neighbours, and even my local grocer. Each year, we refined it further, making it an indispensable guide that reached policymakers, parliamentarians, activists, and media outlets across the country. I poured as much effort into its distribution as I did in its creation, appearing on TV shows and ensuring it reached every corner of Lebanon.

The Citizen Budget quickly became a symbol of empowerment. The real measure of its success came during Lebanon's financial crisis in 2020, when activists flooded our office for more copies, turning the streets of Beirut into a public forum for debates on governance and reform. Later, the Citizen Budget became a vital tool for both parliamentarians and international observers when the Ministry of Finance ceased its regular reporting. One parliamentarian even called to thank me, stating that, for the first time, he felt confident in his understanding of the budget and how it could inform his advocacy.

Amid the twin crises of Lebanon's financial collapse and the COVID-19 pandemic, we shifted to virtual platforms, transforming the Citizen Budget into an interactive dashboard, designed not just to present data but to make it come alive. The dashboard offered real-time insights into government spending, enriched with dynamic graphs and interactive features that allowed users to track fiscal trends.

The dashboard's success was immediate. Civil society organisations, youth groups, and think tanks clamoured for training. Our initiative gained international recognition, being showcased at workshops by the IMF and the International Budget Partnership where it was hailed as a model for improving fiscal transparency in challenging environments.

While the Citizen Budget and dashboard succeeded in amplifying citizens' voices, the lack of effective political response to these concerns highlighted the broader systemic failures. It was also clear that Lebanon's outdated fiscal framework and systemic dysfunction meant there was a limit to what it could achieve on its own. The challenge wasn't just educating the public—it was ensuring that the system would listen and take their concerns seriously.

Bridges of Resilience: Crafting Financial Wisdom Amidst Crisis

As my professional journey deepened and my understanding of public finance in Lebanon and the Arab region expanded, I became acutely aware of a critical gap: the absence of a continuous high-quality, Arabic-language PFM training. I saw this as a unique opportunity to extend the reach of my work, but, as with many of my ideas, it was met with scepticism. I was a woman, after all, from one of the smallest and most turbulent countries in the region. And my endeavour seemed to many a lofty and unrealistic ambition.

However, as I travelled across the region, I saw firsthand how this scepticism stemmed from the very challenges I sought to address. PFM was often treated as an afterthought, relegated to ad hoc external training programmes that failed to meet the systemic needs at hand. These programmes, while often useful to a selected few, were neither continuous nor comprehensive, and they left the vast majority of public financial managers unprepared to navigate the complexities of public budgeting and fiscal oversight. The result was a dangerous combination of a knowledge and skills gap, leaving institutions ill-equipped to manage public finances effectively and responsibly.

Undeterred by the doubters, I crafted a regional portfolio of training and technical assistance services. I also encouraged countries across the region to establish their own 'institutes of finance'—including in Palestine, Morocco, Iraq, Jordan, Djibouti, and Yemen—local, homegrown institutions dedicated to building capacity in PFM. I believed that 'Institutes of Finance,' which often operate at the intersection of three ministries—finance, economy, and civil service—were far more than just training centres. They were spaces where evidence and science-based policy discussions could potentially take place. This collaborative aspect was especially important in countries grappling with significant governance challenges. From my experience, I knew that PFM reforms are rarely successful when imposed top-down; they require broad consensus-building and input from diverse stakeholders. In crisis-prone environments, their action could shift the focus from short-term fixes to a strategic, long-term approach to fiscal governance.

Through tireless advocacy, I worked to convince policymakers of the transformative potential of these institutions. The latter, I argued, would ensure that fiscal reforms were not only technically sound but also politically viable.

My vision extended beyond the borders of any one country: I sought to build a network of expertise across the Arab world, enabling countries to learn from each other's successes and challenges in the pursuit of better fiscal governance. It was an ambitious endeavour, but one I believed in deeply, especially as a woman from the Global South and a fervent supporter of South-South cooperation. Over twelve years, this vision took shape through the Governance Institutes Forum for Training (GIFT-MENA),[7] which helped forge this crucial network across the region.

A Small, but Not Too Small, Victory

As I reflect on my contribution to the fields of governance and public finance, I am poignantly aware of the formidable challenges I have navigated as a female leader in a predominantly male domain, all while Lebanon and the Arab region were attempting to cope with recurrent and increasingly intense crises. The escalating geopolitical tensions have not merely tested my resilience but have also pressed upon me the necessity to innovate and remain steadfast in my mission. The region's toils underscore the critical need for robust public institutions, as the disruptions wrought by conflict threaten the very foundation of the state.

In contemplating the path ahead, a profound question emerges from the depths of my thoughts: amidst the relentless geopolitical tensions, wars, and conflicts, how feasible is it to construct effective public institutions and forge tools that pierce through the fog of financial opacity? And on a more personal note, what will this endeavour mean to me, a non-partisan, non-sectarian woman leading within a predominantly male sphere?

My journey has been marred by systemic biases and scepticism from peers and superiors alike. The weight of my accomplishments was frequently diminished, sometimes by the very minister to whom I report. I recall a poignant moment during a meeting when a male colleague questioned the quality and utility of my work, attributing my success to the support of my French partners rather than acknowledging my skill or vision. Another colleague scrutinised my substantive knowledge and managerial prowess. Numerous times, the initiatives I spearheaded and the projects I launched were perceived as transgressing the boundaries of my mandate. Despite the relentless partiality, I stood resolute, driven by a determination to validate my competence and vision. My forthrightness in confronting male scepticism became a defining pillar of my legacy. I knew time was on my side.

Two decades later, I take immense pride in the work accomplished thus far. But as I ponder the path that lies before us, a multitude of questions linger in the depths of my thoughts. What truly defines success: is it merely our ability to adapt and flourish amidst the unyielding trials that life presents, or does it encompass a more profound essence that eludes the grasp of conventional metrics? How can our collective endeavours sculpt the future of public financial governance and women's leadership, transcending mere tangible outcomes to make a profound imprint on the fabric of society itself? In what ways might we deepen our alliances and synchronise our efforts with regional imperatives to advance our shared vision with greater resonance?

In moments of reflection, I find solace in reading our great Lebanese philosopher Gibran Khalil Gibran. His poetry, so richly evocative, captures the essence of the courage required to lead with unwavering conviction, regardless of the obstacles that lie in our path. Can his profound insights illuminate our journey, helping us transcend the visible barriers that stand before us? How might Gibran's poignant reflection serve as a beacon, guiding our steps with its deep, enduring wisdom as we navigate the complexities of our quest?

Notes

1 The Institute of Finance Basil Fuleihan is a centre of excellence that contributes to capacity development in public financial management and governance through policy research, training and partnership building. The Institute actively contributes to building the financial literacy of youth and facilitating access to information. To that end, it operates a public library. Beyond its national role, the Institute is a platform for regional cooperation hosting the secretariat of the GIFT-MENA network of civil service training schools. It also hosts the regional training centre of the World Customs Organization (WCO).

2 Systematic Country Diagnostic (SCD) for Lebanon, 2016, World Bank, chrome-extension://efaidnbmnnnibpcajpcglclefindmkaj/https://documents1.worldbank.org/curated/en/951911467995104328/pdf/103201-REPLACEMNT-PUBLIC-Lebanon-SCD-Le-Borgne-and-Jacobs-2016.pdf.

3 Angelou, M. (1994). *Wouldn't Take Nothing for My Journey Now.* London: Virago

4 Spending by public corporations and other entities are excluded, leaving over 12 percent of government expenditures unaccounted for, and a staggering 15.5 percent of GDP. https://financially-wise.org/study-off-budget-spending.

5 The Provisional Twelfth Rule, as stipulated in Article 12 of the Public Accounting Law, is a temporary financial mechanism applied when the annual budget is not approved on time. Under this rule, the government may continue spending each month up to one-twelfth of the previous year's budget. This ensures the continuity of public services until the new budget is formally adopted.

6 https://internationalbudget.org/open-budget-survey/country-results/2023/lebanon.

7 Lamia Moubayed Bissat, Sabine Hatem, Carl Rihan (2024), *Governance Cooperation in a Conflict-Ridden Context: The Case of the GIFT-MENA Network*, IIAS Public Governance Series (Vol. 6, 1st ed.), Brussels: IIAS-IISA, 97+vii p.

References

Angelou, M. 1994. *Wouldn't Take Nothing for My Journey Now*. London: Virago.

Moubayed-Bissat, Lamia, Hatem, Sabine, Rihan, Carl. 2024. *Governance Cooperation in a Conflict-Ridden Context: The Case of the GIFT-MENA Network*. IIAS Public Governance Series (Vol. 6, 1st ed.). Brussels: IIAS-IISA, 97+vii p.

World Bank. 2016. *Systematic Country Diagnostic (SCD) for Lebanon*. Washington DC.

Part IV

Reflections and Conversations

Chapter 17

Looking Back, Moving Forward

Diane Elson

Unlike many of the contributors to this book, I did not come to gender budgeting through public financial management but through my research as a feminist economist. I have served for more than 55 years as an academic, advisor to UN agencies and governments, and a civil society activist (most notably in the UK Women's Budget Group).[1]

Feminist Economics, Human Rights and Gender Budgeting

My work on gender budgeting arose in the late 1990s out of my critical analysis of the stabilisation and structural adjustment policies that were conditions for governments in the Global South to access loans from the IMF and the World Bank. These policies entailed cuts to public expenditure on services and social protection income transfers, and rises in consumption taxes (such as VAT), that were supposed to bring down budget deficits and make debt sustainable, though most did not succeed because they held back economic growth and productivity improvements. Analysis by myself and other feminist economists showed that these policies placed disproportionate burdens on women, especially poor women (Elson 1991; Elson 2025). However, no analysis of the gender impact of these policies had been done by the IMF, the World Bank, or governments.

I ignored the advice of a professor in the Manchester University Economics Department where I was employed in the 1990s to forget about gender and focus on trade and development, on which I had already published. I began to think about how we could analyse budgets from a gender equality perspective and propose alternative expenditure and tax policies. I persuaded the London-based Commonwealth Secretariat to begin work on this, that would draw on my own analysis, together with the pioneering work of Rhonda Sharp of the University of South Australia on the Women's Budget in Australia, and that of Debbie Budlender of the Community Agency for Social Enquiry, a leader of the South African Women's Budget Initiative. Our thinking, including the six tools of analysis I developed (drawing on Elson 1998), is summarised in Commonwealth Secretariat 1999.

DOI: 10.4324/9781003732532-21

I persuaded the Commonwealth Secretariat to fund a pilot project on gender budget analysis, working with governments of three Commonwealth countries: South Africa (newly freed from Apartheid), Barbados and Sri Lanka. However, senior economists at the Commonwealth Secretariat blocked the inclusion of taxation as too controversial, and we were only able to discuss expenditure, focusing on the gender impact.[2] This project sowed some seeds, but once the project was over, the three countries did not integrate gender impact analysis into their on-going budgetary policies and processes. We identified challenges that I have continued to see in work with governments, including the view of many officials that gender analysis is an unwelcome addition to an already heavy workload, and the excuse that lack of gender-disaggregated data means they cannot do gender analysis. We concluded that the best condition for a sustainable gender budgeting initiative is an ongoing dialogue between government and civil society, allowing outside-government expertise and scrutiny to play a role.

I was able to extend my work on gender budgeting by taking leave from my academic job at the University of Manchester and spending two years in New York (1998–2000) as special adviser to the Director of UNIFEM. I included a section on gender budgeting in the first UNIFEM report on Progress of the World's Women (Elson (ed) 2000) and helped UNIFEM to develop an international programme on gender budgeting (see for example, Judd (ed) 2002), including a series of workshops with officials, elected representatives, and people from civil society in a wide range of countries. I am pleased to see that UNIFEM's successor agency, UN Women, continues to support work on gender budgeting in a wide variety of countries.

On my return to academic life in the UK in 2000 to a chair in the Department of Sociology at the University of Essex, I began to work on human rights and gender budgeting, in conjunction with UN Women (see Elson 2006). This brought to the fore issues of participation, transparency and accountability, and the possibility of using the human rights reporting system to try to put pressure on governments to design and implement budgets in support of women's rights. This was welcome in a university that had a strong Human Rights Centre, where I could work with law professors who served on UN human rights bodies such as the Committee on Economic, Social and Cultural Rights. I continued this research at Essex University until my retirement from full professor duties in 2011 (when I became an emeritus professor) and sustained it thereafter (see Elson 2017). A focus on budgeting to support the end of all discrimination against women and the fulfilment of the full range of women's human rights guards against a simple focus on narrowing gender gaps. Gender gaps, such as in employment and earnings, can be narrowed through a process in which the employment and earnings of women fall but at a slower rate than falls in men's employment and earnings, a process of equalising down rather than up.

I also became an activist in the UK Women's Budget Group (www.wbg.org.uk) as a member of the Management Committee (2000–10), and as Chair of the Management Committee (2010–2016). WBG operated as a feminist network of academics, policy advisors and activists in women's organisations, producing regular analysis of the gender impact of UK budgets, tax as well as expenditure, and advocating for more gender equitable policies and budgets. In the period when I was chair, we had only one part-time paid worker to coordinate activities and relied on the unpaid work of members. For most of that time we had a productive dialogue with the Labour government, as we had common ground in a shared objective of reducing child poverty. With the support of a woman politician who was a Junior Minister at the UK Treasury, we had regular discussions with Treasury officials and had some impact on policy. For instance, we were able to produce compelling evidence that the design of a proposed new policy to support poor children would have the unintended impact of transferring support from women to men, as it would be paid as a top-up to low wages, excluding all the women not in the labour force—'From the Wallet to the Purse' as we put it. This we backed up with evidence that money going into the hands of women would be more likely to be spent directly on the wellbeing of children than money going into the hands of men. As a result, the policy was changed so that the payment went to the main carer, regardless of employment status. We also persuaded the government that it should conduct and publish a gender equalities impact assessment of each budget, but the government fell before this could be put into law

Resistance and Solidarity

Our experience was very different with the governments in power from 2010 to early 2025, first a coalition between the Conservatives and the Liberal Democrats, and then a Conservative government. These governments were not interested in dialogue, and we had little common ground as they pursued austerity policies, making big cuts to public expenditure and raising VAT (a regressive tax) rather than income tax (a progressive tax). So WBG worked outside government, producing well-researched analyses of the impact of austerity policies, showing the disproportionate impact on poor women and ethnic minority women, with single mothers hardest hit. With the doors to the Treasury closed, WBG engaged with parliamentarians and journalists. For instance, I gave evidence on the gender impact of the budget to the Parliamentary Select Committee on the Treasury in March 2020. My evidence influenced the recommendations made by the Committee which included that the Treasury should publish gender impact assessments. I was also among those interviewed on radio and TV. I talked to journalists and persuaded the mainstream weekly journal *The Economist* to run an article in February 2017 in support of gender budgeting.[3] Our gender budget analysis did have some impact on parliamentarians and the media in the period 2010 to 2025 but it did not change government policy.

Ironically, it was while austerity policies were blocking the adoption of gender budgeting by the UK government that parts of the IMF developed an interest in gender budgeting. I had long been a critic of the IMF's prescription of austerity policies, but I was willing to engage in dialogue if there were people in the IMF who were taking gender analysis seriously. I agreed to serve on the International Advisory Committee for the IMF Project on Gender Budgeting (2015–2016). Some useful reports on gender budgeting in different regions of the world were produced by this project. Subsequently, IMF work on gender budgeting has greatly expanded, and IMF is running workshops for governments, as part of its capacity-building activities. IMF has much more influence with ministries of finance than does UN Women, so more ministries of finance are now introducing a form of gender budgeting.

But I am dismayed to see that what IMF promotes as gender budgeting emphasises a reductionist focus on 'tagging' expenditures that are deemed to be 'for women' or 'for gender equality,' with the aim of producing an estimate of the proportion of expenditure that is 'gender responsive,' with no attention to outcomes. The question of the impact of austerity cannot be raised within this framework. At the same time, the IMF continues to make austerity policies a condition of lending. What began as a feminist initiative was watered down to an accounting exercise, so that the transformational potential of gender budgeting was lost (Elson 2021).

It is easy to lose hope when macroeconomic policies are blocking the adoption of the kinds of gender budgeting that would make substantial progress in fulfilling women's human rights. My hope was kept alive by being able to work with Ailsa McKay (until her untimely death) and Angela O'Hagan on gender budgeting in Scotland where devolution had given the Scottish government a little more autonomy in determining the budget for Scotland. The Scottish government was much more progressive than the UK government and was concerned to address inequality, including gender inequality. I was able to contribute to training on gender budgeting and economic policy for the Scottish government and for Scottish trade unions and to have fruitful discussions with the Chief Economist to the Scottish government. Together with others at the WiSE Centre at Glasgow Caledonian University, we were able to bring ideas from feminist economics into the discussion of public policy in Scotland (see Campbell and Gillespie 2016).

I was also heartened by working with Rhonda Sharp as a Visiting Fellow at the Hawke Research Institute, University of South Australia, in 2009. I learned more about the gains achieved through the Australian Women's Budget Statement produced at the federal level by the Labour government 1984 to 1996, setting out an *ex ante* assessment of the gender impact of the budget. More conservative governments after 1996 preferred to issue a short list of the budget initiatives that they considered of special benefit to women, thus avoiding analyses of the gender impact of austerity measures in the budget. However, the idea of more transformative gender budgeting was kept alive by women's organisations and feminist scholars and some of the state governments. Moreover, AusAid agreed to fund some work on gender budgeting in the Pacific region and I was able to work with Rhonda and other Australian feminist economists on this project. We had a particularly fruitful collaboration with government and civil society in Timor Leste examining the budget for education, its gender impact, and the investments required to increase the enrolment of girls in school to the level of the enrolment of boys (see Austen et al. 2013). By 2024 a Labour government was again in power in Australia, and Australian feminists were ready to assist a revival of gender budgeting at the federal level.

Reasons for Optimism

Gender budgeting in some form is now on the agenda for many governments, as the contributions to this book show. There are two key challenges that must be addressed if the transformational potential of gender budgeting is to be realised. The first is to ensure that the whole budget is addressed, not just those expenditures that are explicitly targeted to gender equality. Investments in water and sanitation, in transport, in clean energy, in health and education services and care services and in social security/welfare benefits, are all capable of reducing inequality gender and improving women's lives if planned and implemented in a gender-responsive way. Similarly, the revenue side of the budget must be addressed—not to introduce special tax breaks for women, but to reform the tax system so that it raises more revenue in ways that are progressive (with the rich paying a higher share of their income and wealth than the poor) and gender equitable.

The second is to address the macroeconomics of the budget. The globalisation of trade, investment and finance has led to a squeeze on fiscal space, restricting the ability of individual governments to raise revenue and manage international borrowing. This has been compounded by governments responding to the rising budget deficits that have been induced by financial crises by cutting public expenditure. Gender analysis can show how this leads not only to increasing gender inequality but also to false economies, preventing public investment that would both support gender equality and increase employment, output, and tax revenues.

When more progressive governments are in power, gender budgeting is implemented in ways that are more likely to have a widespread positive impact. We need to be ready to seize opportunities to work with progressive political forces to secure truly feminist fiscal policies. We need to go beyond expenditure 'tagging' to engage with the design and impact of policies. We need to build on the achievements in *financial* management to transform *economic* management, to engage with the decisions that come prior to the allocation of funding in the budget.

I see several kinds of resources for hope. There is new research on fiscal policy that links gender equality, care and climate change (Grown 2025);

several contributors to this book (Lekha Chakraborty, Amina Bambara, Ayesha Javed, and Trinish Padayachee, among others) also make this point. The UK WBG has grown to be a feminist economics think tank with 14 staff, producing informative and influential briefings on a wide range of economic and social policies, as well as an annual analysis of the implications of the UK government budget for gender equality and women's rights. It engages with the macroeconomics of the budget as well as specific taxes, social security payments and public services, including a feminist critique of the fiscal rules adopted by the first women to be Chancellor of the Exchequer (i.e. minister of finance) (WBG 2025). Civil society budget groups flourish in several other countries, such as the Gender Budget Watchdog Network in the Balkans covering North Macedonia, Albania, Bosnia and Herzegovina, Kosovo, Montenegro, Serbia, and Moldova (https://gbwn.net/en/short-description/). There is a flourishing European Gender Budget Network that brought together researchers, activists, elected representatives, and officials in a conference in Cyprus in March 2026 to consider how to put gender equality at the heart of the next EU budget and how to make gender budgeting more transformative. And we can build on the efforts of women in public financial management documented in this book.

Notes

1 For details see my website www.drdianeelson.com.
2 For more information on this project, see Budlender et al 2002.
3 https://www.economist.com/finance-and-economics/2017/02/23/why-national-budgets-need-to-take-gender-into-account.

References

Austen, S., Costa, M., Sharp, R. and Elson. D. 2013. "Expenditure Incidence Analysis: A Gender-Responsive Budgeting Tool for Educational Expenditure in Timor-Leste?" *Feminist Economics*, 19 (4).

Budlender, D., Elson, D., Hewitt, G. and T. Mukhopadhyay. 2002. *Gender Budgets Make Cents.* London: Commonwealth Secretariat. https://www.thecommonwealthilibrary.org/index.php/comsec/catalog/book/1017.

Campbell, J. and M. Gillespie. (eds.) 2016. *Feminist Economics and Public Policy: Reflections on the Work and Impact of Ailsa McKay.* London: Routledge.

Commonwealth Secretariat. 1999. *Commonwealth Initiative to Integrate Gender into National Budgetary Processes.* https://genderfinancing.unwomen.org/en/resources/a/c/o/a-commonwealth-initiative-to-integrate-gender-into-national-budgetary-processes.

Elson, D. 1991. "Male Bias in Macroeconomics: The case of structural adjustment' in Elson D. ed. *Male Bias in the Development Process.* Manchester: Manchester University Press, reprinted in Elson D. 2025. *The Diane Elson Reader: Gender, Development and Macroeconomic Policy.* Newcastle upon Tyne: Agenda Publishing.

Elson, D. 1998. "Integrating gender issues into national budgetary policies and procedures: some policy options." *Journal of International Development* 10 (7).

Elson, D. ed. 2000. *Progress of the World's Women 2000*. New York: UNIFEM.

Elson, D. 2006. *Budgeting for Women's Rights; Monitoring Government Budgets for Compliance with CEDAW.* New York: UNIFEM. https://gender-financing.unwomen.org/en/resources/b/u/d/budgeting-for-womens-rights-monitoring-government-budgets-for-compliance-with-cedaw-1.

Elson, D. 2017. "Financing for Gender Equality: How to Budget in Compliance with Human Rights Standards" in N. Burn and Z. Kahn (eds.) *Financing for Gender Equality: Realizing Women's Rights through Gender Responsive Budgeting*. London: Palgrave Macmillan.

Elson, D. 2021. "*Gender Budgeting' in G. Berik and E. Kongar (eds.) The Routledge Handbook of Feminist Economics.*" London: Routledge.

Grown, C. (ed.) 2025*Innovations in public finance: A new fiscal paradigm for gender equality, climate adaptation, and care.* Brookings Center for Sustainable Development. https://www.brookings.edu/collection/innovations-in-public-finance-gender-equality-climate-adaptation-care/.

Judd, K. (ed). 2002. *Gender Budget Initiatives.* New York: UNIFEM. https://iknowpolitics.org/sites/default/files/genderbudgetinitiatives_eng.pdf.

Women's Budget Group. 2025. *Rethinking Fiscal Rules. A New Fiscal Framework for Investing in Social Infrastructure and Promoting Gender Equality.* https://www.wbg.org.uk/publication/rethinking-fiscal-rules-a-new-fiscal-framework-for-investing-in-social-infrastructure-and-promoting-gender-equality/.

Chapter 18

Budgeting for Equality from South Africa to Canada

Trinish Padayachee

Introduction

My journey into public finance began in 2009, at the onset of the global financial crisis, when governments prioritised fiscal discipline and macro-economic stability. At the time, the gendered and intersectional impacts of the economic crises received little coverage or analysis. As a young graduate I was trained to prize technical rigour, numerical precision and aggregate outcomes. Public finance priorities and methodologies were long shaped by a narrow group, particularly white men from Anglo-Saxon backgrounds. This lack of diversity fostered a neglect of intersectional perspectives on race, gender, class, and place. Working in public finance reveals how fiscal choices can mirror and perpetuate social inequalities, sharpening disparities in wealth, opportunity, and access to resources. A lack of diversity among decision-makers further reinforces these inequalities. Without diverse perspectives, public finance risks crafting policies that prioritise dominant groups while neglecting the most vulnerable. To address these issues, public finance must be reimagined as a discipline that embeds equality at its core, so fiscal decisions foster fairness and inclusion.

As a public finance professional with experience of working for central budget authorities in the Global South and the Global North, my understanding of inequality has been profoundly shaped by my experiences on the margins. Born in South Africa during Apartheid, my life path was largely dictated by racial classification. In bold block letters, my birth certificate labelled me as 'Indian.' Thirty-three years later, I found myself in Canada, once again assigned a category, as a 'Newcomer.' These two contexts lay bare a universal truth that women shoulder extraordinary barriers in their social, economic, and professional lives. My goal is to contribute to public finance so that gender evidence routinely shapes how policies are designed, and how that impacts everyday life.

DOI: 10.4324/9781003732532-22

Apartheid's Ledger and Life Chances

I was born in Durban, a lush seaside city on the east coast of South Africa. It is a place that winter seems to always ignore, and the perfect climate to cultivate sugar cane. My Indian heritage dates to the late 19th and early 20th centuries, when Indian labourers were brought to South Africa by the British as indentured workers in the sugar cane industry. My community faced the intersection of race, class, and colonialism, first under indenture and then later, under Apartheid. My birth coincided with the state of emergency in the mid-1980s to early-1990s, a period of intense conflict that accelerated the end of the Apartheid regime in South Africa and the country's transition to a democratic dispensation.

The advent of democracy changed my life trajectory, but I was a child at the time, too young to understand what it meant for my future, or to fully comprehend that Apartheid was deliberately designed to prevent me from achieving my full capabilities. Apartheid was a system of indignity, reinforced by state mechanisms such as fiscal policy which maintained racial segregation and economic inequalities. Under the National Party, the Apartheid government allocated a disproportionate share of public funds to the white minority population, ensuring superior education, healthcare, housing, and infrastructure for them at the expense of the majority black population and the smaller coloured and Indian communities. Overall, the intent was to entrench poverty and perpetuate underdevelopment. This was solidified further by the brutal realities of Apartheid geography, enforced through the 1950's Group Areas Act. This law rigidly divided the South African population along racial lines, dictating not only where people could live, but also shaping nearly every aspect of daily life, by determining where people could enjoy leisure, where and what they could study, what economic opportunities they had, and which public services they could access. Under this system, race was not just a social identifier but a determinant of one's quality of life, mobility, and aspirations. The Group Areas Act relegated non-white communities to underdeveloped, resource-starved areas, providing them with substandard infrastructure, healthcare, and education systems that were vastly inferior to those available to white populations. Economic opportunities were deliberately curtailed, confining non-white people to low-paying, menial jobs and barring them from meaningful participation in the broader economy. This racial segregation entrenched cycles of generational poverty and inequality, embedding racial hierarchies into the physical and social fabric of the country—hierarchies whose effects are still evident today.

My earliest understanding of Apartheid and more broadly the concept of social determinants of health was shaped in my childhood, as I witnessed my father battle leukaemia. He underwent treatment in a public hospital designated for people classified as part of the 'Indian Group.' The hospital was appallingly understaffed, and its chemotherapy treatments lagged far behind the advanced care available in hospitals designated for white people. This inadequate access to the care he needed, combined with the immense lifelong stresses he endured under Apartheid, significantly diminished his chances of recovery. His death when I was nine years old, and our subsequent childhood with a single parent, underscored the harsh reality of structural barriers, barriers that often fall heaviest on women who navigate care, work, and safety with fewer choices. My mother was one of ten children, all born into Apartheid. Labour legislation such as the 1956 Jobs Reservation Act and underfunded schools limited tangible socio-economic advancement. She left school at age 16, enrolled in a technical college, and then joined the textile industry in Durban, where limited protections meant low pay and long shifts. Added to that, long, costly commutes consumed a sizable portion of her wages, with constant concerns about time and safety in a country unfortunately known for its disproportionately elevated levels of femicide. That exposure would in the future years be the key focus of my master's research. My mother was well entrenched into her adult life when democracy arrived in South Africa in 1994, after Apartheid formally ended and all South Africans could vote as equal citizens, but there were limited opportunities and too many responsibilities for her to consider re-skilling. Instead, she charted a route for her family to achieve economic successes in ways never attainable to her.

Gender Budgeting Through the Lens of Lived and Comparative Experience

In South Africa, economic success is tied to labour migrancy, and after finishing my studies I faced the reality that to be successful, I had to leave the safety net of my home in Durban and carve out a career in the country's administrative capital, about 600 km away. I remember the day I received two job offers: one from the central budget authority (National Treasury) and the other from the country's National Intelligence Agency (NIA). For a young 20-something year-old, the NIA might have seemed an obvious choice; it offered double the salary, and a permanent role after just a year of training. In contrast, the National Treasury offered a two-year internship with no guarantees, as only the top candidates would be retained. I followed my heart and chose the National Treasury because I was passionate about understanding inequality and how public finance could be leveraged as a tool for change. I called the number listed on the letter and was told that I had to be in Pretoria in four days. It was a hurried, drop-everything move that began my public finance journey at the beginning of 2009, as the global financial crisis's aftershocks were still reverberating.

I was lucky to have had strong support early in my career, largely due to an excellent manager. Although only a few years older than me, she had already worked on three or four budgets and provided mentorship with precision and care. One of my very first tasks was to draft a report on fiscal rules and sovereign wealth funds—a test of my research and writing skills before I progressed to preparing charts for budget publications and providing fiscal-related input for cabinet briefings. The ultimate challenge, however, was updating and running the fiscal framework. This required gathering inputs across macroeconomic, revenue, and expenditure teams and reconciling them into a credible forecast. I remember spending countless hours refining the model, taking notes, studying formulas, and carefully preparing questions for review. Late nights, cold coffee, and the quiet thrill of getting the numbers to balance. I would remain in the Fiscal Policy division for the next decade, progressing from intern to the executive rank within six years. My progression was admittedly very accelerated, driven by a combination of hard work and the support of a strong management team. Several senior managers invested in my growth and advocated for me. Those years of 'growing up' in public finance remain among my happiest and remind me that my path was shaped at critical moments by good mentors.

While I was fortunate to learn from brilliant colleagues, our work at the National Treasury was intensely technical. What was missing was a clear link between public finances and how they affect different groups of citizens, which is crucial in a country as diverse as South Africa, where inequalities are rooted in race, class and gender. The financial crisis of 2009 demanded fiscal consolidation, and protecting social wage expenditure was a priority. Yet our budget documents rarely translated those allocations into lived outcomes, especially for marginalised groups, such as women. After each budget was tabled, I would be sent to parliamentary hearings where various civil society organisations presented their assessment of the budget. These detailed gender-based violence, lack of access to menstrual products, poor literacy outcomes for girls, and life in sprawling urban informal settlements (an enduring legacy of Apartheid geography alluded to earlier). I would diligently take notes, and prepare briefings, but little of it shifted the fiscal choices or narratives. It felt like a perfunctory exercise that had little scope to be advanced at all, as such discussions were often dismissed as veering too far into softer sciences, in a field that favoured technical precision. For me however, these narratives were catalytic. They showed me why gender and diversity (income, age, race, geography etc.) must matter in public finance. Determined to go deeper, I took a one-year hiatus to pursue a master's degree in development economics at University College London.

That year was transformative. It gave me space to reflect on policy practice and the need for evidence. I chose to study transport inequality for women because it shaped the lives of my mother, my friends, and so many women I knew. I asked how reliable, affordable access could change economic outcomes. I conducted fieldwork in one of Johannesburg's largest informal settlements. The finding was stark: limited transport choices sustained social and economic exclusion, especially for women. Safety was integral. Women commuting very late or very early often walked long distances to reach transit, increasing exposure to gender-based violence. The costs of care were also real. A maternal health visit could mean losing a day's wages because travel between clinic and workplace was too long and too expensive. The research was pivotal yet deflating. Why was public finance in South Africa still struggling to connect these lived realities to a more analytical lens to help remedy such inequalities. My restlessness and disappointment were quickly displaced by an unexpected life change. I had met and married a Canadian academic, who after many years living in South Africa was approached for a role back in Canada. I found myself embarking on a journey across continents, much like my ancestors almost 160 years earlier.

I arrived in Canada's capital, Ottawa, in the winter of 2019, unsure how to start over but certain I needed to return to public finance, so when a federal role opened at Environment and Climate Change Canada—linking gender, climate, and budget submissions—I took it. That became my first exposure to gender budgeting in Canada and to Gender-Based Analysis Plus (GBA Plus). A uniqueness of the Canadian system is that each of the line departments in the federal government had its own GBA Plus Centre of Expertise. This was where I worked specifically and advised on the gender and diversity implications of all policies related to the environment and climate change. My South African experience helped more than it hindered. Years of being exposed to spatial inequality, poor service delivery, and the lived experience of economic inequality made it natural to ask who benefits, who bears risk, and how to design equitable policies. The transition still had a learning curve. I had to adjust to Canadian institutions, federal–provincial dynamics, and a distinctions-based approach that centres indigenous partners. Early on, colleagues welcomed the comparative lens but wanted proof that my analysis fit the Canadian evidence base. Once I backed research with Canadian data, incidence logic, and clear fiscal trade-offs, the reception was warm.

Making Equity Routine, Not Optional

Exposure to gender and diversity analysis, and how it was operationalised in Canada prepared me to transition to my next role at the Department of Finance in early 2022, as the lead on gender budgeting. My years in the South African public finance environment had laid a strong foundation for my transition to working in the same field in Canada. South Africa's dynamic, unequal public finance environment gave me a strong foundation in using budgets to tackle systemic issues, with an emphasis on evidence, fiscal discipline, and inclusive growth. The transition was both rewarding and challenging. On one hand, my South African experience equipped me with a deep understanding of public finance as a tool for addressing systemic issues, something that resonates universally. The focus on evidence-based policy-making, fiscal discipline, and inclusive growth in South Africa aligned with many of Canada's priorities. However, adapting to the Canadian context required me to familiarise myself with a new set of institutional structures, cultural nuances, and economic priorities. For instance, Canada's fiscal federalism system presented a steep learning curve, as it differs significantly from South Africa's intergovernmental fiscal arrangements. Colleagues appreciated the focus on evidence-based policy.

I began my public finance journey in Canada, as I had over a decade earlier in South Africa, with a welcoming management team, who valued my experiences of public finance in the Global South and who took time to explain how Canada works. Feeling supported changes what is possible. Soon I was advising on gender budgeting abroad. A full circle moment came when a multilateral institution working in South Africa asked about Canada's gender budgeting approach. I co-presented on a panel with Thoko Madonko, an advocate of gender budgeting who continues to drive gender budgeting efforts in South African public policy discourse (see Chapter 20). It reminded me how interconnected the field of public finance is and how paths often cross in different contexts.

Canada's approach to gender budgeting is distinctive because intersectional analysis is required for every new budget measure, and in fact it stands out for being one of the most rigorous and routinised processes among countries pursuing strategic budgeting. Of course, that level of rigour does take a human toll and many hours, even days to find and analyse disaggregated data, reconcile sources, and carefully articulate every assumption so that gender and diversity analysis can stand on its own. Pushback occurs very often, even in an environment where this is a legislated requirement. The questions are almost always the same—why does this lens matter at all, or assumptions that my job lacks any analytical rigour. My strategy is to keep the focus on gender budgeting as smart economic policy. This is not about adding commentary to a budget. It is about improving fiscal choices, reducing waste from poorly targeted programmes, and raising the return on public spending by reaching the people policy is meant to serve. My experiences in Canada have allowed me to hone my public finance skills. Here, intersectional analysis is baked into budget work, and the question is not whether equity belongs in public finance but how precisely to measure it. I have seen budgets move from programmes on paper to lived outcomes. The Canadian story is not perfect, but it is practical and teachable—build evidence, disclose trade-offs, track results, and keep adapting your approach.

My career has been shaped by the intersection of personal experience and professional growth, from witnessing the systemic inequities of Apartheid South Africa to engaging with the complexities of being a newcomer in Canada. These experiences have reinforced the importance of incorporating diverse perspectives and lived realities into financial decision-making to ensure that public policies meet the needs of all, especially the most vulnerable. Having worked in both a developing and now an advanced economy, I am acutely aware of the unique challenges women and girls face in each context. In South Africa, systemic inequities continue to manifest in severe ways. High rates of gender-based violence, including one of the world's highest femicide rates, create a pervasive climate of fear for women. Poor literacy outcomes for girls, particularly in under-resourced rural areas, limit their opportunities for economic advancement and perpetuate cycles of poverty. Many women face barriers in accessing basic healthcare, safe public transport, and employment opportunities due to the enduring effects of Apartheid-era spatial planning and systemic exclusion. In Canada, the context is different but no less pressing. Indigenous women and girls, for instance, face disproportionately high rates of violence and poverty, as highlighted by the ongoing national crisis of Missing and Murdered Indigenous Women and Girls. Refugee and other newcomer women often arrive in Canada with limited resources, facing economic marginalisation, language barriers, and a lack of access to support networks. Access to affordable childcare, equitable wages, and healthcare, including mental health services, are ongoing challenges for many women in Canada, particularly those in low-income or racialised communities. These issues underscore the need for policies that address intersectional vulnerabilities and create pathways for women to succeed.

Ultimately, whether in Canada, South Africa, or elsewhere, the aim is the same: create conditions for women and girls to thrive. Public finance can do this when it centres intersectional evidence. In Canada, that means building gender and diversity into every decision, publishing the analysis, and tracking who benefits and who is missed. From South Africa I carry the lesson that the absence of a gendered lens in public finance continues to constrain opportunities. Together, these lessons illustrate that gender budgeting, when done consistently, has the power to turn budgets into tools that create meaningful societal change.

Chapter 19

Personalising the Theory

Angela O'Hagan

Introduction and Overview

The women in this volume have shared a range of personal and professional experiences, with a similarly broad spread of conceptual and technical perspectives. These women have had personal and professional lives that span the globe, with all the political, institutional, and cultural differences that entails. That global spread also reinforces the universality of many experiences of attitudes to gender equality policy and in particular gender budgeting, as well as the specifics of individual experiences.

The focus and purpose of this chapter is to draw together these experiences through multiple theoretical and conceptual framings to characterise the shared and highlight the specific. The approach here is an attempt to pull on the threads of these experiences and interweave them into insights from feminist institutionalism, feminist policy analysis and public policy analysis, with of course the foundational origins of gender budgeting in feminist economics and approaches to gender mainstreaming as an institutional turn in feminist public policymaking.

It is very rare for the personal, behind-the-scenes experiences of individuals within public institutions to be revealed in the way approached in this book. As already said, the personal is political, but the personal is also theoretical, by which I mean that we can use the theory both to inform our understanding of the personal, and to use the personal lived experience to inform theoretical development. In that spirit, it is the hope of this volume to inspire further research in this field that surfaces women's experience in public institutions, public financial management (PFM), and the multiple relational, professional, and discipline-specific elements that are relevant.

There are four sections in this chapter: following this brief overview, the chapter summarises the historical and conceptual origins of gender budgeting, locating the experiences of the contributors in this context; it then explores their stories from the perspective of feminist institutionalism and institutional structures and processes intended to advance gender equality. The final section draws from the aspirations and inspirations of the contributors to this volume, with

DOI: 10.4324/9781003732532-23

some insights from research on the realities and ongoing gaps in gender equality and the representation of women in policy institutions.

In *Out of the Margin*, 30 years ago, Kuiper and Sap (1995) sought to surface a key concern which has echoed down the years and pulses through the experience and efforts of the contributors to this book:

> Feminists have found much of concern in the way the economics has written women out of its history, built its theories around masculinist values, failed to take proper account of women and their work when measuring the economy and ignored most of the policy issues that press most heavily upon women.

At the time, feminist economics was emerging as an academic discipline and propositions for gender budgeting, named as gender responsive budgeting (GRB), were beginning to appear at the international level, and separate from the growing presence PFM beginning to take hold in international institutions. It was also a time, as Lekha Chakraborty reminds us in her chapter of useful context, "before any global goals on human development: it was all about numbers, with GDP as the policy outcome. 'Beyond the GDP' paradigm was a tough ask. The global goals like UN's MDGs (Millenium Development Goals) and SDGs (Sustainable Development Goals) came later."

Thirty years on, that challenge to the discipline of economics remains. This book contains the testimonies of women economists and women working in public finance and economic policy, bearing witness to the ongoing closed nature of the discipline conceptually as well as the character of many public finance departments and organisations. The women in this volume, also and importantly, demonstrate where they individually have introduced new approaches to public finance, including for some gender budgeting, that have challenged the status quo, and where their own experiences of sexism and other forms of discrimination, and for some additional demands, have resulted in a transformation for them individually and for the organisational practices in which they are engaged.

Locating Experience in the Conceptual and Aspirational Context of Gender Budgeting

Feminist economists generally, and the women in this book, along with advocates of gender budgeting have consistently argued and evidenced that gender is relevant to economic policy and that "Gender analysis is central to the formulation of economic policy and the implementation of gender equality outcomes as public policy objectives at programme and project level" (Klatzer and O'Hagan, 2020: 64).

This is a radical proposition and one which exposes the inherent weaknesses in the established practices which result in the maintenance and exacerbation of unequal outcomes for women's economic status and security, and which Italian feminist economist Annalisa Rosselli has informally described it as "a powerful instrument for feminist transformation" (Klatzer and O'Hagan, 2020: 64).

As the women in this volume have exemplified in their work,

> Demonstrating the deficiencies of 'gender-blind' economic policy has provided evidence and demand for improved gendered analysis in public policy and the need to integrate questions of resource allocation into policy rationale and objectives.
>
> (Klatzer and O'Hagan, 2020: 65)

In applying Kuiper and Sap's characterisation of feminist economics as moving "from the margins to the mainstream," Klatzer and O'Hagan (2020) described:

> Gender budgeting, or gender budget analysis, is the examination, from a gender perspective, of the potential impacts of benefits of public spending and revenue decisions, including at the macroeconomic level. It incorporates a gender equality perspective in economic policies and budget processes and aims at restructuring these in order to promote gender equality.
>
> (p. 64)

Elson (2006) characterised it as an important tool for determining the differential impact of expenditures on women and men to help ensure the equitable use of existing resources. This positioning of the budget as part of the policy process has not been a usual description of either the budget setting or policymaking process, with conceptual and practical efforts to keep the elements separate in academic analysis and in the practice of government. In 2015, citing respectively Kay (2005) and Sen (2000) on the construction of the budget as a "policy institution" having no influence or impact over the status of women, O'Hagan again argued that "Gender budgeting challenges these norms by locating the budget as central to the policy process" as a method to reveal and eliminate the "built-in gendered assumptions" in government approaches to policymaking and resource allocation (O'Hagan, 2015: 234).

Early feminist economists, including Marilyn Waring in her exploration of national accounts, and separately advocates of gender budgeting, were clear to reinforce the interrelated nature of policy and public finance, and to highlight not only the possibility but the necessity of bringing the two together. Waring discusses the concept of value and what is valued, contrasting the focus on GDP with the everyday of women's lives and the social infrastructure of care. She asks us:

> Can you imagine the nation's annual budget becoming a realistic description of the wellbeing of the community and its environment, a reflection of real wealth and different values? The budget would answer all of the following. Who does what work and where—paid and unpaid? What is the position of the nation's children and the aged? Who is not housed adequately? Who has the poorest health...?
>
> (Waring, 1988)

Describing the innovation of the Women's Budget in South Africa, and in her expression since, former parliamentarian and lifelong campaigner Pregs Govender has variously characterised the budget as the principal expression of a government's priorities, who it values and who it does not, whose work it values and whose it does not. In the instructive UN Women publication (2002) edited by Karen Judd, Govender makes the challenge to budgets and key concepts in public finance:

> 'Budgets,' 'Economics,' 'Financial Governance': none of these are neutral terms. The question is: Who defines their meaning and in whose interests do they operate? What are the priorities? What is the agenda? Who determines these?
>
> (Govender, 2002:58)

So far, we are building up a picture that gender budgeting as a concept in itself has existed for 30 years in international institutional policy and before that in the 1980s with the early 'women's budgets' of the Australian federal government and then the women's budgets of South Africa. As the years have passed, there is evidence to reinforce that in the fields of public policy and administration, including public finance, the budget has been quietly considered as a part of the policy process. This reality is core to the 'project' of gender budgeting and furthermore reaffirms that public finance has not been ignorant of the link but has rather perhaps chosen not to accept it as readily as advocates would hope, as exemplified in so many of the experiences of the women in this volume.

In rather guarded observations, Klatzer and O'Hagan observed in 2020 that "GB has moved from the margins to the mainstream of public finance over more than 30 years," arguing that

> The understanding and situating of gender responsive budgeting (GRB) has changed considerably [including] a gradual shift whereby the radical nature of GB is potentially being lost to increasingly bureaucratised processes of 'doing GRB' within institutionalised process which themselves do not change.
>
> (2020: 64)

This challenge not to dilute the potential of gender budgeting as feminist policy change has been central to many experiences of the women in PFM in the contributions in this volume. These women are all clear on the transformational character of gender budgeting and concerned to preserve and advance progress, alert to the pontential for dilution of its feminist intent and original character as "GB gains increasing validation as a tool of modern public finance management (PFM) and becomes more widely implemented" (Klatzer and O'Hagan, 2020: 64). There is an inherent risk here that the transformational intent and potential become muted or undermined in the face of institutional resistances and the dominance of gender-blind ways of thinking and doing. However, the experiences detailed in this volume clearly evidence individuals working within and against institutional norms to advance gender equality and to alter the established path dependencies and introduce alternative conceptual and analytical approaches to PFM. In their narratives, most women in this book address different aspects of gender in budgeting, or gender within or outside the institutions and processes of public finance—and all the challenges, visible and less visible—to bring actual feminist transformation in the way budgets are being discussed and developed.

In her chapter, Ermira Lubani discusses the move to shift economics as the 'hard science,' to a "more accessible and effective approach that could be adapted to our context," explicitly seeking to dilute the dominance of 'orthodox' economics (as developed by white (dead) men) and the entrenched assumption of the neutrality of the budget process in which gender is regarded as not relevant to the budget process. Trinish Padayachee reinforces this learning and application of economic thinking and gender equality objectives in her chapter:

> The link between budgets and policies was not yet clear to me, and I had to learn how public finances relate to the real-life outcomes we see in society. It was an overblown concept at first, but I was determined to understand and bring gender considerations into discussions on public finances.

There are multiple learning points for us all as advocates of gender budgeting in Trinish's open reflections—that there is both learning for us all to work through, and a caveat to avoid the 'overblown': to take others with you and keep the focus on another realisation that "Budgets were not just about numbers, they were about people's lives and affected women and men in different ways." Maja Bosnić reflects on the resistance of government officials to embrace gender analysis in their work, even when it clearly leads to a better understanding of who benefits from public funds (and who does not). Trinish's comments again echo across the literature with her challenge that experiences on the margins must be the mainstream of policymaking, overturning the orthodoxy that "The budget was an essential government policy, too important to be 'complicated' with gender issues." Understanding these resistances is central to devising ways to challenge and overturn them, as well as to explaining/characterising the experiences detailed in this volume. One theoretical framing that offers routes into this understanding is feminist institutionalism which is explained in further detail in the following section.

Unpacking Lived Experience Through a Feminist Institutionalist Lens

Contributors to the book reflect on their own experiences, which are often influenced by the institutions and institutional frameworks they work in. This context gives rise to the key question and focus of reflection for the contributors, the reader, and for us collectively in the operation of institutions and the advancement of gender equality: can institutions that are non-feminist in their core implement feminist concepts externally?

Throughout the 2000s, the field of feminist institutionalism (FI) has been growing in strength in terms of the scope of analysis as well as its scholarly and global reach. FI is concerned with the "rules of the game" (Krook and Mackay, 2011: 1) in political institutions, and how these rules, both formal and informal, are gendered—in their established norms, approach to policy-making and legislation, and as an alternative to how institutions might adopt more gender-aware and proactively gender-equal norms including increasing women's representation in decision-making and elected politics.

For Madsen, "Feminist institutionalism takes its point of departure in the assumption that institutions are gendered rules, norms and processes" (Madsen, 2019: 74). The core propositions or toolkit for analysing institutions from an FI perspective include:

- Institutions are gendered: the established ways, or rules, that set institutional norms and practices often privilege men or masculine-coded behaviours.
- Tension of change within continuity: whereby change can occur even within institutions resisting gendered reforms.
- Importance of 'critical actors': the individuals or groups within institutions who are key to the promotion of gender equality despite the structural barriers in place.
- 'Rules of the game': the formal vs. informal rules which include both written laws and the unwritten norms at play, all contribute to shaping gender outcomes.

It is clear from the experiences detailed in this book, and as explored across FI literature and more widely, that there are institutional resistances to gender analysis and advancing gender equality at work within and externally to public (and private) institutions.

FI scholarship has also sought to explore the causes and responses to "resistance, reproduction and obstruction of positive change around gender issues in institutions" and to better understand why it is that "some gendered changes are obstructed" (Thomson, 2018:178). Discussed across FI literature more widely, and in relation to gender budgeting specifically, forms of institutional resistances have been variously described, including as wilful ignorance (Franzway et al., 2009) and, more broadly, deliberate opposition, sometimes ideological, and a lack of basic knowledge or understanding of the concept and willingness to become more informed. As is obvious from the testimonies in this volume, the women here are used to institutional resistance, which as Trinish observed as "pushback" which "occurs very often, even in an environment where this is a legislated requirement." Consistent with the FI analysis that change can still be engendered from within and in the face of resistance, Lamia Moubayed's response arguably characterises the collective in this volume who remain "undeterred by the doubters."

While political, geographic, and other contextual factors are of course important, as Catharina Schmitz highlights, "All PFM systems are of course shaped and influenced by the specific context in which they are being implemented." If that context is one of "stereotypical expectations" which Catharina and Ana Patricia Muñoz underscored as present among and co-workers as well as elected members of parliament/ministers, then introducing gender analysis as well as having women in male-dominated organisations have not been straightforward, to say the least.

At the conceptual level, the disregard of the relevance of gender to economic policy has been a backdrop for the introduction of gender budgeting. This is compounded by what a number of the women describe here as a lack of diversity within institutions, the tendency to talk down to women—particularly women of colour and not from countries with a predominantly white population from which the men that dominated in international finance institutions (IFIs) come. The very nature of institutions and the expert world of PFM appear to be "dominated by white, native English-speaking men" as Maja reflects, a sentiment echoed by Trinish. The dominant male norms characterise communication styles, including tipping into 'mansplaining' on economics as Catharina highlights, to the geo-political contexts of women's home countries, as gently but firmly articulated by Manal Fouad. Lamia reveals the stark character of institutional norms which led her to feel "marred by systemic biases and scepticism from peers and superiors alike. The weight of my accomplishments was frequently diminished, sometimes by the very minister to whom I report."

The disregard for women's role as child-bearers and care givers that has formed part of the experiences of many of the women as narrated in this book, characterise to varying degrees —and with a scattering of resilient humour, including candid stories about breast-feeding while pushing for institutional change—further evidence the women's capabilities for multi-tasking (if that were necessary).

What they are talking about are the 'rules of the game,' formal in the sense of the economic models and institutional processes as evidenced in the programmes, and informal in the low-level attritions of diminishing women's knowledge and skills bases. Trinish observes the impact of this lack of diversity on the content and impact of policies; she is clear that "Without diverse perspectives, public finance risks crafting policies that prioritise dominant groups while neglecting the most vulnerable."

Many of the women, including Manal, Trinish, Ayesha Javed, and Ana Patricia highlight the importance of positive role models, especially women as role models in management and the significance of different, more inclusive leadership styles, and in modelling that behaviour to others/the next generation. They celebrate their co-workers and younger colleagues in the teams they lead, and the importance of modelling the good behaviour they have benefitted from and applauding the innovation of the next generation and the challenge they bring to traditional expectations. For many of the women, their family life has been an integral part of their professional progression, including the gendered expectations they have experienced working against them. These accounts reinforce the reality of the support women need and why and how that is different for women, and for the support networks that men have—which are often provided by women from men's support networks. All of which underscores the need for men to be more supportive of women, and for institutions as employers to be more alert to and less tolerant of discrimination in the workplace.

Narratives in this volume demonstrate the importance of taking the long view. The temporal context is pivotal to the successful adoption, implementation and sustainability of gender budgeting. Annual budget cycles are very short for introducing the long-term process and conceptual change required, and parliamentary cycles mean a constant threat on undoing progress and even underpinning legislation for gender budgeting. The "Framework for Favourable Conditions" that I highlight in Chapter 13 provides a roadmap for the existing conditions to ensure lasting success.

A further part of the long view is weathering the fluctuations in the health and stability of gender equality policy and the supporting legislative and institutional architecture at different levels of government and governance of institutions. Catharina, among others, emphasises the importance of gender equality policy being formalised in state policy as an important lever and support for change. But also one which, as others have pointed out too, cannot be taken for granted as a permanent feature of government and institutional vision and practice.

Allowing for the reality that, as Madsen states, "A high degree of institutional inertia may exist, and the gendered institutional barriers might be very persistent and difficult to change" (Madsen, 2019:74), the gendered nature of organisations can still be re-gendered, which is clearly core to the objectives of the women in this book who have been critical actors in organisational change. The testimonies of Ayesha, Amina Bambara, Nordia Campbell, Hajar Ben Ameur, Urška Zrinski, Oksana Tsiupa, and all the other contributors here reveal multiple barriers to advancing their ideas and the pushback they experienced, often in highly gendered ways to devalue their presence, proposals, and their potential.

In working through the testimonials, FI also offers a helpful typology of the different types of institutional change, based on Mahoney and Thelen (2010) and their framework for models of gradual institutional change which also allow for the historical and temporal dimensions that inform feminist institutionalism. These types are layering, displacement, drift, and conversion.

- The form of change most in evidence from these experiences, following Mahoney and Thelen's model, are '*layering*' which is the process of attaching new rules to existing ones through revision, attachment and amendment and is by nature less radical as it works to create change within the existing system. Many of the women have moved into and through PFM, introducing incremental change, building networks and support, learning to read the political opportunities as they emerged.
- '*Displacement*' seeks to replace existing rules, and that has not been the explicit objective or way of working of the advocates of gender budgeting in this volume. The long build of a career and internal support networks is clearly set out in Urška's story of what led to the displacing innovation of the PEFA framework, and in many others of the women who have replaced existing systems for fraud (Nordia), development goals (Ayesha), and many others who have changed the rules, processes and structures of PFM in their own or other countries, and in international institutions as Maja, Manal and others do or did.
- Similarly, a strategy of '*drift*' where change is a form of resistance to external factors and changes, has not been an approach in evidence here, as the women have been proactive in their efforts to change institutional practice. Drift has clearly not been an option for the women in this book. They have not allowed their commitment to social, economic, and gender justice to drift, and they have not accepted drift from the institutions and systems within which they have worked.
- The remaining type, '*conversion*', is where actors seek to bend the original rules towards other ends—in this case the advancement of gender equality through gender budgeting. In this category, the women in this book are champions—in all senses. They have worked within existing systems to introduce sustainable change, bending decision-making processes towards economic justice and more gender equal outcomes, as

> leaps off the pages of the chapters from Lekha, Ayesha, Nordia, Amina, Manal, Urška, and many more.

For Waylen (2014), layering and conversion can be more effective in securing gendered institutional change as they are

> gradual, endogenous and potentially more achievable when actors have sufficient power to create some new rules or use existing rules in creative ways, but not enough to displace these existing rules.
>
> (Waylen, 2014: 8)

Madsen characterises this as gender actors having to "manoeuvre strategically to promote institutional change" (Madsen, 2019:74).

Many of the women in the book discuss the country and institutional contexts in which they have been introducing and nurturing gender budgeting, including the provenance of formal mechanisms in domestic legislation, international policy and legal frameworks. Oksana talks about the importance of embedding gender in budget frameworks and documents. Structural supports for these policies include named ministries and government departments, national gender equality bodies funded by the state, and well-functioning civil society organisations with whom the state engages effectively. These structures are vulnerable to political and regime change, again as the experience of many contributors has revealed.

Multiple contributors throughout their accounts have discussed the importance of effective engagement with civil society organisations, and the importance of the intersectional analysis that should be part of government analysis which is often brought to government by external organisations. They also reflect that often the perspectives on women's everyday realities presented by non-governmental organisations often not 'cutting through' as Trinish describes. There are welcome contrasts to this provided by Lamia on the positive example of Ministry of Finance working with civil society on budget literacy and the introduction of the Citizens' Budget, and on the exciting example of mainstream television programmes as innovation in government engagement that Amina pioneered.

A central theme is also the core support and drive from international bodies—and the interventions and direction from UN Women, IFIs, and international funding bodies. For some countries,[1] the technical know-how and engagement from external bodies have been hugely significant in building capacity and progress domestically, and providing much needed reinforcement to local civil society organisations as well as leverage for government action. Still, as many contributors explain, even when supported by outside bodies, a lot of convincing, mostly data-driven, is needed to ensure government ownership of the approach to gender budgeting, as discussed by Ermira, Oksana, Amina and others. International knowledge exchange, support from established experts, and the development of networks feature prominently in the experiences of many women.

The importance of academic, practitioner, and research communities is well established in feminist public policy literature, and the stories of these women brings the theory alive on the page. Maya Rostanty talks warmly of first accessing the work of Debbie Budlender and then having the direct engagement of Diane Elson (also featured in this book) and Rhonda Sharp and the difference that made to building support for gender budgeting. They offer many more examples that contribute to the international evidence base and develop further theories on the application of knowledge exchange, the deepening of knowledge bases, how feminist knowledge builds into praxis, and how that integrates into system change within organisations.

Within the international influence and leverage, a key element is the knowledge exchange through feminist networks—academic and civil society—and the policy learning and transfer that this engagement supports. The influence of feminist movements in legislative and institutional reform in established and emerging democracies in this volume is highlighted in the experiences of women in Sweden, South Africa, Canada-South Africa, and the Balkan countries, among others in this volume. Catharina highlighted an important example of policy learning from Global South to North, in "the groundbreaking work in Southern Africa inspired the Nordic countries, which, in turn, contributed to shaping the GRB methodology." Both give further importance to being able to apply 'evidence-based' proposals and arguments for gender budgeting as cited by Catherina and Ana Patricia, with her emphasis on the importance accorded to evidence-based policy making in PFM. Hajar, Lekha, and Urška among many others tell of how being around other women working on the same topic created complicity, comfort, and support in important testimony on the power of the presence and co-operation of women. Nordia raises a different point on the importance of bringing forward a generation of men concerned with women's equality, with Oksana among others citing the importance of support from male colleagues. The stories of support and men opening up closed paths also contrast with the other experiences of the institutionalised permissions to undermine women —their presence, the values, and the ideas they bring. Urška recounts the seared memory of a senior male colleague dismissing her legitimacy as an economist—and disparaging cultural expression—confident in the established behaviours which have allowed these gendered attacks to pass unchallenged.

It is clear throughout the personal testimonies that being the pioneers and 'policy entrepreneurs' these women have encountered significant challenges throughout their careers, which for some have been exacerbated by other life moments. These include the state violence referenced by Ana Patricia and the personal violence experienced by her family, and personal trauma that affected Lekha. For Ermira, the emergence from communist rule to the 'freedoms' of democracy while not always violent, contrasts with the peaceful constitutional reform in the UK at the end of the 1990s described by Angela.

Framing Futures in Feminist Public Finance

Throughout this volume, the contributors have repeatedly returned to the human, the stories of their everyday and life experiences. Inside institutions across the globe, these women have described what it has been like to be or feel feminist in neoliberal institutions such as public finance institutions. I have heard this feeling described elsewhere, including in the neoliberal world of universities as "being in a holding pattern to keep hope alive."

In their professional lives, many of the contributors have recalled the importance of strong and compassionate role models, other women—and some men—who have taken the time or the deliberate step to offer positive feedback or an encouraging word. Modelling this feminist ethic of care is central to the concept of this book and its intention to consciously value the contributions of others. The most common thread in all these testimonies, beyond and separate from those that can be discussed through different theoretical lenses is humanity. The unifying character and belief in humanity, and the potential for and desire for change for a better life for all is present throughout this volume. These women are united in a passion for social justice and a compassionate state.

In concluding, I echo Trinish's clear call to action that "Public finance must be reimagined as a discipline, that embeds equality at its core, so fiscal decisions foster fairness and inclusion." Across the years of agency and advocacy by the women in this volume, it is clear that they are succeeding in this endeavour, and that the institutional support is emerging. Combatting institutional resistance to gender equality and gender policy as feminist policy change has been a shared experience for the women in this book, impacting their professional standing and personal life.

Gender as a legitimate analytical focus as well as political goal can remain elusive in practice, despite institutional policy commitments. Clear recommendations for evidence of need to drive budget decisions rather than political interests underscore the efforts and potential for learning from the work of the women in this volume to bring about the necessary institutional change and underpinning knowledge to sustain gender analysis in public finance management and budgetary processes.

What is clear though, is that women can and are changing the world. The determination to innovate, drive change, produce the evidence and analysis, and introduce new approaches to policymaking and PFM decisions that challenge the established path dependencies and knock through entrenched institutional resistances course through all the contributions in this volume. The evidence and experiences here can be explored through myriad theoretical frameworks around feminist change, and here we have focused on feminist institutionalism.

As scholars and practitioners continue to reveal and analyse women's experience in policy making, this overview offers a number of future directions for research, considering how gender *in* budgeting, PFM, and public policymaking create opportunities for alternative policy outcomes, and gives clear direction to institutions on the internal changes that are essential to remake organisations with a new set of norms that value and sustain a commitment to gender equality and the women—and men—who are committed to securing it.

Note

1 This is explained clearly outside this volume in describing the development of gender budgeting at municipal level in Turkey (Yucel et al., 2025).

References

Elson, E. 2006. "Budgeting for women's rights." *Monitoring Government Budgets for Compliance with CEDAW.* New York: UNIFEM.

Franzway, S., Sharp, R., Mills, J.E. and Gill, J. 2009. "Engineering ignorance: The problem of gender equity in engineering." *Frontiers: A Journal of Women Studies*, 30 (1): 89–106.

Govender, P. 2002 in Judd, K. (ed.) *Gender Budget Initiatives: Strategies, Concepts and Experiences. UN Women.* Available at: https://www.unwomen.org/en/digital-library/publications/2002/1/gender-budget-initiatives-strategies-concepts-and-experiences.

Kay, A. 2005. "A Critique of the Use of Path Dependency in Policy Studies." *Public Administration*, 83 (3): 553–571.

Klatzer, E. and O'Hagan, A. 2020. "Moving Boundaries with Gender Budgeting: From the Margins to the Mainstream" in Maria Cristina Marcuzzo, Ghislain Deleplace, Paolo Paesani (eds.), *New Perspectives on Political Economy and Its History.* London: Palgrave Macmillan.

Krook, M.L. and Mackay, F. 2011. "Introduction: Gender, Politics, and Institutions." In *Gender, Politics and Institutions: Towards a Feminist Institutionalism* (pp. 1–20). London: Palgrave Macmillan UK.

Kuiper, E. and Sap, J. eds. 1995. *Out of the Margin: Feminist Perspectives on Economics.* Psychology Press.

Madsen, Diana Højlund. 2019. "Gender, Power and Institutional Change – The Role of Formal and Informal Institutions in Promoting Women's Political Representation in Ghana." *Journal of Asian and African Studies*, 54 (1): 70–87.

Mahoney, J. and Thelen, K. (2010) *Explaining Institutional Change – Ambiguity, Agency and Power.* Cambridge: Cambridge University Press.

O'Hagan, A. 2015. "Favourable conditions for the adoption and implementation of gender budgeting: insights from comparable analysis." *Politica Economica / Journal of Political Economy*, vol. XXXI (2): 233–252.

Rubery, J. 2005. "Reflections on gender mainstreaming: An example of feminist economics in action?" *Feminist Economics*. 11 (3): 1–26.

Sen, G. 2000. "Gender mainstreaming in finance ministries." *World Development*, 28 (7): 1379–1390.

Thomson, J., 2018. "Resisting gendered change: Feminist institutionalism and critical actors." *International Political Science Review*, 39 (2): 178–191.

Waring, M. and Steinem, G., 1988. *If Women Counted: A New Feminist Economics.*

Waylen, G. (2014) "Informal institutions, institutional change, and gender equality." *Political Research Quarterly* 67 (1): 1–12.

Yucel, Y., Yakut-Cakar, B., Yakar-Onal, A. and Gunluk-Senesen, G., 2025. "Global to Local: Translation of UN Women's Gender Responsive Budgeting Framework into Municipalities in Türkiye." *Global Policy.*

Chapter 20

Public Finance, Feminism, and Resistance

A Conversation

Marine Destrez, Sepideh Labani, Thokozile Madonko, Scherie Nicol, Sureni Weerathunga and Maja Bosnić

Introduction

We wanted to close the book with a conversation, because that is how the stories we share usually happen: in the unmoderated, generous spaces we meet, exchange and share. When there is no script, institutional filter, or 'proper' sequencing of ideas. We wanted to reproduce the intimate, genuine, and spontaneous conversations we have when a group of women gets together, the quick 'sisterhood' that results, and the bonding that it creates. This chapter is a minimally moderated conversation by Maja Bosnić between five women whose trajectories in public financial management (PFM) and gender budgeting are both diverse and intersected:

- **Marine Destrez**, the French lawyer and former diplomat turned anti-corruption and public finance specialist whose career has taken her from Eastern Europe to Pakistan and the Pacific and who currently steers multi-country reform processes connected to the political economy of budgeting and accountability institutions.
- **Thokozile Madonko** (Thoko), the South African activist-scholar who has spent two decades challenging the economic orthodoxy that renders women invisible.
- **Sepideh Labani Motlagh,** the Iranian-Belgian, who, since her life-changing discovery of gender studies, dedicates her career to gender mainstreaming and gender budgeting worldwide, working at the intersection of policy, finance and social change with international organisations, public institutions and grassroots civil society.
- **Scherie Nicol**, the Scottish economist who started her career in government, then as a parliamentary staff where she helped set up a new Financial Scrutiny Unit, and is now at the OECD working on a variety of public finance issues; and
- **Sureni Weerathunga**, the Sri Lankan economist and graduate student at University of Glasgow whose early PFM work has been shaped by her

DOI: 10.4324/9781003732532-24

experience internationally and working amid the economic crisis in her home country.

Starting the Conversation: Us in this Space

Maja: It is such a pleasure to join this group and to see us all in one space—joining from many different time zones. Thank you for agreeing to meet and exchange, share your story, experience and what you're passionate about in the public finance and gender budgeting world.

Let's begin our conversation today, with talking about your own experiences—in PFM, but also within the broader landscape of public policy. We all come from different backgrounds and trajectories. What experience has followed you, shaped you, or stayed with you—something you would truly like to share?

Scherie: To start the discussion, I've been reflecting on how my perspective on gender equality has evolved over time. For example, for many years my work in gender budgeting was primarily framed as an exercise in sound economic and fiscal policy rather than from an explicitly values-driven standpoint.

That view began to shift a few years ago, influenced by personal and professional experiences. Becoming a parent brought new insights into the challenges new mothers face when balancing work and family responsibilities. In highly competitive environments, even short absences can create vulnerabilities, and returning to work often requires significant adjustment. These dynamics are not unique to any one organisation—they reflect broader structural issues that many professional women encounter.

Navigating these realities deepened my understanding of why this work matters beyond technical budgeting. It reinforced for me that what we do helps shape real lives and careers. That experience was transformative for me and sparked a renewed commitment to advancing gender equality. From that point onward, I realised why for so many people gender budgeting is deeply values-driven. To me, it is both. The systems we design and maintain must make economic sense, but they can also ensure people benefit in fair and equitable ways. That requires more than technical accuracy—it requires intention, awareness, and a commitment to justice.

So, that is a part of my professional journey, how my understanding and approach to gender budgeting changed fundamentally once my own lived experience forced me to confront the inequalities embedded in the systems we work within every day.

Sepideh: This is such an important reflection, Scherie. I sometimes think that many of us are born feminists—some simply haven't discovered it yet, though I hope they eventually will. I come from an Iranian background and a traditional family. There was a fairly traditional vision of women's and girls' roles. But at the same time, I grew up in Belgium, in a social environment with very different expectations, opportunities, and possibilities for women.

Whenever I questioned why things were done differently in my family compared to what I saw around me in Belgium, the answer was always: "This is how they do it in Belgium; we are Iranian, and we do things differently." Yet there was another contradiction within my family: my father was deeply invested in my education. He insisted that I study, go as far as I wanted, travel wherever necessary, and, ideally, return with a PhD. That encouragement was a strong push, and it shaped my early understanding of feminism and activism. It taught me that men can be important allies, and we should acknowledge that in our journeys. At the same time, I was also deeply influenced by powerful female role models. In particular, my great-aunt—an extraordinary woman—left a lasting mark on me. She was independent and free, highly educated, politically engaged, married for love, worked and ran her own business in the Tehran bazaar at a time—the 1960s—when this was almost unthinkable in such a traditional environment. She commanded respect, was involved in theatre, and lived fully on her own terms. She was not only a role model, but also a source of validation for my personal and professional choices, long before I had the language to name them as feminist.

When I later moved to Spain and began studying gender studies, everything clicked for me. It felt like I had been handed a magnifying glass—a way to analyse all the things that had always felt 'not normal' but for which I had no conceptual language. I remember being a child in school, learning French. Marine will know this well: the grammar rule '*le masculin l'emporte*,' literally: masculine dominates. Even if a classroom has forty girls and one boy, the grammar becomes masculine. And I also remember the boys' reaction when the teacher explained this rule. They would look at the girls and laugh. It was subtle, almost banal, but very powerful. A quiet sense of dominance on one side, and a feeling of inferiority on the other—something that seeps in very early, long before we have the words to question it. And as a child, I remember thinking: Why? How is this considered 'normal'?

Gender studies gave me the theoretical tools to make sense of these systemic patterns. It was a profound revelation—academically, professionally, and personally. Coming back to Maja's question, what has been most important for me in working in PFM and gender budgeting is the connection between personal experience and technical work. PFM is seen as extremely technical, and gender budgeting even more so. But personal experience can illuminate what the technical language obscures.

For instance, I have worked in many countries, such as Morocco, where the family structure is essential and women play a central role in the domestic economy. Women manage household finances on a daily basis. In my own family, my mother did not work outside the home, but she was responsible for managing the money my father provided—deciding how best to allocate it to meet everyone's needs. That is gender budgeting in practice.

Every time we talk about gender budgeting, someone inevitably says, "Why are you bringing gender into PFM? PFM is just about numbers, about technical tools." But these personal stories are powerful because they connect the technical with what is fair, what requires change, and what tools we can use—and PFM is indeed one of the most powerful tools we have to achieve de facto gender equality.

Bringing personal experience into the conversation when I work on gender budgeting, has become my method—my 'magic tool.' Across all levels of hierarchy, in government, NGOs, and civil society, personal stories open doors. They make people speak about their own lives, and through that, they understand the importance, relevance, and necessity of bringing gender equality into budget discussions.

Sureni: Listening to Sepideh made me realise how much her story resonated with my own childhood. When I was around 12, I got my first period. Just before that, my mother had bought me a beautiful pair of shorts that I loved. I used to ride my bicycle everywhere—there was a small shop nearby and I would cycle there often. My father and grandfather taught me to ride a bike when I was in grade four or five, and it became one of my favourite things to do. I am the eldest child, and I think my father raised me a bit 'like a boy,' at least in my early years.

But as soon as I started menstruating, everything changed. I come from South Asia, where relatives often feel they have a say in your life—something I now find intrusive and, in many cases, toxic, and most of which I have cut off as an adult. But at that age, I had no voice and little control. The tradition was that once you start your period, you stay inside a room for five to seven days, without seeing a single male, and you are given a long list of instructions about how to live 'modestly' from that point on. It felt sudden and absurd. I was 12—I couldn't understand why the way I had lived so far was suddenly 'wrong.'

My beloved shorts were taken away by an elderly relative, and I hated it. My mother became very protective. Even if I wanted to go to the shop, she didn't want me to ride the bike anymore. But I didn't want to walk either, because of the catcalling that is so common, even for girls as young as I was. These experiences pushed me into a kind of internal rebellion. I began arguing for myself at home, asserting my rights, resisting what felt unfair and arbitrary.

When I started working, my first boss was a woman, and a lawyer. My very first assignment was to read about the gender wage gap, and it was transformative. Until that moment, I had assumed everyone was paid according to qualifications, because that is what job requirements suggested. I didn't realise gender itself could determine your salary. That reading changed my life. I became consumed by the question: Why should gender make such a difference?

Later, when I joined the IMF, I somehow ended up working on gender budgeting. I spoke with ministries around the world, reviewed their survey responses, and processed huge volumes of country data. To my surprise—

and disappointment—so many governments saw gender budgeting as something 'nice to have,' not a serious structural reform. Even when they lacked systems or laws, they would produce some random report to tick the box and say, "We're doing this, so it counts." It made my blood boil. I couldn't understand why something so important was treated as optional.

After returning to Sri Lanka, I met with a government officer (a woman) working in public finance. Because of my work on the IMF gender budgeting database, I knew exactly where Sri Lanka stood in the Gender Budgeting Index, and I wanted to explore ways to move things forward. During our short conversation, she fully acknowledged the need for gender budgeting. But she also openly acknowledged the deeply entrenched patriarchy and the hierarchical constraints within government institutions. She explained that they had "more urgent problems": dealing with the economic crisis, debt restructuring, and economic instability. Gender was simply not a priority.

I asked her: If it has never been a priority before, and it is not a priority now, when will it ever become one? She had no answer. Gender budgeting remains consistently sidelined—deemed nice to have, but not essential. Recently Sri Lanka opened the railway sector to women—after 165 years. If it takes that long for something so basic, I can't imagine how long it will take for gender budgeting to become normalised.

To this day, I feel somewhat traumatised by how dismissively these issues are treated. And, as if to underscore it, the official I spoke with told me she didn't even like the term 'gender budgeting.' She suggested calling it 'inclusive budgeting' instead. That, to me, was deeply sad—a sign of how uncomfortable people still are with the idea of naming gender explicitly.

On Not Being 'One of the Boys'

Maja: I'm really noticing a common thread running through our stories on gender budgeting: we very quickly go to the personal. We talk about becoming mothers, getting our first periods, the encouraging words our fathers gave us—these deeply formative experiences. And this, I think, is what makes gender budgeting fundamentally different from other budget reforms—such as accrual accounting, debt management, or performance budgeting, for example…

You don't reach back into your personal experiences to decide whether accrual accounting is a good idea. But you do reach back into your personal experiences—your childhood, your identity, your relationships, your body—when you start engaging with gender budgeting. Because this reform is technical, yes, but it is also inseparable from the personal and from how gender norms and identities have shaped our lives.

Thoko: I have two stories that come to mind. Listening to everyone's beautiful reflections made me think about a fundamental question: when did I first realise I was a gender? My earliest memory of that awareness involves a family friend. I was a rough-and-tumble child—always in shorts, always hanging out with boys. I must have been about twelve when we were preparing to go swimming with family friends. An aunt pulled me aside and said, "No, you're not one of the boys."

It was a moment strikingly similar to what Frantz Fanon describes about becoming aware of race, suddenly realising, Oh. I'm a girl. And what does that mean? That moment has stayed with me, especially because the world of budgeting and public finance is such a male-dominated space. And economics—the so-called dismal science—has shaped so much of the language we now use to talk about gender equality: efficiency, equity, good budgeting. These concepts often end up rendering women invisible or 'neutral.' It's a kind of technical way of saying:" You're not one of the boys."

I've been very fortunate to work with people such as Debbie Budlender and Diane Elson as key voices in early days of gender budgeting. Debbie especially opened my eyes to how fiscal policy, monetary policy, and macroeconomics are built on implicit assumptions about women. Women are taken for granted in economic models and policy decisions; whatever choices are made, women become the shock absorbers of those decisions. That shows up in the form of unpaid labour—caring for the sick, the elderly, children, doing food provisioning and emotional labour. Women are always there in the background, doing this essential work, but never explicitly counted.

Working with activists and policymakers, I have often found myself putting these decisions under scrutiny: the choices made in rands and cents—or dollars—have different impacts on different genders. Asking these questions makes people uncomfortable, because it forces them to confront the consequences of their decisions.

A very current example: in South Africa, we've just reduced the inflation target to 3 percent. That means an extremely constrictive monetary policy, which will hurt small and medium enterprises, reduce access to employment, and limit economic opportunities. And who picks up the tab when households struggle because of these macroeconomic choices? Women. Every time.

When you trace the logical conclusion of these powerful decisions—decisions mainly made by men or shaped by ways of thinking dominated by men—you see clearly how the burden shifts onto women. This is why gender-responsive budgeting (GRB) is so vital. It shows that alternatives exist: the well-being economy, approaches that move beyond GDP, frameworks that count women and make their contributions visible, drawing on the 5Rs of care we need to Recognise, Reduce, Redistribute, Reward, and Represent care to achieve gender equality.

But it's not all bleak. South Africa has examples of real feminist victories. Our Child Support Grant, one of the most important social protection policies in the country, was championed by feminist economists and GRB advocates such as Debbie Budlender. It has demonstrably reduced poverty. Our multi-billion-rand HIV/AIDS programme is also highly gender-responsive and has saved countless lives and families. These successes show what is possible when gender is taken seriously in budgeting.

But then we face setbacks. Our Treasury recently published a gender statement that was only seven pages long—actually five after accounting for blank placeholders. It was embarrassing. It did not reflect the lived reality of gender inequality in one of the most unequal countries in the world. And this was despite years of support, technical assistance, and having someone like Debbie—a global expert—right here in the country.

So, this work is a pattern of winning small battles while still facing a very long war. And I know it's not very feminist to use a military metaphor—but sometimes it feels like the only one that fits.

Marine: I find all of this wonderful—and very familiar. I've just come back from maternity leave, and I carry a whole catalogue of experiences that could make anyone even more feminist than they already are. What gives me hope, though, is recognising that these experiences—and our refusal to accept the status quo—can become catalysts for change. It is well documented[1] that anger, when understood and channelled, is one of the strongest motivators for reform. It comforts me to think that all of us here may be 'angry' in that sense, making us reformers and change-makers with powerful personal and professional experiences and emotional investment. Listening to our stories, this is clearly a common thread.

What is interesting to me is that my journey has been almost the opposite of what others have described. I was raised intellectually and conceptually as a feminist—theoretically, philosophically, academically. I believed I was ready to go out into the world, change things, fight inequality, confront discrimination. I had read the books. I knew the theories. And then I stepped into the real world… and it made me angry.

Because you think that being raised a feminist prepares you, but it doesn't. No one can prepare you for the lived reality of discrimination, or the inequality that operates on so many different levels, across so many different dimensions of identity. And I say this knowing that I also personally experience privileges on a daily basis, as a white, educated woman currently working in a multilateral organisation.

When Sepideh spoke about language, it brought me back to my time starting my PhD in Turkey in 2013. I was learning Turkish, and any introductory language course uses simple tropes to teach basic sentences: "Mum is in the kitchen," "Dad is in the car." And suddenly, there it was—the same old gendered assumptions. It made me angry all over again.

There are countless examples from my personal life, but what it all comes back to for me is this: anything that does not actively centre equality and equity is simply funding the status quo. It reinforces the structures already in place. And because all of us here work, in one way or another, on governance, we know that governance is fundamentally about designing the processes that lead to an end goal. The way you design the process shapes the outcomes you get.

So, when all our systems were built inside a patriarchal framework, how could we possibly expect them to produce unbiased results? I think about this every day in my work at the UN. When I am asked to draft a gender specific budget, and I am told, "Our target is 20 percent gender," all I can think is: So, 80 percent is non-gender? In other words, 80 percent is simply the status quo. And that feels like we are walking backwards.

Maja: What strikes me listening to all of us is how similar the pattern is: privately, and then professionally, we each discovered that we are not 'one of the boys.' As children, we simply wanted to belong—to be part of a community. And then, as young girls, suddenly there was that moment when we realised we are 'the others.' It was usually in our early youth when our bodies changed, we got our period, we wanted to compete in sports—and we realised we were no longer being treated the same way. Society sends very clear messages: you must now find 'your place,' and that place is not in all arenas.

I was recently writing about this because the memory came back so vividly. It wasn't that I wanted to be 'one of the boys' because boys were somehow better. It was because they were privileged. They had more freedom, more opportunity, a broader world available to them.

And this carries directly into the professional sphere—the second moment when you realise you are not one of the boys. In my case, being one of the boys professionally meant not talking about gender, and certainly not working on gender budgeting. When I was first assigned gender budgeting, I resisted it: No, no, no. I'm an economist. I work on the serious things. Gender budgeting, I feared, would weaken my status, my legitimacy, my credibility as an expert. Which says a lot about the hierarchy of knowledge in our field.

Challenging Orthodoxies, Opening up Economics and the Public Finance Landscape

So, this brings me to my next question: Have you had that moment professionally? The moment when you realised that mainstream economic thought sits on one side, and that by engaging with gender budgeting you might be putting yourself at a disadvantage.

Thoko: I can respond quickly, because this has been very real for me. I recently transitioned into a new unit, and although I do not have a formal economics background—mine is in political economy and anthropology, I have worked in PFM and GRB for a very long time.

Suddenly, I found myself in a team of four where the others were all economists, all former Treasury officials, including a very senior one. I sat there listening to them and realised that I didn't think they were speaking English. I simply could not understand what they were talking about. Part of me was excited: this was a chance to learn a whole new world. But at the same time, I began doing my own reading.

I went back and read Keynes, and then Blanchard, and all the major figures—most of them men. And I discovered that Keynes did write in plain English and was actually very accessible. It's only in more recent decades that economics has become a highly technical language, one that keeps people out unless they have been specifically trained in it.

Political economist Clara Mattei has written about this shift in the 2020s, when economics moved from being a deeply political exercise to a deliberately technical one. And suddenly you realise: the discipline has created a boys' club—exclusive, insular—and the language is the gatekeeping tool.

Meanwhile, GRB is often treated as "soft and fluffy." Something peripheral. Something you let the women do. And yet, as Debbie Budlender and others have always argued, this work is not about women as a category: it is about gender equality, about values, about race, class, and the structural dynamics embedded in our budgets. It is far more nuanced than setting a 20 percent target or creating a few women-focused programmes.

I have struggled with this dynamic a great deal. Then I read Robert Skidelsky's *What's Wrong with Economics*,[2] and it made me feel so much better. He argues exactly this—that modern economics is a political project that keeps people out unless they have been formally trained in its language. Of course, not all economists are the same—there are brilliant feminist economists and heterodox thinkers—but the dominant neoclassical, neoliberal framework has systematically excluded women. Or, alternatively, women must become 'one of the boys,' speak the language, fit in, and avoid asking uncomfortable questions.

I'll give one example. In South Africa, there was a proposal to increase the value-added tax (VAT) by three percentage points. Everyone acknowledges VAT is regressive and harms poor households far more than wealthy ones, but it is a politically easy way to raise revenue.

My colleagues made only the efficiency argument: it raises revenue quickly and neatly. When I raised the equity argument—asking what this meant for poor households and for women who absorb the shock—they treated me as though I were mad. As if equity simply did not belong in the conversation. That experience reinforced for me how economics, as currently practised, marginalises the very questions GRB insists on asking.

Scherie: I've often been associated with areas of public finance that are seen as more avant-garde or innovative, such as gender budgeting, green budgeting, public engagement, and transparency. These are important topics, and I approach them with the same analytical rigour as any other area of public finances.

But externally, I notice a very clear difference between how my gender budgeting work is received versus my green budgeting work. For example, I find many economists are enthusiastic about exploring climate issues. But they show less interest in gender. And yet, the modelling in the gender space is just as interesting: growth accounting, the economic contribution of gender equality, analyses showing how closing gender gaps produces tangible economic benefits. The technical content is there. But it is somehow often not as 'exciting.'

I think semantics play a major role. The term gender budgeting carries connotations and pre-judgments that hold it back. Ideally, we would live in a world where these terms didn't trigger preconceived ideas about the people who work on them—or about their value. But we do not. And the phrasing does shape how we are perceived professionally.

Marine: I was thinking about what you said, because my experience is slightly different. I am not formally associated with gender budgeting in the work I do; my title is more generic, and my portfolio is broad. I am the PFM expert in the UNDP office in the Pacific, and my counterparts are ministries of finances and revenue agencies but also parliamentarians, auditors, civil society, and other oversight actors in 16 countries. So, when I sit at PFM stakeholder roundtables, I am already positioned as the 'nice' person—the one who talks to the non-Ministry of Finance groups.

At first, that actually worked to my advantage. I was non-threatening. I was the person engaging the public on debt issues, promoting openness, supporting citizen budgets—all the things that are seen as positive and harmless, and that help governments 'tick the box' and look good on assessments such as PEFA. It was comfortable for everyone.

But then something changed. I've now been in the Pacific long enough that leaders of the opposition—the people I used to work with on parliamentary budget analysis, reviews of loans, and oversight—have become ministers of finance. They know and trust the technical support we have been providing for years and want to continue engaging us as they take on ministerial portfolios. This shift means I am no longer focusing on public finance oversight but core reforms. This is space is in more direct competition with other technical advisors.

Suddenly, I am no longer the 'nice' and non-threatening person to invite for coffee or to stakeholder roundtables. I've become a competitor—someone whose influence needs to be contained. And when you become a competitor, the rhetoric changes. Instead of open collaboration, there is subtle discrediting, territorialism, and pushback.

As such this is not a challenge, and some might say it is the price of relevance, but it goes hand in hand with a deeper pattern which should raise concerns in the public finance community. Most of us have strong assumptions about what constitutes essentials vs 'nice to have' fiscal capacity and processes. Modern FMIS?[3] Essential. Cross-cutting policy budget data? Nice to have. Macro fiscal projections? Essential. Getting feedback on allocative efficiency? Nice to have. Many of us have referred to this classification implicitly in this conversation. While I entirely agree with the need to prioritise reform—advising on such prioritisation is central to my work—I am concerned by the assumptions and values we bring into these exercises. These past years have shown me that once you step into the political centre of

PFM, dynamics shifts and tools meant to advance inclusion are used as excuses to shut down deeper conversations about equity and biases of the frameworks.

Sepideh: We have been facing resistance for as long as I can remember—throughout my entire 25 years of working in this field. What Scherie said earlier reminded me that we could probably write an entire book, or several books, filled with the things people have said to us to discourage gender budgeting work. In the end, the resistance and the arguments people use against gender are always the same.

I remember once being in a meeting in Morocco—it was a very tough meeting with enormous resistance. Everything I said was challenged. We had long, difficult exchanges. And when we finally stepped out, the team leader of the project looked at me and said, "You have a reply for everything." I laughed and said, "Let's just say I've heard them all before." The first time you hear them, you might feel unsure; the second time, you start thinking; by the third time, you know exactly how to respond. That is what I call everyday challenge to resistance in our work. We are trained. We have tools. We have studied. We have read countless books. Many of us have PhDs. And we also have lived experience—years of testing theory in practice, in real contexts. We know how to analyse and deconstruct every argument thrown at us.

What worries me now, however, is that the setting and the framework are changing. Until very recently, we were fortunate—people working on gender issues were on the crest of the wave. There was momentum. There were global structures supporting gender equality. There were constitutions and human rights frameworks we could rely on. But now, we are sliding down the wave. There is a shift—and it has come like a punch in the face.

When USAID cut funding for gender, the impact was immediate and devastating. I see it in the field all the time: offices closing, teams dismantled, gender-based violence units saying, "We have no funding anymore." This is not the small everyday resistance we are trained to handle. This is a larger, structural, institutional backlash. And although this is not the first time in history and we know these cycles, I believe we must think together about new strategies, just as we once did for the smaller resistance. This backlash is bigger and more dangerous because the frameworks that supported us are weakening.

Colleagues in many countries tell me the same thing: they are asked to change the wording in documents, to avoid words like gender or equality because they are no longer 'suitable' or 'acceptable.' They are told that using these terms will create resistance. This is happening across organisations. And yes, it is destabilising. But coming from an Iranian background, with its long history of political constraint and coded discourse, this logic is not unfamiliar to me. I grew up with an awareness of how language is shaped, negotiated, and sometimes disguised in order to move forward. As we say in Spanish, "to call a rabbit a cat"—to name something else in order to survive. Across different contexts, we have often had to frame our work in ways that avoid backlash while still pursuing the same goals. That is a strategy many of us recognise. But the scale of the current backlash demands something more collective.

One of the most destabilising (and painful) aspects is that some of the resistance comes from women themselves. Maja mentioned the 'boys' club,' but that club contains women who want to belong to it, women who resist us when we bring up gender. And of course, the men in the boys' club love this. They say, "Look, even the women disagree." We understand where this comes from and why certain women align with the boy club, but it still hurts.

In my own case, because I am a gender expert, I didn't face the boys' club as directly in my earlier work—most of us working on gender were women, and our project managers were also women. Only recently have we started seeing men working in gender, and you can count them on one hand. But entering the PFM world was a shock; there, I confronted the everyday reality of walking into meetings where every panel member was male. That was the norm.

What truly worries me now is the institutionalised resistance: the way gender and gender budgeting are becoming unacceptable topics while other areas like green budgeting are considered 'safer' and 'better.' This is not only a concern for my own job or survival—although that is real—but for the projects I see on the ground: teams with no resources, initiatives being shut down, entire areas of work collapsing. We assumed that GRB was about fairness and equality, and that 'good budgeting' was inherently aligned with those same values.

But now we are seeing a major shift. We are increasingly surrounded by governments whose political agendas no longer prioritise fairness, equality, inclusiveness, or diversity. Under such governments, the definition of good budgeting changes. It no longer includes gender equality or equity. That means GRB becomes more political than ever before. In the past, we could navigate this tension: we could switch between being the technical PFM expert and being the activist committed to gender equality. But that is becoming much harder. We are no longer simply challenging budgeting practices, we are challenging a new set of political values that openly reject equality.

Where is Gender Budgeting Now?

Maja: Often in my own career, I have heard the question: Why are we calling it gender budgeting? People say, "If you called it social budgeting, everyone would love it more because it would feel less threatening, less political." That has always struck me, because it reveals a deeper tension: Are we working toward gender equality, or are we working toward gender budgeting? That is one thread of this discussion—the politics of naming the work itself.

The second thread is gender in budgeting, which connects directly to what we've been calling the 'boys' club.' We keep circulating manuals, frameworks, and reference texts that remain overwhelmingly shaped by the same demographic: white men from privileged, elite backgrounds, largely from English-speaking countries. I highlight the racial and class dimensions deliberately, because this is not incidental; it is part of the structural problem. From the 1800s to today, economics has been shaped by this narrow group, and we continue to operate inside the dogmas they created.

So, my question here is about what is really happening to gender budgeting right now, especially in the context of the new strategic frameworks emerging in PFM—these priority-based budgeting categories, thematic budgeting initiatives, and the attempts to 'package' gender budgeting within them. What I am seeing, and I wonder if you see it too, is a kind of picking and choosing among priorities. What are you seeing in your own work—the challenges, the shifts, the implications?

Sureni: I think that in general—whether in society, in professional spaces, or in everyday interactions—people are afraid of certain words. It's not only 'gender budgeting.' The moment you say feminism, many assume you are attacking men or trying to elevate women above others. They don't understand that feminism isn't about women alone; it is about social equality. But the word itself scares people.

There have been many times when I felt that if changing the terminology helps us get the work done—then fine, let's change the word. If the outcome is achieved, the label is secondary. But something I've consistently noticed is that when men use words like feminism or speak about gender issues, they are praised as progressive—as though they are doing charitable work for 'vulnerable groups.' Yet when women speak about feminism, rights, or equality, it is perceived as an attack, as though we are demanding something we shouldn't have. I have felt this repeatedly whenever I speak about gender or feminism.

Even in my personal life, I have been very direct about these issues. I have been married for four years, and before saying yes to my husband, I was very clear: I am a woman with a career, and I will not stop working after marriage. I would love to have a child one day, but motherhood still scares me deeply. Listening to all the experiences shared in this conversation today, the challenges, the loss of opportunities, the struggles, it terrifies me. I want to experience motherhood, but the fear of everything it might take away from what I've built for myself is very real.

People only see the joyful images—the happy photos, the celebrations—but not the difficult nights, the exhaustion, the lack of support, the professional setbacks. And I don't want to find myself in a situation where I lose what I've worked so hard to achieve. Even now, when my husband and I talk about planning for a child in the next two or three years, I worry. What if his mindset changes? What if one day he says, "Someone needs to stay home with the baby, can you do it?" My answer is no. That possibility frightens me because I do not want to give up my ambitions or my independence.

There is also the implicit assumption that women are the caregivers: they cook, they manage the household. These are the expectations we are constantly fighting, both at home and in the professional world.

And on the 'economic boys' club,' I've had my own very direct experiences. During my last two years in Sri Lanka, I was essentially the public face of the think tank where I worked. Sri Lanka was under an IMF-supported programme at the time, and the reforms were the centre of national debate. I was the one going on television and radio often explaining what the programme required, what targets were set, and what policy changes were expected.

Budgeting is an extremely male-dominated field in Sri Lanka, and for nearly two years I was one of the few women regularly engaging in public discussions on national budgeting issues. My own specialisation was budget implementation, so I was constantly commenting on what the government was doing—and not doing.

After many of my interviews, I would receive calls on Messenger or strange messages from unknown numbers. The tone was often threatening. I ignored them—there are many unbalanced people out there—but the fact that so many people later asked me, "Have you received threats? Is it safe for a woman to speak like that?" said everything. I was constantly told I shouldn't be "so direct" or "so outspoken," as if identifying gaps or failures in policy was an act of aggression.

When a man spoke critically, it was treated as normal professional analysis. But when a woman said the same, it was often treated as aggressive, inappropriate, or 'attacking.' Having a strong voice and a clear opinion as a woman—and a young woman—in Sri Lanka added a double layer of pressure. The moment I opened my mouth in a room full of senior experts, there was this underlying assumption that because I was young, I didn't know enough or wasn't adding real value.

There is an experience in my work in public finance that has stayed with me, not because it was exceptional, but because it revealed how expertise is often quietly gendered. I was invited to participate in a senior-level budget discussion alongside policymakers and established experts. I was the only woman on stage—one woman and 11 men—and by far the youngest. I felt intimidated, but also proud to represent women in that space.

As the discussion unfolded, a pattern became apparent: men were to answer questions on tax policy, revenue, macroeconomic targets, and expenditure management, and women those about education, health, and 'soft' sectors. It was as though the place of a woman was predetermined: She was the person to talk about the 'social' issues, not the 'technical' ones, even though her work focused on PFM law, systems, and implementation.

It offended me deeply. Not because education or health aren't important, they are essential, but because this framing makes it clear that a woman is being categorised as someone who could not comment on the technical core of public finance. Despite being the only woman in the room, and grateful to have a seat at the table, I was also aware of how narrow that seat was expected to be.

Marine: I am trying to answer in my head the very complex question you raised, Maja, about the strategic budgeting initiatives—gender versus climate, versus child, versus social, versus whatever the newest trend is. I can't even remember the latest one I heard. And I think that's important to say: we are trying to change the system. We are not collecting gender data simply for the sake of collecting gender data or doing gender analysis simply to produce a report. There is a genuine power-shift agenda behind this work—a change process that goes well beyond the technicalities, and beyond gender.

And so the question becomes: What is the right narrative? What is the framing that will actually make this change happen—and make it acceptable, even compelling, to others? That is what we have been circling around throughout this discussion.

At the same time, there is a parallel conversation happening inside ministries of finance: What data do they want? What data do politicians want? How do we facilitate conversations around the priorities of the government of the day? And I increasingly feel that this is almost a separate discussion. I had the most wonderful exchange with the Minister of Finance of a country I work with at the moment: they want to design tools that allow them to engage with policy priorities current and future. Producing the information that governments need on cross-cutting policies and providing the data that align with the political priorities of a particular administration, is one thing. That is the technical requirement, the service delivery function.

But the change agenda is something different. It is about shifting where power sits within the PFM machinery. It is about questioning what we centre: are we centring traditional ideas of budget balance, rigidity, and fiscal orthodoxy? Or are we centring equity, social justice, and the real lived impacts of fiscal decisions? We recently spent a week with representatives of governments, the IMF and the World Bank debating this very question and it was a lively discussion. For me, this distinction is crucial. It is the difference between multiplying and de-multiplying the power of the data we produce—between simply generating numbers within the chart of accounts and using those numbers to shift the outcomes, the priorities, and the structures that budgeting supports.

Where Do We Go Next?

Maja: So what do we see as the way forward?

Scherie: I'll choose optimism. I really do feel hopeful, because when I look back, I can see how much progress has been made over the years. I think about my family when I was growing up, and the constraints my mother faced: raising a family while trying to build a career that was interesting, meaningful, and decently paid. It was a struggle for her, and she did an extraordinary job.

But the opportunities I've had simply did not exist for her generation. My life today is unimaginable compared to what was available to women then. In my own family, for example, I am the main breadwinner, and I have a partner who stays at home and looks after our child.

So yes, I am hopeful for the next generation. My son will grow up seeing a version of family life where gender roles are not fixed, where a woman can travel the world for her work, where a man can cook (even if he doesn't particularly like it), care for a child, and run a household. He will not carry the same expectations into adulthood with any future partner he may have. And really, that is what we can do: model the world we want them to inherit, so that the opportunities we struggled for become the baseline for them.

Thoko: I think Sepideh's earlier point is crucial: the political moment we are living through is profoundly unfriendly to any form of progressive thinking. Whether you work on climate, gender, race, or class, there is backlash everywhere. The environment is broadly hostile to anything that challenges existing structures of power. From my own experience, one thing that makes a difference—especially for women in PFM—is having strong networks. Finding other women who support you, mentor you, and understand the terrain is essential.

We constantly have to rethink how we name this work, how we frame it, and how we articulate it. Language shapes perception; naming shapes acceptance. This is fundamental for keeping our politics vibrant, alive, and intellectually honest. Staying connected to civil society and grassroots actors is equally important. Without that grounding, it is easy to become trapped in the ivory towers of treasuries, parliaments, and policymaking spaces; spaces where decisions are made far away from lived realities. Staying close to grassroots organisations keeps us honest. It forces us to translate technical or theoretical analysis into concrete, human terms: is there funding for HIV treatment? What does an increase in VAT mean for poor households?

Grounding PFM in people's lived experiences makes the work meaningful and powerful. There is also a kind of irony in how we fragment ourselves. Right now, gender-budgeting experts argue that climate budgeting is gender budgeting, while climate experts contest that. There is a turf war. But in reality, these issues are deeply interlinked. This is why it is essential to build the climate–gender nexus rather than splitting ourselves into narrow silos that make the work weaker rather than stronger.

Another thing that has kept me grounded is the commitment to read widely, beyond the dominant canon. Decolonising our thinking means reading Latin American economists, South Asian thinkers, African feminist scholars, and heterodox PFM practitioners from across the world. These perspectives expand our frameworks and remind us that economics and PFM are not neutral—they are deeply political disciplines with histories of inclusion and exclusion.

Finally, I want to emphasise something championed by the International Association for Feminist Economics: we need to cite each other. We need to reference each other's work. The boys' club has always done this instinctively—they cite each other endlessly, reinforcing their authority. But we, as women in PFM and GRB, often fail to cite our peers because we're busy referencing the 'canonical' (mostly male) authors. This book is part of that effort: it shows that we are a community, and that our expertise deserves to be named, cited, and recognised.

Marine: Listening to everyone, I realised I have three hopeful stories I want to share. And Scherie, your point about setting an example really resonated with me.

The first story is from my daughter. She is six now, but when she was four, we met a new couple in Fiji. She looked at me, very puzzled, and said: "Mom, the dad is working." I said yes, of course. And she replied: "He's allowed to work?" That was the moment I realised that in our little world, our bubble of friends and families, the women were the ones going to the office, travelling for work, leading careers, and the fathers were the ones staying home or working from home. That was the model she saw everywhere. So encountering a different arrangement was a revelation for her. It gave me hope to see how her sense of normality had already shifted.

The second hopeful story is what I'm seeing among activists and advocates in the Pacific. Many of the grassroots and community-level women we've been working with, particularly those engaged in care economy issues, are now starting to talk openly about entering politics. I've heard so many women saying recently: "I'm going to stand for election," "I want to be part of the political conversation—not just an outside influence." They are moving from feminist activism and technical advocacy into formal political spaces. It's a reaction, I think, to the backlash we've been discussing—the realisation that if they want to defend certain values, they must take their place inside political institutions. I'm seeing this momentum everywhere in the Pacific. It would be fascinating to know if similar shifts are happening in other regions.

And the third story is that there is an extraordinary network of women in PFM across the Pacific, and I was fortunate to be welcomed into it. In several ministries of finance, these networks are multigenerational: women mentoring women, grooming their successors, creating continuity and confidence in each other. Almost all the heads of budget divisions are women. They mentor each other formally and informally. In Fiji, the past three heads of budget still have a WhatsApp group with the future heads—they encourage one another, share advice, offer support, and help each other navigate politically complicated environments. Seeing this network in action, women lifting each other, protecting each other, preparing each other for leadership roles, gives me enormous hope. It shows the power of solidarity among women in PFM, especially in contexts where political conditions are difficult and unpredictable. These three moments remind me that change is not only possible: it is already happening in small, powerful ways.

Sepideh: I want to try to summarise a few things that emerged from our conversation, points that I deeply agree with. The first is about the next generation of experts. We have a responsibility now to mentor younger professionals who want to work in PFM or in gender studies. I try to do this every chance I get. We are navigating a difficult period, and passing the torch is essential.

The second point is about role models, and not only for our children. What Scherie and Marine said reminded me that we all have similar anecdotes. When my son was about six, I was preparing a short video for a training—something about gender roles and domestic work. The video said that women perform, on average, three more hours of unpaid housework every day. I wanted to see if my son could understand it, so I showed it to him. When we reached that part, he said, "That's not correct." I asked him why, and he replied, "Because at home, Dad is doing everything. You're not doing anything." I burst out laughing. Of course, I am doing things—I travel constantly for work—but from his perspective, the model of gender roles at home is completely reversed. Seeing his father as the primary caregiver shapes his understanding of what a man can be.

Another crucial point is the need to make ourselves visible. We have been conditioned for so long to be discreet, quiet, modest, 'nice.' But we need to claim our space. It is important to assert our expertise: we have decades of experience, we have worked in dozens of countries, we hold PhDs, we have contributed to fundamental reforms. We must verbalise that.

Finally, I want to come back to networking, which is absolutely essential. If you'll allow me, I want to read a sentence by Marcela Lagarde, a feminist and former member of Parliament in Mexico. She wrote: "What would have become of women in patriarchy without the network of women around us, beside us, behind us, ahead of us—guiding the way, holding on together? What would become of us without our women friends? What would become of women without the love of other women?"[4]

Every time I read that, I become emotional. Our strength lies in each other. The network of women around us is not optional; it is the solution. It is how we survive, how we resist, and how we move forward.

Sureni: Listening to all of you, what I hear throughout this roundtable is what I would call a butterfly effect: each of us doing something in our own lives to change, unlearn, resist, or break away from the patterns we inherited from our parents, relatives, communities, and older generations.

In my own life, over these 32 years, I've unlearned so much. I've cut ties where I needed to. I've grown. But when I look to the future, I still feel fear. Not about my career or capabilities, because I know I can manage those. What scares me is my biology: the things that will happen to me simply because I am a woman. And if society continues to discriminate against us on that basis, then that fear becomes even sharper. So it has been inspiring to listen to all of you, to hear how each of you has grown as women and as professionals. Your stories make me feel more grounded.

Maja: Thank you, Sureni. I want you to know that it is going to be okay.

Thank you all for sharing your reflections, experiences, for this exchange. I certainly hope we will continue this conversation and expand to include more colleagues, because as we all agree, these are the topics that need to be discussed more and in wider, more 'mainstream' settings. And we will make it happen, together.

Note

The conversation between Marine, Scherie, Sepideh, Sureni, and Thoko, was filled with laughs, some more personal stories and some tears—we did not include it all in this conversation, but it was clear how much we all enjoyed speaking about our stories, our experiences and our worlds that always collide. We promise to continue this and similar conversations soon because not only are they fun and cathartic, but they are important and timely. They are our stories of Gender *in* Budgeting.

Notes

1 Read for instance the work of Daniel Goleman, Harvard University, or Marc Brackett, Yale University.
2 Skidelsky, R. (2020). *What's Wrong with Economics?: A Primer for the Perplexed.* Yale University Press. doi:10.2307/j.ctvxkn7jq.
3 Financial Management Integrated System.
4 Lagarde M. (2006) Pacto entre mujeres. Sororidad. Recuperado de https://www.asociacionag.org.ar/pdfaportes/25/09.pdf.

Afterword

Opening Essential Conversations

Maja Bosnić and Manal Fouad

Closing this book does not mark the end of the stories of women in public financial management (PFM) nor the discussion about gender in budgeting. Rather, we imagine this book as an opening, an invitation to sustain the conversations on more inclusive public finance and broaden it to historically marginalised groups.

PFM remains a deeply patriarchal field, shaped by norms and systems that limit who is heard and whose knowledge counts. Challenging these structures is not only a matter of gender equality; it is essential for building economic systems that serve societies more fairly and inclusively. This volume serves as an important record of institutional memory, particularly in the current international context where progress on gender equality, and consequently gender budgeting, remain politically fragile and at risk of reversal.

Read together, the 20 chapters in this volume constitute a collective intellectual project that documents lived institutional histories while also advancing a substantive argument: that lived experience, grounded in economic realities, the political economy of care and labour markets, can reveal broader structural dynamics that are often overlooked in traditional economic analysis. Insider perspectives serve not only as personal testimony, but as wider evidence demonstrating how gender budgeting contributes to more inclusive, accountable, and equitable fiscal outcomes, reinforcing the personal experiences as a legitimate source of economic insight.

As such, the book bridges academic thinking on GRB with the realities of practice, focusing deliberately on what happens *inside* PFM systems. It offers one step, among many still to come, towards narrowing the distance between research and reform, between conceptual frameworks and the everyday impact of PFM reforms.

Finally, the process of co-creating this book deserves reflection of its own. The collaboration behind it was marked by solidarity, trust, and a strong sense of safety and sisterhood that impressed all of us, women used to hierarchies, deadlines, and criticisms, in a professional world not designed for us. It offers lessons not only in substance, but in how we work together—lessons

DOI: 10.4324/9781003732532-25

that we hope to carry forward into future collaborations, reforms, and shared efforts to open up the world of public finance.

In the same spirit, we hope this book sparks further critical conversation, inspires new research and writing, and motivates stronger collective action.

Onwards!

Index

For Product Safety Concerns and Information please contact our EU
representative GPSR@taylorandfrancis.com
Taylor & Francis Verlag GmbH, Kaufingerstraße 24, 80331 München, Germany

www.ingramcontent.com/pod-product-compliance
Ingram Content Group UK Ltd.
Pitfield, Milton Keynes, MK11 3LW, UK
UKHW020008200926
475702UK00015B/2545
9781041202134